MISSION COLLEGE
LEARNING RESOURCE SERVICE

DATE DUE

DEMCO 38-297

Other books by Jean Carper
Ask your bookseller for the books you have missed.

THE ALL-IN-ONE CALORIE COUNTER
THE ALL-IN-ONE CARBOHYDRATE COUNTER
THE BRAND NAME NUTRITION COUNTER—Revised Edition
JEAN CARPER'S TOTAL NUTRITION GUIDE: THE
   COMPLETE OFFICIAL REPORT ON HEALTHFUL
   EATING
THE FOOD PHARMACY

The
All-In-One
Calorie
Counter

By Jean Carper

2nd Revised Edition

BANTAM BOOKS

NEW YORK · TORONTO · LONDON · SYDNEY · AUCKLAND

THE ALL-IN-ONE CALORIE COUNTER

A Bantam Book / published by arrangement with
Workman Publishing Co., Inc.

PRINTING HISTORY

Bantam edition / January 1974

2nd printing........ May 1974	8th printing ..... August 1977
3th printing ..... August 1974	9th printing .... October 1977
4th printing....... April 1975	10th printing .... January 1978
5th printing ... December 1975	11th printing .... January 1978
6th printing......... July 1976	12th printing ...... May 1978
7th printing ... November 1976	13th printing .. November 1979

Revised Bantam edition / July 1980

15th printing .. September 1980	19th printing .... October 1983
16th printing .... June 1981	20th printing........ July 1984
17th printing .... June 1982	21st printing ... February 1985
18th printing .... January 1983	22nd printing..... August 1985

23rd printing... March 1986
2nd revised edition / March 1987

All rights reserved.
Copyright © 1974, 1980, 1987 by Jean Carper.
No part of this book may be reproduced or transmitted
in any form or by any means, electronic or mechanical,
including photocopying, recording, or by any information
storage and retrieval system, without permission in writing
from the publisher.
For information address: Bantam Books.

ISBN 0-553-26326-9

Published simultaneously in the United States and Canada

Bantam Books are published by Bantam Books, a division of Bantam
Doubleday Dell Publishing Group, Inc. Its trademark, consisting of
the words "Bantam Books" and the portrayal of a rooster, is Registered
in U.S. Patent and Trademark Office and in other countries. Marca
Registrada. Bantam Books, 666 Fifth Avenue, New York, New York
10103.

PRINTED IN THE UNITED STATES OF AMERICA

O   12 11 10 9 8 7 6 5

Contents

Introduction

"Counting calories is not just the best way to long-term weight maintenance—it's the only way," says internationally known nutritionist Dr. Jean Mayer of Tufts University. It is that unit of energy—the calorie—that determines how much weight you put on and take off, he says. And certainly there are hundreds of thousands of successful calorie-counting dieters who would agree. Take in fewer calories than you burn up each day, and you're bound to shed pounds.

But how to do it? Unfortunately, there aren't any mysterious secrets for making dieting actually fun. But in this book you'll find loads of information that I hope will take some of the monotony out of dieting, boost your chances of success, enable you to eat some foods on your diet you never dreamed possible and clear up some misconceptions you may have about which foods are high in calorie content and which aren't. For example, many calorie-conscious persons avoid potatoes and spaghetti like the plague (which by themselves are fairly low in calories) and load up on "protein" foods such as beef (which is comparatively much higher in calories). At the same time I have heard people say Japanese sushi (rice and vegetables or raw fish) is high in calories. It is not, as you will see in this book.

In the case of potatoes and pasta, it is not the basic food itself but the way it is prepared or the embellishments that make the caloric difference. A medium-sized boiled potato weighs in with only 104 calories, whereas only ten French fries have 137 calories. Of course, if you want to splurge occasionally and eat French fries or load up your baked potato with butter and sour cream cheese sauce, why shouldn't you as long as you consider the calorie difference?

And why shouldn't you eat a Mars bar if you want one? Or a slice of Sara Lee's rich cake? Or Jeno's pizza? If you don't exceed your daily limit. Dieting—even if you are counting calories—doesn't have to be a monklike experience—ascetic and uninteresting. However, overindulging in sweet or high-fat foods at the expense of well-balanced nutrition is not in your best interest.

The only stumbling block may be that you don't know how many calories are present in food products. For unlike pure, fresh foods, when the ingredients get into a company chef's kitchen, they are all mixed any which way according to the company's special recipe. Only the company can tell you how many calories are in their foods. And that's the kind of information you will find in this book: a comprehensive listing of not only all common "generic-type" foods, but also commercially prepared foods—from Apple Jacks to Mrs. Paul's fried, frozen zucchini sticks.

You will see that the number of calories in similar grocery products can vary greatly, and you will find that simple knowledge can trim calories off a product quickly. For example, it is almost startling to realize that one cup of Chicken of the Sea light tuna in oil contains 550 calories, but that one cup of the same brand tuna canned in water has only 200—a saving of 350 calories!

If you've bought or are thinking of buying this book, you're probably already committed to losing or maintaining your weight, so there's no use wasting time telling you why you should be weight-conscious, or all about the terrible medical problems you may confront if you aren't. But there are some facts about calories that you may find valuable. A calorie is a unit of energy in foods. Technically, it is the amount of heat needed to raise the temperature of one liter (about a quart) of water by one degree centigrade. The body constantly takes in calories through food and expends them through activity.

Theoretically, if you took in precisely as many calories in a day as you used up in energy, you wouldn't gain or lose a smidgen of an ounce that day. But when you take in more calories than your body can use, you store them as fat. The rule of thumb is that a moderately active person needs about 15 calories per day per pound of body weight to "stay as is."

That is, if you weigh 120 pounds and want to stay that way, you should consume about 1800 calories a day. If you're happy at 150 pounds, you should take in 2250 calories a day. (Of course, this assumes a constant level of exercise. If you increase your level of activity, as experts advise as part of a weight-loss program, you expend additional calories.) If you want to get rid of some of that stored fat by counting calories, the calorie intake should dip considerably. How much you want to lose and how fast are up to you.

According to the American Medical Association, there are about 3500 calories in each stored pound of fat. So if you want to take off a pound, you have to get rid of that 3500 somehow. One way to do it is to shave 500 calories a day for seven days off your caloric intake. Thus, if you're 120 pounds and want to take off a pound a week, you would cut your regular 1800 calorie daily count to 1300; and if you weigh 150, you would want to go down from 2250 calories daily to 1750. Theoretically, that's the formula that should work for most people. Your scales will track your own success.

As far as giving you the basic facts necessary to follow your diet, you'll find in this book the calorie counts on all kinds of foods—both fresh and processed (by brand name, of course) —from A to Z. Included also for the first time, in this new edition, is a special section on calorie counts of restaurant foods. New surveys show that Americans now eat about 50 percent of their meals outside the home—in restaurants of all types, including fast-food chains. It is not easy to know the exact calorie counts in general restaurant foods, but we have obtained approximate figures from the U.S. Department of Agriculture, used in its national nutritional surveys and compilations. We consider these figures an exciting addition to this book, making it even more comprehensive and helpful.

A word about the figures in the book: This book was first published in 1974 and has been an enormous success. It was completely revised and updated in 1980. Hundreds of people have written to say how much it helped them lose weight, and it is used in numerous organized weight-loss clinics. We are convinced it is the most comprehensive and easy-to-use guide available. It has sold over a million copies. Since the last revision, some of the calorie counts have changed because of new analyses or reformulation of products and new products have been introduced. We simply did the book over from start to finish. Of course, some of the calorie counts are the same or similar, since the calories in many basic foods, such as milk, cheese, bread, as well as alcoholic drinks, don't change much. However, we have greatly expanded some of the fresh food sections, such as fish, poultry and meat to make it even easier for you to determine calories in fresh foods. A few companies we contacted did not have new information; thus we used their previous figures.

The figures bearing brand names in this book were provided by food companies and are the latest the company advised us were available. Only a few companies we contacted declined to send available information; a few companies reported they did not have such information and a few said they were in the process of doing new analyses that were not ready at the time of publication.

In virtually all cases we used the serving sizes indicated by the companies; in a few cases we changed the serving size and corresponding calorie counts. For example, we converted a "serving size" of two slices of bread or bacon to one slice.

We used the calorie figures as provided by the companies. Many companies, notably those using nutritional labeling, provide calorie counts rounded off. For example, a food with 109 calories, according to a chemical analysis, may be rounded up to 110. On the other hand, many companies still report figures without rounding off, which accounts for more precise counts. Since similar foods may vary slightly—by a few calories—anyway, such rounding off is insignificant. Some companies have asked us to point out that their figures are the best average calculations or analyses they have on specific products, but because of normal variations beyond their control, there may be ever-so-slight variations from batch to batch for the same manufacturer. Even such factors as seasonal conditions or soil composition may influence final food nutritional values.

More companies are now putting nutritional labels on their foods. Still, it is difficult to make comparisons among various brand name foods without running all around the supermarket. Thus, one benefit of this book: you can pick out the lower calorie items *before* you go shopping.

Most calorie counts remain exceedingly stable over the years. However, occasionally a food maker will change the composition of a product, changing the calorie count. In that case, if the food is labeled, the calorie count on the label will differ from that in this book. To avoid confusion, if such contradictions exist, you should assume the food composition has changed and the label is correct. The accuracy of a food company's labeling and dissemination of nutritional information is regulated by the federal Food and Drug Administration, and a company would be subject to severe penalties for putting out a food label that is grossly inaccurate.

All the calorie counts without any brand name or company attribution are from the U.S. Department of Agriculture. Here, too, some calculations were done to make sure the figures were in the most convenient form.

To sum up, the new revised *All-In-One Calorie Counter* will provide you with the latest, most accurate, comprehensive data available about fresh foods, processed foods and restaurant foods.

Jean Carper

How To Use This Book

The most important organizational fact about *The All-In-One Calorie Counter*, as you will quickly see, is that it is alphabetized for easy use according to food categories. That is, you don't have to look in the front of the book under B for bean soup and then flip to the T's to find out if tomato soup is lower in calories. The supermarket portion of the book runs through the alphabet, starting with baby food and ending with yogurt. After that, you will find our new, special section on restaurant foods, including fast-food chains.

All the breads are listed together in the B section, all the fruits are grouped together under F, the vegetables under V and so on. Simply by looking at the Contents in the front of the book, you can quickly spot which category a food is in and turn directly to that section. You will then find the foods alphabetized within the sections. Some foods, to be sure, just don't fit easily into categories, and rather than force them into some artificial grouping, we have listed them alphabetically too, even though there may be only one or two of a kind; for example, baking powder and thickeners have listings of their own.

In other words, the book is akin to a dictionary—with headings at the top of each page, too, to help you out. If you get stuck and can't decide where a food might be, just consult the index.

We have tried to standardize the language and the serving sizes as much as possible to make them useful, but here again we haven't strained the point. We have tried to be practical. For example, under cereals you won't find all of them in either 1-cup or ½-cup portions. The reason: Cereals vary greatly in their density and weight. Thus, the typical 1-ounce serving size for cereals varies in cup measurements, depending on the type of cereal. An ounce of puffed rice will fill a 1-cup measuring cup, but an ounce of heavier All-Bran fills about ⅓ of a measuring cup. In all cases, we have followed the manufacturers' recommendations and provided single-serving sizes they believe appropriate.

For listings using the word "prepared," the calories are based on the assumption that the food has been prepared according to the manufacturer's directions. If you alter the preparation, for example, by adding meat drippings instead of water to a gravy mix or using milk when water is called for on the package or adding other embellishments of your own, you must figure in these extras. Whenever milk is called for in a preparation, we assume it is whole milk—not skim or nonfat or condensed milk. If you use other ingredients—either raising or lowering the calorie content in the finished product—you should make provision for them.

In most cases, companies prefer to tell you how many calories are in the finished prepared product—for example, a cup of pudding from a pudding mix—because it is rare that the powder would be used in any other way. But in some instances you will find the calorie count for the dry mix only—before preparation. That way, if you want to add another ingredient to your mix, you can do so and add up the extra calories. Also on this note: Whenever you merely add water to a mix, you are not adding calories—for example, when you prepare a Lipton's dry mix soup. If you use the dry soup mix in any other fashion, say as a dip mix, there are the same number of calories in the dry mix as in the cup of prepared soup.

In keeping with our determination to make this book easy to use, we have taken due note of the power of identity of brand names. Whenever possible, without interfering with the organization, we have used brand names for quick identification. Thus, when you look up a certain cookie, cracker or cereal, you don't have to peruse the whole list searching for a description of your cookie. We don't have Cheez-Its listed under "Crackers, cheese"; it is alphabetized simply under Cheez-Its. Similarly, we have Oreo cookies under O and not under "Chocolate creme sandwich." The same goes for Froot Loops (under F in the cereal section). At the same time, it was not always possible to do this without creating a chaotic organization, and in many cases the only identifying factor is a description of the product (chocolate chip cookies, for example) and the name of the manufacturer.

Within the listings, we repeat the measurements frequently. However, on items such as cookies, crackers and frozen dinners, where the portion size is almost always one cracker, cookie or complete dinner, we have simply noted the portion at the head of the section. This has also been done on fairly short listings.

To avoid confusion, whenever possible, we have stated the measurement in the most easily used terms: cups, tablespoons and fluid ounces for liquids and items such as canned fruits and vegetables; and weight ounces for items such as cheese and frozen fish filets. On some of the candy bars, we have noted the calories per ounce, so you can figure calories if the sizes of the candy bars change. Since many candy companies report calories for their current-size bars, we urge you to check the weight of the candy bar on the wrapper to be sure it corresponds with the weight noted in this book.

A few other words of advice: On certain basic products, even though the brand names differ, the calorie counts are essentially the same. For example, the caloric content of milk, cheese, butter and oils depends primarily on the fat content. That is why all standard margarines have the same calorie count: 100 per tablespoon. Cheeses of the same type, for example cheddar, have virtually the same fat content no matter who makes it. Thus, you can assume that the calorie counts for such basic natural cheeses are standard despite the brand name. On the other hand, when companies make their own cheese products or low-calorie cheeses and spreads, the calorie count depends upon their special recipes.

In this revision, we have retained our "health foods" section, even though such foods have become increasingly popular and widely purchased. The line between such "health and natural" foods and general foods is growing less clear, as Americans become more nutrition-conscious and many food companies respond by formulating and promoting so-called "health foods." Even so, some companies and some ingredients, such as carob, are still closely associated in the public's mind with "health and natural" foods and we think it is easier for readers who want to find those products to look them up in a special section. Some of the products are still sold only in specialty or "health food" stores. However, we have to admit that some such foods may have slipped over into other sections. So if you don't find them one place, check elsewhere.

For our readers who have used the previous editions, here is what's new about this revision. It has many more items both by brand name and generic. We are listing nearly 9000 foods compared with 5500 in our last edition. The sections on fish, meat, poultry, candy, beers and wine, snacks of all types, doughnuts and "health and natural" foods have been especially expanded. We are listing calorie counts from a different database at the U.S. Department of Agriculture than we used previously, thus drawing in hundreds of generic foods, such as raw tuna for sushi lovers and Cornish game hens as well as chicken prepared many different ways.

For the first time, we are listing the Harmony brand name candies and snacks commonly found in supermarket bins; the pre-prepared specialty salads made by the Orval Kent Company and often found in supermarket deli sections; Haagen Dazs ice cream and the tofu-based frozen dessert called Toffuti; a long list of regional as well as national brand beers; and the Pritikin low-calorie, low-fat products. And most exciting, we have added a whole new section on restaurant foods, made up of an expanded list of fast-foods chains, including for the first time Wendy's, Ponderosa, Jack in the Box and Roy Rogers, as well as common dishes, such as all kinds of sandwiches, chicken cacciatore, Japanese sushi and crab imperial, found in a variety of types of restaurants, American as well as ethnic. We believe that this section alone gives our readers a monumental plus in their calorie-counting capabilities.

Despite our best efforts, there is no way we can save you from doing some figuring on your own, simply because no one, including yourself, wants to eat the food company's designated serving size all the time. And obviously, when you use your own recipes, you can obtain the calorie counts for only the basic ingredients. You have to take it from there.

For doing your own conversions, here is an equivalency table that may help:

$$1 \text{ tablespoon} = 3 \text{ teaspoons}$$
$$2 \text{ tablespoons} = 1 \text{ fluid ounce}$$
$$4 \text{ tablespoons} = \tfrac{1}{4} \text{ cup}$$
$$5\tfrac{1}{3} \text{ tablespoons} = \tfrac{1}{3} \text{ cup}$$
$$16 \text{ tablespoons} = 1 \text{ cup}$$
$$1 \text{ cup} = 8 \text{ fluid ounces}$$
$$= 1 \text{ pint}$$
$$2 \text{ pints} = 1 \text{ quart}$$
$$1 \text{ pound} = 16 \text{ ounces}$$

Happy calorie counting!

Abbreviations

art	artificial
diam	diameter
fl	fluid
in	inch
lb	pound
med	medium
oz	ounce
pkg	package
swt	sweetened
tbsp	tablespoon
tsp	teaspoon
unswt	unsweetened
w	with
wo	without

Baby Food

BAKED GOODS

	CALORIES
1 piece:	
Biscuits / **Gerber**	50
Cookie, animal shaped / **Gerber**	30
Cookie, arrowroot / **Gerber**	25
Pretzel / **Gerber**	25
Zwieback toast / **Gerber**	30

STRAINED BABY FOODS

Cereal: 1 jar

Mixed w apples and bananas / **Heinz**	100
Mixed w applesauce and bananas / **Beechnut** Stage 2	80
Mixed w applesauce and bananas / **Gerber**	90
Oatmeal w applesauce and bananas / **Beechnut** Stage 2	90
Oatmeal w applesauce and bananas / **Gerber**	80
Rice w applesauce and bananas / **Beechnut** Stage 2	90
Rice w apples and bananas / **Heinz**	110
Rice w applesauce and bananas / **Gerber**	100

CALORIES

Cereal, Dry: ½ ounce unless noted (½ ounce is about 6 tablespoons dry)

Barley / **Beechnut** Stage 1	50
Barley: 4 tbsp / **Gerber**	60
Barley / **Heinz**	50
Brown rice / **Health Valley**	50
Hi-Protein / **Beechnut** Stage 2	50
High Protein: 4 tbsp / **Gerber**	50
Hi-Protein / **Heinz**	50
High Protein w apple and orange: 4 tbsp / **Gerber**	60
Mixed / **Beechnut** Stage 2	50
Mixed: 4 tbsp / **Gerber**	60
Mixed / **Heinz**	60
Mixed w banana: 4 tbsp / **Gerber**	60
Oatmeal / **Beechnut** Stage 1	50
Oatmeal: 4 tbsp / **Gerber**	50
Oatmeal / **Heinz**	50
Oatmeal w banana: 4 tbsp / **Gerber**	60
Rice / **Beechnut** Stage 1	60
Rice: 4 tbsp / **Gerber**	60
Rice / **Heinz**	60
Rice w banana: 4 tbsp / **Gerber**	60
Sprouted baby cereal / **Health Valley**	50

Desserts: 1 jar

Apple Betty / **Beechnut** Stage 2	90
Banana apple dessert / **Gerber**	100
Cottage cheese w pineapple / **Beechnut** Stage 2	110
Dutch apple dessert / **Gerber**	110
Dutch apple dessert / **Heinz**	90
Fruit dessert / **Beechnut** Stage 2	100
Fruit dessert / **Gerber**	100
Fruit dessert / **Heinz**	90
Hawaiian Delight / **Gerber**	120
Mixed fruit yogurt / **Beechnut** Stage 2	110
Peach cobbler / **Gerber**	100
Peach cobbler / **Heinz**	110
Peaches and yogurt / **Beechnut** Stage 2	100

CALORIES

Pineapple dessert / **Beechnut** Stage 2	100
Pineapple-orange / **Heinz**	90
Pudding	
Apple custard / **Beechnut** Stage 2	100
Banana / **Heinz**	120
Banana custard / **Beechnut** Stage 2	90
Cherry vanilla / **Gerber**	100
Chocolate custard / **Gerber**	110
Custard / **Heinz**	100
Orange / **Gerber**	120
Vanilla custard / **Beechnut** Stage 2	100
Vanilla custard / **Gerber**	110
Raspberry dessert w nonfat yogurt /	
Gerber	80
Tutti-frutti / **Heinz**	100

Fruit: 1 jar

Apples and apricots / **Heinz**	70
Apple blueberry / **Gerber**	80
Apples and cranberries / **Heinz**	90
Apples and grapes / **Beechnut** Stage 2	110
Apples, oranges and bananas / **Beechnut**	
Stage 2	90
Apples, peaches and strawberries / **Beechnut**	
Stage 2	100
Apples and pears / **Heinz**	80
Apples, pears and bananas / **Beechnut** Stage 2	100
Apples, pears and pineapples / **Beechnut**	
Stage 2	100
Apples and strawberries / **Beechnut** Stage 2	100
Applesauce	
Gerber	70
Heinz	70
Beechnut Stage 1	60
and apricots / **Beechnut** Stage 2	60
and apricots / **Gerber**	80
and bananas / **Beechnut** Stage 2	60
and cherries / **Beechnut** Stage 2	70
w pineapple / **Gerber**	60
Apricots w tapioca / **Beechnut** Stage 2	80

CALORIES

Apricots w tapioca / **Gerber**	100
Apricots w tapioca / **Heinz**	80
Bananas	
Beechnut Stage 1	100
w tapioca / **Gerber**	100
w tapioca / **Heinz**	110
w tapioca and pineapple / **Beechnut**	
Stage 2	80
w pineapple and tapioca / **Gerber**	70
w pineapple and tapioca / **Heinz**	90
Guava w tapioca / **Beechnut** Stage 2	100
Island Fruits / **Beechnut** Stage 2	90
Mango w tapioca / **Beechnut** Stage 2	90
Peaches	
Gerber	100
Heinz	50
Beechnut Stage 1	60
Pears	
Gerber	70
Heinz	70
Beechnut Stage 1	70
and pineapple / **Beechnut** Stage 2	100
and pineapple / **Gerber**	80
and pineapple / **Heinz**	80
Plums w tapioca	
Beechnut Stage 2	100
Gerber	100
Heinz	80
Prunes w tapioca	
Beechnut Stage 2	100
Gerber	110
Heinz	120

Juices, Strained: 1 jar or can unless noted

Apple	
Beechnut Stage 1	60
Beechnut Stage 2 / 4 fl oz	60
Gerber	60
Heinz	60
Apple-apricot: 4.2 fl oz / **Heinz**	70

CALORIES

Apple-banana / **Gerber**	60
Apple-cherry / **Beechnut** Stage 2	50
Apple-cherry / **Gerber**	60
Apple-cherry: 4.2 fl oz / **Heinz**	60
Apple-cranberry / **Beechnut** Stage 2	60
Apple-grape / **Beechnut** Stage 2	60
Apple-grape / **Gerber**	60
Apple-grape: 4.2 fl oz / **Heinz**	70
Apple-peach / **Beechnut** Stage 2	60
Apple-peach / **Gerber**	60
Apple-peach: 4.2 fl oz / **Heinz**	60
Apple-pineapple: 4.2 fl oz / **Heinz**	60
Apple-plum / **Gerber**	60
Apple-prune / **Gerber**	60
Apple-prune: 4.2 fl oz / **Heinz**	70
Grape / **Beechnut** Stage 1	80
Juice Plus / **Beechnut** Stage 2	60
Mixed fruit / **Beechnut** Stage 2	60
Mixed fruit / **Gerber**	70
Mixed fruit: 4.2 fl oz / **Heinz**	70
Orange / **Beechnut** Stage 2	60
Orange / **Gerber**	70
Orange: 4.2 fl oz / **Heinz**	60
Orange-apple / **Gerber**	70
Orange-apple-banana: 4.2 fl oz / **Heinz**	60
Orange-apricot / **Gerber**	70
Orange-pineapple / **Gerber**	80
Pear / **Beechnut** Stage 1	60
Tropical blend / **Beechnut** Stage 2	70

Main Dishes, Strained: 1 jar

Beef Dinner Supreme / **Beechnut** Stage 2	120
Beef and egg noodles / **Heinz**	60
Beef noodle w vegetables / **Beechnut** Stage 2	90
Beef and noodles w vegetables / **Gerber**	90
Beef w vegetables / **Gerber** High Meat Dinner	120
Beef w vegetables / **Heinz** High Meat Dinner	100
Cereal and egg yolk / **Gerber**	70
Chicken and noodles / **Gerber**	80
Chicken-noodle / **Heinz**	70

Chicken-noodle w vegetables / **Beechnut** Stage 2	80
Chicken-rice w vegetables / **Beechnut** Stage 2	90
Chicken w vegetables / **Gerber** High Meat Dinner	130
Chicken w vegetables / **Heinz** High Meat Dinner	110
Chicken soup / **Heinz**	70
Chicken soup, cream of / **Gerber**	80
Cottage cheese w pineapple / **Gerber** High Meat Dinner	130
Ham w vegetables / **Gerber** High Meat Dinner	100
Macaroni and cheese / **Gerber**	90
Macaroni, tomato and beef / **Beechnut** Stage 2	90
Macaroni-tomato w beef / **Gerber**	80
Macaroni, tomatoes and beef / **Heinz**	70
Turkey	
Beechnut Stage 2	100
and rice w vegetables / **Gerber**	80
and rice w vegetables / **Beechnut** Stage 2	70
and rice w vegetables / **Heinz**	60
w vegetables / **Gerber** High Meat Dinner	130
w vegetables / **Heinz** High Meat Dinner	120
Veal w vegetables / **Gerber** High Meat Dinner	80
Vegetables	
and bacon / **Gerber**	100
and bacon / **Heinz**	80
and beef / **Beechnut** Stage 2	90
and beef / **Gerber**	80
and beef / **Heinz**	70
and chicken / **Beechnut** Stage 2	90
and chicken / **Gerber**	70
dumplings and beef / **Heinz**	70
and ham / **Beechnut** Stage 2	80
and ham / **Gerber**	80
and ham / **Heinz**	60
w noodles and chicken / **Heinz**	90
w noodles and turkey / **Heinz**	60
and lamb / **Beechnut** Stage 2	80
and lamb / **Gerber**	80

CALORIES

and lamb / **Heinz**	60
and liver / **Gerber**	60
and turkey / **Gerber**	70

Meat and Eggs: 1 jar

Beef / **Gerber**	90
Beef and beef broth / **Beechnut** Stage 1	120
Beef and beef broth / **Heinz**	130
Beef w beef heart / **Gerber**	90
Beef liver / **Gerber**	90
Chicken / **Gerber**	140
Chicken and chicken broth / **Beechnut** Stage 1	110
Chicken and chicken broth / **Heinz**	130
Egg yolks / **Gerber**	180
Ham / **Gerber**	110
Lamb / **Gerber**	100
Lamb and lamb broth / **Beechnut** Stage 1	130
Lamb and lamb broth / **Heinz**	150
Liver and liver broth / **Heinz**	90
Pork / **Gerber**	110
Turkey / **Gerber**	120
Turkey and turkey broth / **Beechnut** Stage 1	120
Turkey and turkey broth / **Heinz**	120
Veal / **Gerber**	90
Veal and veal broth / **Beechnut** Stage 1	120
Veal and veal broth / **Heinz**	130

Vegetables: 1 jar

Beets / **Gerber**	50
Beets / **Heinz**	50
Carrots / **Gerber**	35
Carrots / **Heinz**	25
Carrots / **Beechnut** Stage 1	40
Corn, creamed / **Beechnut** Stage 2	70
Corn, creamed / **Gerber**	90
Corn, creamed / **Heinz**	90
Garden / **Beechnut** Stage 2	60
Garden / **Gerber**	50
Green beans / **Gerber**	40
Green beans / **Heinz**	40

CALORIES

Green beans / **Beechnut** Stage 1	40
Mixed / **Beechnut** Stage 2	50
Mixed / **Gerber**	60
Mixed / **Heinz**	60
Peas / **Gerber**	60
Peas, creamed / **Heinz**	80
Peas / **Beechnut** Stage 1	70
Peas and carrots / **Beechnut** Stage 2	60
Spinach, creamed / **Gerber**	60
Squash / **Beechnut** Stage 1	30
Squash / **Gerber**	40
Squash / **Heinz**	45
Sweet potatoes / **Beechnut** Stage 1	70
Sweet potatoes / **Gerber**	80
Sweet potatoes / **Heinz**	90

JUNIOR BABY FOODS

Cereal: 1 jar

Mixed w applesauce and bananas / **Gerber**	140
Oatmeal w applesauce and bananas / **Gerber**	130
Rice w mixed fruit / **Gerber**	170

Desserts: 1 jar

Banana / **Beechnut** Stage 3	160
Banana-apple / **Gerber**	170
Cottage cheese w pineapple / **Beechnut** Stage 3	180
Dutch apple / **Gerber**	160
Dutch apple / **Gerber** Chunky	140
Dutch apple / **Heinz**	150
Fruit / **Beechnut** Stage 3	170
Fruit / **Gerber**	170
Fruit / **Heinz**	160
Hawaiian Delight / **Gerber**	190
Mixed fruit yogurt / **Beechnut** Stage 3	180
Peach cobbler / **Gerber**	160
Peach cobbler / **Gerber** Chunky	140
Pineapple-orange / **Heinz**	140

Pudding
Banana custard / **Beechnut** Stage 3	170
Cherry vanilla / **Gerber**	160
Custard / **Heinz**	170
Vanilla custard / **Beechnut** Stage 3	150
Vanilla custard / **Gerber**	190

Raspberry w nonfat yogurt / **Gerber**   150
Tutti-Frutti / **Heinz**   150

Fruit: 1 jar

Apples
and apricots / **Heinz**	110
and blueberries / **Gerber**	120
and cranberries w tapioca / **Heinz**	140
and grapes / **Beechnut** Stage 3	190
mandarin oranges and bananas / **Beechnut** Stage 3	150
peaches and strawberries / **Beechnut** Stage 3	160
and pears / **Heinz**	130
pears and bananas / **Beechnut** Stage 3	160
pears and pineapples / **Beechnut** Stage 3	160
and strawberries / **Beechnut** Stage 3	160

Applesauce
Gerber	100
Heinz	110
and apple bits / **Beechnut** Stage 3	100
and apricots / **Beechnut** Stage 3	90
and apricots / **Gerber**	110
and bananas / **Beechnut** Stage 3	110
and cherries / **Beechnut** Stage 3	110

Apricots w tapioca / **Beechnut** Stage 3   140
Apricots w tapioca / **Gerber**   160
Apricots w tapioca / **Heinz**   150
Bananas
w tapioca / **Beechnut** Stage 3	130
w tapioca / **Gerber**	150
w tapioca / **Gerber** Chunky	130
w tapioca / **Heinz**	180
w pineapple and tapioca / **Gerber**	120

CALORIES

w pineapple and tapioca / **Heinz**	150
Island fruits / **Beechnut** Stage 3	150
Peaches / **Beechnut** Stage 3	150
Peaches / **Gerber**	160
Peaches / **Heinz**	90
Pears	
Gerber	120
Heinz	120
Beechnut Stage 3	140
and pineapple / **Beechnut** Stage 3	160
and pineapple / **Gerber**	120
Plums w tapioca / **Gerber**	170
Prunes w tapioca / **Gerber**	180

Fruit Juices: 4 fluid ounces

Apple / **Gerber** Toddler	60
Apple-cherry / **Gerber** Toddler	60
Apple-grape / **Gerber** Toddler	60
Mixed fruit / **Gerber** Toddler	60

Main Dishes: 1 jar

Beef	
Beechnut Stage 3	190
w noodles and vegetables / **Gerber**	140
w noodles and vegetables / **Gerber** Chunky	120
w noodles and vegetables / **Beechnut** Stage 3	140
Stew / **Beechnut** Table Time	130
w vegetables / **Gerber** High Meat Dinner	130
w vegetables and cereal / **Heinz** High Meat Dinner	130
Cereal and egg yolk / **Gerber**	110
Chicken	
and noodles / **Gerber**	120
and noodles / **Heinz**	150
and noodles w vegetables / **Beechnut** Stage 3	130
w vegetables / **Gerber** High Meat Dinner	130
w vegetables / **Heinz** High Meat Dinner	120

CALORIES

Soup w stars / **Beechnut** Table Time	180
Egg noodles and beef / **Heinz**	120
Ham w vegetables / **Gerber**	
High Meat Dinner	110
Macaroni	
and cheese / **Gerber**	140
w tomatoes and beef / **Beechnut** Stage 3	150
w tomatoes and beef / **Gerber**	130
w tomatoes and beef / **Heinz**	110
Noodles and chicken / **Gerber** Chunky	110
Pasta squares in meat sauce / **Beechnut**	
Table Time	150
Spaghetti	
Rings in meat sauce / **Beechnut**	
Table Time	150
w tomato and beef / **Beechnut** Stage 3	150
w tomato sauce and beef / **Gerber**	150
w tomato sauce and meat / **Heinz**	130
Split peas with ham / **Gerber**	150
Turkey	
Beechnut Stage 3	180
and rice w vegetables / **Gerber**	140
and rice w vegetables / **Beechnut** Stage 3	120
and rice w vegetables / **Heinz**	110
w vegetables / **Gerber** High Meat Dinner	130
w vegetables / **Heinz** High Meat Dinner	130
Veal w vegetables / **Gerber** High Meat Dinner	90
Vegetables	
and bacon / **Beechnut** Stage 3	180
and bacon / **Gerber**	170
and bacon / **Heinz**	130
and beef / **Beechnut** Stage 3	130
and beef / **Gerber**	140
and beef / **Gerber** Chunky	120
and beef / **Heinz**	120
and chicken / **Beechnut** Stage 3	130
and chicken / **Gerber**	110
and chicken / **Gerber** Chunky	120
dumplings and beef / **Heinz**	110
and ham / **Gerber**	140
and ham / **Gerber** Chunky	120

CALORIES

and ham / **Heinz**	120
and lamb / **Gerber**	130
and lamb / **Beechnut** Stage 3	140
and liver / **Gerber**	90
w noodles and chicken / **Heinz**	140
w noodles and turkey / **Heinz**	110
Soup / **Beechnut** Table Time	70
Stew w chicken / **Beechnut** Table Time	160
and turkey / **Gerber**	90
and turkey / **Gerber** Chunky	120

Meat: 1 jar

Beef / **Gerber**	100
Beef and beef broth / **Heinz**	130
Chicken	
Gerber	140
and chicken broth / **Heinz**	130
Sticks / **Gerber**	120
Ham / **Gerber**	120
Lamb / **Gerber**	100
and lamb broth / **Heinz**	150
Meat sticks / **Gerber**	110
Turkey / **Gerber**	130
Turkey sticks / **Gerber**	120
Veal / **Gerber**	100
Veal and veal broth / **Heinz**	130·

Vegetables: 1 jar

Carrots / **Beechnut** Stage 3	60
Carrots / **Gerber**	60
Carrots / **Heinz**	55
Corn, creamed / **Gerber**	130
Corn, creamed / **Heinz**	160
Garden / **Beechnut** Stage 3	100
Green beans / **Beechnut** Stage 3	60
Green beans, creamed / **Gerber**	100
Green beans, creamed / **Heinz**	90
Mixed / **Beechnut** Stage 3	90
Mixed / **Gerber**	90
Peas / **Gerber**	140

CALORIES

Peas, creamed / **Heinz**	140
Potatoes, scalloped / **Beechnut** Stage 3	160
Squash / **Gerber**	70
Sweet potatoes / **Beechnut** Stage 3	120
Sweet potatoes / **Gerber**	140
Sweet potatoes / **Heinz**	140

Baking Powder

CALORIES

Canned: 1 tsp / most brands	5

Beer, Ale, Malt Liquor

CALORIES

12 fluid ounces

ALE

Duke	138
Koehler	138
McSorley's Cream Ale	176
Red Cap	160
Scheidt 20th Century	176
Tiger Head	176

BEER

Amstel Light	95
Andeker	160
Bavarian	138
Bavarian Light	98
Bergheim	138

CALORIES

Black Label	148
Break L.A.	116
Budweiser	145
Budweiser Light	108
Busch	145
Christian Schmidt Classic	140
Christian Schmidt Select	150
Coors	140
Coors Light	105
Duke	138
Erlanger	162
Gablinger's Light	98
George Killian's Irish Red	173
Goebel	138
Golden Lager (**Coors**)	147
Heilman	145
Heileman Light	93
Heileman Near Beer	60
Heileman Premium	155
Herman Joseph's	158
Kaier's	138
Knickerbocker	138
Koehler	138
L.A. (Anheuser Busch)	110
L.A. (Miller)	86
Meisterbrau	149
Meisterbrau Light	116
Michelob	162
Michelob Light	134
Miller High Life	150
Miller Lite	96
Milwaukee's Best	132
Natural Light	110
Old Milwaukee	145
Old Milwaukee Light	120
Olde Pub	138
Olympia	140
Olympia Gold Light	70
Otlieb's	138
Pabst Blue Ribbon	150
Pabst Extra Light	70

CALORIES

Pabst Light	100
Piels Draft Style	138
Plank Road	150
P.O.C.	138
Primo	142
Prior Double Dark	175
Reading	138
Rheingold	148
Rheingold Extra Light	98
Rock & Roll	138
Schaefer	138
Schaefer Light	112
Schaefer Low Alcohol	92
Scheidt	138
Schlitz	145
Schlitz Light	96
Schmidt's	148
Schmidt's Light	98
Schmidt's Bock	172
Signature	166
Silver Thunder	190
Strohs Light	115
Strohs Premium	142
Tuborg USA	148
U Save A Lot (USA)	138
Valley Forge	138

MALT LIQUOR

Coqui 900	193
Golden Hawk	168
Heilman	155
Schlitz	177

Biscuits

	CALORIES
Mix: 2 oz / **Arrowhead Mills**	100
Mix: 2 oz / **Bisquick**	240

BISCUITS, REFRIGERATED

1 biscuit

Ballard Oven Ready	50
Hungry Jack Butter Tastin' Flaky	90
Hungry Jack Flaky	85
Merico Butter Flavored	95
Merico Butter-Me-Not	95
Merico Homestyle	50
Merico Mountain Man	95
Merico Texas Style	95
Merico Texas Style Butter Flavored	105
Merico Texas Style Flaky	110
1869 Brand	100
Pillsbury Country Style	50
Pillsbury Good 'n Buttery Big Country	95
Baking Powder / **1869 Brand**	100
Baking Powder / **Pillsbury** Tenderflake	55
Butter / **Pillsbury**	50
Buttermilk	
Ballard Oven Ready	50
1869 Brand	100
Hungry Jack Extra Rich	55
Hungry Jack Flaky	85
Hungry Jack Fluffy	90
Merico Weight Watchers	45
Pillsbury	50
Pillsbury Big Country	100
Pillsbury Big Premium Heat 'n Eat	140
Pillsbury Extra Lights	55

	CALORIES
Pillsbury Heat 'n Eat	85
Pillsbury Tenderflake	55
Weight Watchers	40
Wheat / **Merico** Weight Watchers	45
Wheat / **Weight Watchers**	40

Bread

1 slice unless noted

	CALORIES
Apple w cinnamon / **Pepperidge Farm**	70
Barley bran / **Earth Grains**	70
Bran w diced raisins / **Pepperidge Farm**	70
Bran 'N honey / **Country Hearth**	70
Bran'nola / **Arnold**	90
Bran'nola Hearty / **Arnold**	105
Brown, canned: ½-in slice / **B & M**	80
Brown, canned w raisins: ½-in slice / **B & M**	80
Buckwheat	
Butternut	80
Weber's	80
Buttermilk	
Butternut	80
Country Hearth	80
Country Hearth Old Fashioned	70
Eddy's	80
Millbrook	80
Sweetheart	80
Weber's	80
Cinnamon / **Pepperidge Farm**	80
Cinnamon apple and walnut / **Pepperidge Farm**	80
Cinnamon-raisin / **Butternut**	80
Corn and molasses / **Pepperidge Farm** Thin Sliced	70
Dark / **Hollywood**	70
Date and nut loaf: 1 oz / **Crosse & Blackwell**	65
Date walnut / **Pepperidge Farm**	75
Earth bread / **Earth Grains**	70

European butter sesame / **Country Hearth**	70
French / **Earth Grains**	70
French: 2 oz / **Pepperidge Farm**	140
French: 2 oz / **Pepperidge Farm** Brown & Serve	140
French / **Wonder**	75
French style: 2 oz / **Arnold Francisco**	160
French style: 2 oz / **Pepperidge Farm**	150
Granola / **Country Hearth**	70
Honey bran: 1½-lb loaf / **Pepperidge Farm**	95
Honey and buttermilk / **Earth Grains**	80
Honey grain	
Colonial	70
Kilpatrick's	70
Rainbo	70
Honey and oat / **Country Hearth**	70
Honey oatberry / **Earth Grains**	70
Honey wheatberry / **Arnold**	90
Honey wheatberry / **Earth Grains**	70
Honey wheatberry / **Home Pride**	70
Honey wheatberry / **Pepperidge Farm**	70
Honey whole grain	
Butternut	80
Eddy's	80
Millbrook	80
Sweetheart	80
Weber's	80
Italian: 2 oz / **Pepperidge Farm Brown & Serve**	150
Low protein: about 1.1 oz /	
Nutri-Dyne Aproten	78
Multigrain	
A&P	70
Earth Grains	70
Pepperidge Farm Very Thin Sliced	40
Oat / **Bran'nola** Country	110
Oatmeal	
Pepperidge Farm 1½-lb loaf	70
Pepperidge Farm Thin Sliced	70
Onion / **Pepperidge Farm** Party Slices	15
Orange and raisin / **Pepperidge Farm**	75
Potato	
Eddy's	70

CALORIES

Sweeetheart	70
Protein / **Thomas'**	50
Pumpernickel	
Arnold	75
Levy's Real	85
Pepperidge Farm Family	80
Pepperidge Farm Party Slices	18
Raisin / **Earth Grains**	80
Raisin w cinnamon / **Pepperidge Farm**	75
Raisin tea / **Arnold**	70
Rye	
Butternut	70
Country Hearth Deli	70
Earth Grains Light	70
Earth Grains Light, Very Thin	70
Earth Grains Party: 1 oz	70
Earth Grains Pumpernickel Rye	70
Eddy's	70
Millbrook	70
Pepperidge Farm Family	85
Pepperidge Farm Party	15
Pepperidge Farm Sandwich 1½-lb loaf	95
Pepperidge Farm Very Thin Sliced	45
Sweetheart	70
Dijon mustard / **Pepperidge Farm**	55
Dill, seeded / **Arnold**	75
Jewish / **Pepperidge Farm**	90
Jewish, seeded / **Arnold**	75
Jewish, seeded / **Levy's** Real	80
Jewish, unseeded / **Arnold**	75
Jewish, unseeded / **Levy's** Real	80
Melba thin / **Arnold**	50
Seedless / **Pepperidge Farm**	80
Weight Watchers	40
Seven grain / **Home Pride**	70
Sour dough	
DiCarlo	70
Earth Grains Mini Loaf	40
Sour dough French / **Earth Grains**	70
Vienna / **Pepperidge Farm**	75
Vienna French: 2 oz / **Arnold** Francisco	160

Wheat

Arnold Brick Oven 1-lb loaf	60
Arnold Brick Oven 2-lb loaf	80
Arnold Brick Oven Small Family 8-oz loaf	60
Arnold Measure Up Whole Wheat	40
Butternut	70
Colonial	70
Colonial Whole Wheat	70
Country Hearth Butter Split Top	70
Country Hearth Nature's Wheat	70
Country Hearth Sandwich	70
Country Hearth 7 Whole Grain	80
Earth Grains Gold 'N Bran	70
Earth Grains Lite 35	70
Earth Grains 100% Whole Wheat	70
Earth Grains Very Thin	70
Eddy's	70
Fresh Horizons	50
Fresh & Natural	70
Home Pride Butter Top	75
Home Pride 100% Whole Wheat	70
Kilpatrick's	70
Kilpatrick's Whole Wheat	70
Pepperidge Farm 1½-lb loaf	95
Pepperidge Farm 2-lb loaf	70
Pepperidge Farm Sandwich	55
Pepperidge Farm Thin Sliced Whole Wheat	65
Pepperidge Farm Very Thin Sliced Whole Wheat	45
Rainbo	70
Rainbo Whole Wheat	70
Roman Meal	70
Sweetheart	70
Weber's	70
Weight Watchers Thin Sliced	40
Wonder Family	75
Wonder 100% Whole Wheat	70

Wheat, cracked

Butternut	70
Earth Grains	70
Earth Grains Mini Loaf	70

	CALORIES
Eddy's	70
Pepperidge Farm Thin Sliced	70
Sweetheart	70
Weber's	70
Wonder	75
Wheat, honey	
Home Pride	70
Wheat, light fiber	
Butternut	50
Millbrook	50
Sweetheart	50
Wheat, sprouted	
Arnold	65
Pepperidge Farm Sliced	70
Wheat, stoneground	
Earth Grains	70
100% Whole Wheat / **Arnold**	55
100% Whole Wheat / **Country Hearth**	70
Wheatberry	
Country Hearth	70
Home Pride	70
Wheat germ / **Pepperidge Farm** Thin Sliced	65
White	
Arnold Brick Oven 1-lb loaf	65
Arnold Brick Oven 2-lb loaf	85
Arnold Brick Oven Small Family: 8 oz	65
Arnold Country White	95
Arnold Hearthstone	85
Arnold Measure Up	40
Bran'nola Old Style / **Arnold**	105
Butternut	70
Colonial	70
Colonial Country Meal	80
Country Hearth Butter Split Top	70
Country Hearth D'Italia	70
Country Hearth Old Fashioned	70
Earth Grains Country White Mini	70
Earth Grains Lite 35	70
Earth Grains Salt Free Sandwich	80
Earth Grains Very Thin	80
Fresh Horizons	50

CALORIES

Hillbilly	70
Hollywood Light	70
Home Pride Butter Top	75
Kilpatrick's	70
Kilpatrick's Country Meal	80
Pepperidge Farm 1½-lb loaf	95
Pepperidge Farm Large Family	75
Pepperidge Farm Sandwich	65
Pepperidge Farm Thin Sliced	75
Pepperidge Farm Very Thin Sliced	45
Pepperidge Farm Toasting White	85
Rainbo	70
Rainbo Country Meal	80
Sweetheart	70
Weber's	70
Weight Watchers Thin Sliced	40
Wonder	70
w buttermilk / **Wonder**	75
w cracked wheat / **Pepperidge Farm**	95
Light, fiber / **Butternut**	50
Low sodium	
Butternut	80
Eddy's	80
Wonder	70
Yogurt bran / **Earth Grains**	70

BREAD AND CRACKER CRUMBS

Pepperidge Farm Premium: 1 oz	110
Herb Seasoned: 1 oz / **Pepperidge Farm** Premium	110
Seasoned: 1 rounded tsp / **Contadina**	35
Toasted: 2 oz / **Old London** Regular Style	210
Corn flake crumbs: ¼ cup / **Kellogg's**	110
Cracker meal: 1 cup / **Nabisco**	440

BREAD MIXES

Prepared unless noted

Applesauce spice: 1/12 loaf / **Pillsbury**	150
Blueberry nut: 1/12 loaf / **Pillsbury**	150

CALORIES

Carrot nut: ¹⁄₁₂ loaf / **Pillsbury**	150
Cherry nut: ¹⁄₁₂ loaf / **Pillsbury**	170
Corn	
Arrowhead Mills: 1 oz baked	100
Aunt Jemima Easy Mix: 1.7 oz baked	205
Ballard: ⅛ recipe	
Dromedary: 2 × 2 in sq	130
Fearn: 1.6 oz dry	147
Cranberry / **Pillsbury**	160
Date: ¹⁄₁₂ loaf / **Pillsbury**	160
Multigrain: 2 oz baked / **Arrowhead Mills**	150
Nut: ¹⁄₁₂ loaf / **Pillsbury**	160
Rye: ½-in slice / **Pillslbury** Poppin' Fresh	110
Wheat: ½-in slice / **Pillsbury** Poppin' Fresh	110
Wheat: 1-in slice / **Pillsbury** Pipin' Hot	80
White: ½-in slice / **Pillsbury** Poppin' Fresh	110
White: 1-in slice / **Pillsbury** Pipin' Hot	80
Whole wheat: 2 oz baked / **Arrowhead Mills**	120
Whole wheat, stone ground: 2 oz or ½ cup / **Elams**	200

BREAD STICKS

1 stick

Stella D'Oro	43
Stella D'Oro Dietetic	43
Onion / **Stella D'Oro**	40
Sesame / **Stella D'Oro**	52
Sesame / **Stella D'Oro** Dietetic	57
Soft / **Pillsbury**	100
Whole wheat / **Stella D'Oro**	40

STUFFING MIXES

½ cup prepared unless noted

Bells Ready Mix Stuffing	223
Kellogg's Croutettes	150
Stove Top Americana New England, prepared w butter	180
Stove Top Americana San Francisco, prepared w butter	170

CALORIES

Beef, prepared w butter / **Stove Top**	180
Chicken, prepared w butter / **Stove Top**	180
Chicken, pan style: 1 oz dry / **Pepperidge Farm** 6-oz pkg	110
Chicken-flavored / **Bells**	197
Chicken-flavored w cornbread / **Uncle Ben's**	189
Corn bread: 1 oz dry / **Pepperidge Farm** 8-oz or 16-oz pkg	110
Corn bread, prepared w butter / **Stove Top**	170
Cube: 1 oz dry / **Pepperidge Farm** 7-oz or 14-oz pkg	110
Cube, unseasoned: 1 oz dry / **Pepperidge Farm** 7-oz or 14-oz pkg	110
Herb-seasoned: 1 oz dry / **Pepperidge Farm** 8-oz or 16-oz pkg	110
Pork, prepared w butter / **Stove Top**	170
Seasoned, pan style: 1 oz dry / **Pepperidge Farm** 6-oz pkg	110
Turkey, prepared w butter / **Stove Top**	170
w rice, prepared w butter / **Stove Top**	180

CROUTONS

½ oz

Bacon and cheese / **Pepperidge Farm**	70
Blue cheese / **Pepperidge Farm**	70
Cheddar and Romano cheese / **Pepperidge Farm**	60
Cheese and garlic / **Pepperidge Farm**	70
Dijon mustard rye and cheese / **Pepperidge Farm**	70
Onion and garlic / **Pepperidge Farm**	70
Seasoned / **Pepperidge Farm**	70
Sour cream and chive / **Pepperidge Farm**	70

Butter, Margarine and Oils

BUTTER

	CALORIES
Regular: ½ cup (¼-lb stick)	815
1 tbsp	100
Whipped: ½ cup	540
1 tbsp	65

MARGARINE

1 tablespoon unless noted

Imitation	
Blue Bonnet Diet	50
Fleischmann's Diet	50
Mazola Diet	50
Weight Watchers Cooking Spray:	
1-second spray	2
Regular and Soft	
Ann Page	100
A&P Corn Oil	100
A&P Premium	100
A&P Soft	100
Blue Bonnet	100
Blue Bonnet Soft	100
Country Morning	100
Dalewood	100
Empress	100
Fleischmann's	100
Fleischmann's Soft	100
Hain	100
Imperial	100
Imperial Soft	100
Land O Lakes	101
Mazola	100

CALORIES

Mother's	100
Mrs. Filbert's	100
Mrs. Filbert's Reduced Calorie	50
Nucoa	100
Nucoa Soft	90
Scotch Buy	100
Weight Watchers, stick	30
Weight Watchers, tub	33
Spread	
Autumn	80
Blue Bonnet	80
Empress, tub	80
Fleischmann's	80
Imperial	70
Imperial Light	80
Imperial Light, Soft	60
Mrs. Filbert's Family	70
Mrs. Filbert's Spread 25	80
P & Q 60% Vegetable	80
Promise	90
Scotch Buy, 52% oil tub	70
Promise Soft	90
Whipped	
Blue Bonnet	70
Country Morning	50
Fleischmann's	70
Imperial	50

Cakes

FROZEN

	CALORIES
Apple walnut: ⅛ cake (1⅜ oz) / **Pepperidge Farm** Old Fashion	150
Black forest: ⅛ cake / **Sara Lee**	190
Boston cream: ¼ cake (2⅞ oz) / **Pepperidge Farm** Supreme	290
Butter pound: ⅒ cake (1 oz) / **Pepperidge Farm** Old Fashion	130
Butterscotch pecan layer: ⅒ cake (1⅝ oz) / **Pepperidge Farm**	160
Carrot: ⅛ cake (1⅜ oz) / **Pepperidge Farm** Old Fashion	140
Carrot: 2.6 oz / **Weight Watchers**	150
Cheesecake	
Sara Lee: ⅙ cake	350
Weight Watchers: 4 oz	170
Black cherry: 4 oz / **Weight Watchers**	160
Cherry, individual: 1 (6 oz) / **Morton's** Great Little Desserts	460
Chocolate chip: ⅙ cake / **Sara Lee**	420
Cream, individual: 1 (6 oz) / **Morton's** Great Little Desserts	480
French cream: ⅛ cake / **Sara Lee**	260
Pecan praline: ⅙ cake / **Sara Lee**	430
Pineapple, individual: 1 (6 oz) / **Morton's**	

27

CALORIES

Great Little Desserts	460
Strawberry: 4 oz / **Weight Watchers**	150
Strawberry French: ⅛ cake / **Sara Lee**	250
Strawberry, individual: 1 (6 oz) / **Morton's**	
Great Little Desserts	470
Chocolate: ¼ cake (2⅞ oz) / **Pepperidge Farm**	
Supreme	310
Chocolate chip pound: ⅒ cake / **Sara Lee**	130
Chocolate fudge layer: ⅒ cake (1⅝ oz) /	
Pepperidge Farm	180
Chocolate mint layer: ⅒ cake (1⅝ oz) /	
Pepperidge Farm	170
Chocolate mousse Bavarian: ⅛ cake / **Sara Lee**	250
Coconut layer: ⅒ cake (1⅝ oz) /	
Pepperidge Farm	180
Coffee cake, pecan: ⅛ cake / **Sara Lee**	160
Coffee cake, walnut: ⅛ cake / **Sara Lee**	170
Devil's food layer: ⅒ cake (1⅝ oz) /	
Pepperidge Farm	180
German chocolate layer: ⅒ cake (1⅝ oz) /	
Pepperidge Farm	180
Golden layer: ⅒ cake (1⅝ oz) /	
Pepperidge Farm	180
Lemon coconut: ¼ cake (3 oz) /	
Pepperidge Farm Supreme	280
Pineapple cream: ¹⁄₁₂ cake (2 oz) /	
Pepperidge Farm Supreme	180
Raisin walnut pound: ⅒ cake / **Sara Lee**	140
Spice: 2.6 oz / **Weight Watchers**	160
Strawberry cream: ¹⁄₁₂ cake (2 oz) /	
Pepperidge Farm Supreme	190
Strawberry shortcake: ⅛ cake / **Sara Lee**	190
Vanilla layer: 1⅝ oz / **Pepperidge Farm**	190
Walnut: ⅒ cake (2½ oz) / **Pepperidge Farm**	300

MIXES

Prepared according to package directions
¹⁄₁₂ cake unless noted

Angel food	
Duncan Hines	140

CALORIES

Chocolate / **Betty Crocker**	150
Confetti / **Betty Crocker**	160
Lemon chiffon / **Betty Crocker**	190
Lemon custard / **Betty Crocker**	150
Raspberry / **Pillsbury**	140
Strawberry / **Betty Crocker**	150
White, traditional / **Betty Crocker**	140
White / **Betty Crocker**	150
White / **Pillsbury**	140
Apple / **Duncan Hines**	260
Apple cinnamon / **Betty Crocker** SuperMoist	260
Applesauce raisin: ⅑ cake / **Betty Crocker** Snackin' Cake	180
Applesauce spice / **Pillsbury** Plus	250
Banana / **Betty Crocker** SuperMoist	260
Banana / **Pillsbury** Plus	250
Banana / **Duncan Hines**	260
Banana walnut: ⅑ cake / **Betty Crocker** Snackin' Cake	190
Bundt: ¹⁄₁₆ cake	
Boston cream / **Pillsbury**	270
Chocolate macaroon / **Pillsbury**	250
Fudge / **Pillsbury** Tunnel of Fudge	270
Fudge nut crown / **Pillsbury**	220
Lemon / **Pillsbury** Tunnel of Lemon	270
Lemon blueberry / **Pillsbury**	200
Marble / **Pillsbury**	250
Pound / **Pillsbury**	230
Butter recipe / **Pillsbury** Plus	240
Butter brickle / **Betty Crocker** SuperMoist	260
Butter pecan: ⅑ cake / **Betty Crocker** Snackin' Cake	190
Butter pecan / **Betty Crocker** SuperMoist	250
Butter recipe / **Betty Crocker** SuperMoist	260
Carrot / **Betty Crocker** SuperMoist	260
Carrot / **Duncan Hines**	250
Carrot nut: ⅑ cake / **Betty Crocker** Snackin' Cake	180
Carrot w cream cheese frosting: ⅙ cake / **Betty Crocker** Stir n' Frost	230
Carrot and spice / **Pillsbury** Plus	260
Cheesecake: ⅛ cake / **Jello**	300

CALORIES

Cherry chip / **Betty Crocker** SuperMoist	180
Cherry / **Duncan Hines**	260
Chocolate: ⅒ cake / **Dia-Mel**	100
Chocolate: ⅒ cake / **Estee**	100
Chocolate chip / **Betty Crocker** SuperMoist	190
Chocolate chip / **Duncan Hines**	260
Chocolate chip w chocolate frosting: ⅙ cake / **Betty Crocker** Stir 'n Frost	230
Chocolate chocolate chip / **Betty Crocker** SuperMoist	250
Chocolate chocolate chip w chocolate chocolate chip frosting: ⅙ cake / **Betty Crocker** Stir n' Frost	230
Chocolate devil's food w chocolate frosting: ⅙ cake / **Betty Crocker** Stir n' Frost	230
Chocolate fudge / **Betty Crocker** SuperMoist	250
Chocolate fudge chip: ⅑ cake / **Betty Crocker** Snackin' Cake	190
Chocolate fudge w vanilla frosting: ⅙ cake / **Betty Crocker** Stir 'n Frost	230
Chocolate mint / **Pillsbury** Plus	260
Coconut pecan: ⅑ cake / **Betty Crocker** Snackin' Cake	190
Coffee cake	
Aunt Jemima: 1.3 oz	160
Apple cinnamon: ⅛ cake / **Pillsbury**	240
Butter pecan: ⅛ cake / **Pillsbury**	310
Cinnamon streusel: ⅛ cake / **Pillsbury**	250
Sour cream: ⅛ cake / **Pillsbury**	270
Cupcake: 1 piece / **Flako**	150
Dark chocolate / **Pillsbury** Plus	260
Deep chocolate / **Duncan Hines**	280
Devil's food / **Betty Crocker** SuperMoist	270
Devil's food / **Duncan Hines**	280
Devil's food / **Pillsbury** Plus	250
Fudge / **Duncan Hines** Butter Recipe	270
Fudge marble / **Duncan Hines** Deluxe	260
Fudge marble / **Pillsbury** Plus	270
Fudge peanut butter chip: ⅑ cake / **Betty Crocker** Snackin' Cake	200
German Black Forest / **Betty Crocker**	180
German chocolate / **Betty Crocker** SuperMoist	260

German chocolate / **Pillsbury** Plus	250
German chocolate coconut pecan: ⅑ cake / **Betty Crocker** Snackin' Cake	180
Gingerbread: ⅑ cake / **Betty Crocker**	210
Gingerbread: 2-×-2-in square / **Dromedary**	100
Gingerbread: 3-in square / **Pillsbury**	190
Golden / **Duncan Hines**	270
Golden chocolate chip: ⅑ cake / **Betty Crocker** Snackin' Cake	190
Golden vanilla / **Duncan Hines**	260
Lemon / **Betty Crocker** SuperMoist	260
Lemon: ¹⁄₁₀ cake / **Di-Mel**	100
Lemon: ¹⁄₁₀ cake / **Estee**	100
Lemon / **Pillsbury** Plus	260
Lemon / **Duncan Hines** Deluxe	260
Marble / **Betty Crocker** SuperMoist	260
Milk chocolate / **Betty Crocker** SuperMoist	250
Mint fudge chip: ⅑ cake / **Betty Crocker** Snackin' Cake	190
Oats and brown sugar / **Pillsbury** Plus	260
Orange / **Betty Crocker** SuperMoist	260
Orange / **Duncan Hines** Deluxe	260
Pineapple / **Duncan Hines** Deluxe	260
Pineapple upside-down: ⅑ cake / **Betty Crocker**	270
Pound: ¹⁄₁₀ cake / **Dia-Mel**	100
Pound: ¾-in slice / **Dromedary**	210
Pound, golden / **Betty Crocker**	200
Pudding, chocolate: ⅙ cake / **Betty Crocker**	230
Pudding, lemon: ⅙ cake / **Betty Crocker**	230
Sour cream chocolate / **Betty Crocker** SuperMoist	260
Sour cream chocolate / **Duncan Hines**	280
Sour cream white / **Betty Crocker**	180
Spice / **Betty Crocker** SuperMoist	260
Spice: ¹⁄₁₀ cake / **Dia-Mel**	100
Spice / **Duncan Hines** Deluxe	260
Spice w vanilla frosting: ⅙ cake / **Betty Crocker** Stir n' Frost	280
Strawberry / **Betty Crocker** SuperMoist	260
Strawberry / **Pillsbury** Plus	260
Strawberry / **Duncan Hines** Deluxe	260
Streusel:	

Banana / **Pillsbury**: 1/16	260
Butter, rich / **Pillsbury**: 1/16	260
Cinnamon / **Betty Crocker**: 1/6	260
Cinnamon / **Pillsbury**: 1/16	260
Dutch apple / **Pillsbury**: 1/16	260
Fudge marble / **Pillsbury**: 1/16	260
German chocolate / **Betty Crocker**: 1/6	240
German chocolate / **Pillsbury**: 1/16	260
Lemon / **Pillsbury**: 1/16	270
Pecan, brown sugar / **Pillsbury**: 1/16	260
Swiss chocolate / **Duncan Hines** Deluxe	280
White / **Betty Crocker** SuperMoist	250
White / **Duncan Hines** Deluxe	250
White: 1/10 cake / **Estee**	100
White / **Pillsbury** Plus	240
Yellow / **Betty Crocker** SuperMoist	260
Yellow / **Duncan Hines** Deluxe	260
Yellow / **Pillsbury** Plus	260
Yellow w chocolate frosting: 1/6 cake / **Betty Crocker** Stir n' Frost	230

SNACK CAKES

1 piece

Chip Flips / **Hostess**	330
Coffee cake / **Drake's**	220
Creamie, chocolate / **Tastykake**	195
Crumb cakes / **Hostess**	130
Cupcakes	
Buttercream, cream-filled / **Tastykake**	130
Chocolate / **Dolly Madison**	170
Chocolate / **Hostess**	170
Chocolate / **Tastykake**	120
Chocolate, cream-filled / **Tastykake**	125
Orange / **Hostess**	150
Dessert cups / **Hostess**	60
Devil Dogs / **Drake's**	170
Ding Dongs / **Big Wheels**	170
Fruit Loaf / **Hostess**	400
Funny Bones / **Drake's**	160

CALORIES

Ho-Ho's / **Hostess**	120
Hostess-O's / **Hostess**	240
Junior chocolate / **Tastykake**	355
Junior coconut / **Tastykake**	330
Kandy Kake, chocolate / **Tastykake**	95
Kandy Kake, coconut / **Tastykake**	105
Kandy Kake, mint / **Tastykake**	100
Kandy Kake, peanut butter / **Tastykake**	105
Koffee Kake / **Tastykake**	330
Koffee Kake, cream-filled / **Tastykake**	150
Krimpet, butterscotch / **Tastykake**	120
Krimpet, cream-filled, chocolate / **Tastykake**	150
Krimpet, cream-filled, vanilla / **Tastykake**	150
Krimpet, jelly / **Tastykake**	100
Krump Kake, apple-filled / **Tastykake**	135
Lil' Angels	90
Peanut Putters, filled	360
Peanut Putters, unfilled	410
Ring Ding Jr. / **Drake's**	160
Sno Balls / **Hostess**	150
Suzy Qs, banana / **Hostess**	240
Suzy Qs, chocolate / **Hostess**	240
Teen, chocolate / **Tastykake**	260
Tempty, chocolate / **Tastykake**	100
Tiger Tail / **Hostess**	210
Twinkies / **Hostess**	160
Yankee Doodles / **Drake's**	110

Candy

CALORIES

Almond Joy, bar: 1.6 oz	220
Almond Roco: 1 piece (½ oz)	58
Almonds, sugar-coated: 8 pieces (1 oz) / **Jordan**	130
Breath candy: 1 piece	
Breath Savers, sugar free / **Life Savers**	7
Certs, clear	8

CALORIES

Certs, pressed	6
Clorets Mints	6
Dentyne Dynamints	2
Trident Mints	8
Baby Ruth: 1 oz	140
Bit-O-Honey: 1 oz	105
Bonkers!: 1 piece	23
Boston baked beans: 1 box (1¾ oz)	230
Bridge mix, chocolate: 1 oz / **Deran**	130
Butterfinger: 1 oz	140
Butter toffee peanuts: 1 oz / **Harmony**	140
Candy corn / **Curtiss**	4
Caramello bar: 2 oz / **Cadbury**	280
Caramel Nip: 1¾ oz / **Pearson**	220
Charleston Chew: 1¾-oz bar	200
Chocolate bars	
Cadbury Dairy Milk: 2 oz	300
Ghirardelli Milk: 1⅛ oz	172
Ghirardelli Dark: 1⅛ oz	171
Hershey's: 1.45 oz	220
Hershey's: miniature bar	55
Hershey's Special Dark: 1.05 oz	160
Hershey's Special Dark: 4 oz	610
Nestlé's: 1¹⁄₁₆ oz	160
Nestlé's: miniature	53
w almonds: 1⅛ oz / **Ghirardelli**	175
w almonds: 1.45 oz bar / **Hershey's**	230
w almonds: miniature bar / **Hershey's**	55
w almonds: 1 oz / **Nestlé's**	150
w brazil nuts: 2 oz / **Cadbury**	310
w fruit and nuts: 2 oz / **Cadbury**	300
w hazel nuts: 2 oz / **Cadbury**	310
w munchy malt: 1⅛ oz / **Ghirardelli**	170
w raisins: 1⅛ oz / **Ghirardelli**	163
Chocolate-covered nuts and fruit	
Almonds, dark chocolate: 1 oz / **Harmony**	150
Almonds, milk chocolate: 1 oz / **Harmony**	160
Apricots: 1 oz / **Harmony**	110
Bridge mix: 1 oz (about 14 pieces) / **Nabisco**	135
Cashews: 1 oz / **Harmony**	150
Cherries: 4 pieces / **Nabisco**	290

	CALORIES
Macadamias: 1 oz / **Harmony**	170
Peanuts: 1 oz / **Brach**	155
Peanuts: 1 oz / **Harmony**	160
Peanut Snackums: 1 oz / **Harmony**	140
Pecans: 1 oz / **Harmony**	170
Pistachios: 1 oz / **Harmony**	150
Raisins, dark chocolate: 1 oz / **Harmony**	120
Raisins, milk chocolate: 1 oz / **Harmony**	130
Raisins: 1 oz / **Deran**	120
Raisins: 1 box (2½ oz) / **Nabisco**	330
Raisins: 1 oz / Raisinets	115
Walnuts: 1 oz / **Harmony**	160
Chocolate crisp: 1⅛ oz / **Ghirardelli**	168
Chocolate mint: 1⅛ oz / **Ghirardelli**	165
Chocolate mint square: ⅜ oz / **Ghirardelli**	55
Chocolate parfait: 1¾ oz / **Pearson**	240
Chocolate stars: 1 box (2¼ oz) / **Nabisco**	360
Chuckles	
Cherry: 7 pieces (1⅞ oz)	185
Cinnamon softee: 1 box (1⅞ oz)	200
Coconut squares: 4 pieces (2 oz)	270
Jelly beans: 1 box (1¾ oz)	190
Jelly candy: 5 pieces (2 oz)	200
Jelly mint softees: 11 pieces (1⅞ oz)	190
Jelly rings: 6 pieces (2¼ oz)	220
Ju Ju Softees: 1 box (1½ oz)	155
Licorice jellies: 6 pieces (2 oz)	200
Licorice softees: 1 pkg (1⅞ oz)	200
Orange slices: 1 pkg (2 oz)	210
Spearmint leaves: 1 pkg (1½ oz)	165
Spice drops: 1 pkg (1½ oz)	160
Spice sticks: 18 pieces (2 1/16 oz)	210
Chunky, regular, bar: 1 oz	130
Chunky, pecan, bar: 1 oz	130
Clark, bar: 1 oz	130
Coffee Nip: 1¾ oz / **Pearson**	220
Coffioca: 1¾ oz / **Pearson**	240
Cotton candy: 1 cone	80
Cough drops: 1 drop / **Beech-Nut**	10
Cough drops: 1 drop / **Pine Bros.**	8
Crispy / **Switzer Clark:** 1 oz	150

CALORIES

Crows: 1 piece	11
Crunch / **Nestlé's:** 1¹⁄₁₆ oz	160
1 oz	150
Dots: 1 piece	10
Golden Almond, bar / **Hershey's:** 1 oz	160
Good & Plenty: 1 box	136
Good 'n Fruity: 1 box	136
Hard candies	
Butterscotch disc: 1 piece	23
Red Hot dollars: 1 oz	108
Sour bites: 1 piece	38
Sweet Tarts: 1 piece	4
Red Hots: 1 ball	30
Root beer barrel: 1 piece	39
Candy cane: 1 cane (½ oz)	58
Candy hearts: 1 piece	23
Christmas candy: 1 cup	790
Jawbreakers: 1 piece	8
Fudge bar / **Nabisco:** 2 bars (1⅜ oz)	170
Halvah, plain	147
Halvah, chocolate-covered	147
Heath bar, English toffee, 1¹⁄₁₆ oz	150
Hot Tamales: 1 piece	7
Jelly beans: 10 pieces (1 oz)	105
Junior Mints / **Nabisco:** 1 pkg (1.43 oz)	170
Jumbo Block / **Nabisco:** 1 oz	150
Kisses / **Hershey:** 1 oz (6 pieces)	150
Kit Kat, bar: 1.5 oz	210
Krackel, bar: 1.45 oz	220
Krackle, bar, miniature	52
Licorice Nip / **Pearson:** 1¾ oz	220
Life Savers roll candy, fruit flavors: 1 drop	10
Life Savers, mint: 1 piece	7
Life Savers, sours: 1 piece	10
Lollipop: **Life Savers,** fruit, swirled: 1 lollipop	45
M & M's, plain: 1.7 oz	235
M & M's, peanut: 1.7 oz	240
Mallo Cup: 1.2 oz cup	115
Maltballs / **Harmony:** 1 oz	140
Malted milk balls: 1 oz / **Deran**	140
Mars, bar: 1.9 oz	255

   CALORIES

Marshmallows: 1 large	22
1 cup miniatures	147
10 miniatures	23
Marshmallows: 2 large or 24 mini / **Campfire**	40
Marshmallow, chocolate-covered egg: 1 small egg	23
Marshmallow, chocolate-covered egg: 1 medium egg (⅓ oz)	42
Marshmallow, chocolate-covered rabbit: 1 rabbit (about ½ oz)	53
Mary Jane: 1 piece	26
Marzipan paste: 1 oz	144
Milk chocolate, bar / **Switzer Clark**	155
Milk Duds: 1 oz	115
Milk Maid caramels / **Brach:** 1 oz	110
Milky Way, bar: 2 oz	270
Mint parfait / **Pearson:** 1¾ oz	240
Mounds, bar: 1.65 oz	230
Mr. Goodbar, bar: 1.65 oz	250
Mr. Goodbar, miniature	54
Nut fudge squares / **Nabisco:** 4 pieces (2 oz)	260
Nutcracker / **Switzer Clark:** 1 oz	160
$100,000; bar: 1½ oz	200
$100,000; bar: ¾ oz	100
Payday, bar	250
Peanut brittle: 1 oz	120
Peanut candy: 1 oz / **Planters** Old Fashioned (vacuum can)	140
Peanut caramel clusters, chocolate: 1 oz	145
Peanut clusters, chocolate: 1 oz / **Brach**	155
Peanut clusters, chocolate: 1 oz / **Deran**	150
Pecan nut cluster: 1 piece (1 oz) / **Heath**	130
Pecan roll: 1 oz	148
Peppermint patties: 4 pieces (2 oz) / **Nabisco**	220
Pom Poms: 1 box (1.48 oz)	180
Powerhouse, bar: 2.2 oz	290
Reese's Peanut Butter Cup, plain or crunchy: 2 pieces (1.6 oz)	240
Reese's peanut butter–flavored chips: ¼ cup	230
Reese's Pieces: 35 pieces (1 oz)	140
Reggie: 2-oz bar	290
Rocky Road: 1 oz	155

CALORIES

Rolo: 5 pieces (1 oz)	140
Royals: 1 oz / **Brach**	120
Rum wafers: 1 oz / **Deran**	150
Salt water taffy: 1 piece	18
Sesame crunch: 1 piece / **Sahadi**	10
Skittles bite-size: 1.7 oz	200
Slo-Poke: 1 oz	120
Snickers, bar: 2 oz	275
Special Dark Bar: 1.45 oz / **Hershey's**	220
Starburst Fruit Chews: 2.1 oz	245
Sugar Babies: 1⅝ oz	180
Sugar Daddy: 1⅜ oz	150
Sugar Mama: 1 piece	90
Summit: .7 oz	115
3 Musketeers: 2.3-oz bar	280
Thin mints: 6 pieces (1⅞ oz) / **Nabisco**	220
Toffees: 1 oz / **Brach**	120
Tootsie Pop, caramel, chocolate, flavored:	
.49-oz pop	55
Tootsie Pop drop: 1 oz	113
Tootsie Roll: 1 oz	115
Tootsie Roll: 1¼-oz roll	145
Tootsie Roll, .23-oz midgee	26
Twix Caramel: 1 oz	130
Twix Peanut Butter: .9 oz	130
Twizzler, cherry, chocolate, strawberry: 1 oz	100
Twizzler, licorice: 1 bar	175
Twizzler, licorice: 1 stick	38
Whatchamacallit, bar: 1.4 oz	210
Whoppers	
York Mints: 1.5 oz	180
Zagnut, bar: 1 oz	130

DIETETIC CANDY

Chocolates, boxed or pieces	
Peanut butter cups: 1 piece / **Estee**	45
Raisins, chocolate-covered: 6 pieces	30
T.V. mix: 4 pieces / **Estee**	35
Estee-ets: 5 pieces	35
Chocolate bar: 2 squares / **Estee**	60

CALORIES

Crunch: 2 squares / **Estee**	45
Gum drops: 4 pieces / **Estee**	12
Hard candies: 2 pieces / **Estee**	25
Lollipops: 1 / **Estee**	12
Mints: 1 piece / **Estee**	4

Cereals

COLD, READY TO SERVE

CALORIES

Measurements vary according to what companies consider appropriate one-serving sizes. The servings generally are one ounce in weight.

All-Bran: ⅓ cup	70
All-Bran w extra Fiber: ½ cup	60
Alpha-Bits: 1 cup	110
Almond Delight: ¾ cup	110
Amaranth w bananas: 1 oz / **Health Valley**	110
Arrowhead Crunch: 1 oz / **Arrowhead Mills**	120
Bran: 1 oz / **Loma Linda**	60
Bran w apples and cinnamon: 1 oz / **Health Valley**	105
Bran w raisins: 1 oz / **Health Valley**	100
Bran flakes, 40%: ⅔ cup / **Kellogg's**	90
Bran flakes, 40%: ⅔ cup / **Post**	90
Bucwheats: ¾ cup	110
C-3PO's: ¾ cup	110
Cap'n Crunch: ¾ cup	121
Cap'n Crunch's Crunchberries: ¾ cup	120
Cap'n Crunch's Peanut Butter Cereal: ¾ cup	127
Cheerios: 1¼ cup	110
Cheerios, Honey Nut: ¾ cup	110
Cinnamon Life: ⅔ cup	105
Cinnamon Toast Crunch: ⅔ cup	120
Cocoa Krispies: ¾ cup	110
Cocoa Puffs: 1 cup	110

C

CEREALS

40

CALORIES

Cookie Crisp, chocolate chip or vanilla wafer:
1 cup — 110
Corn bran: ⅔ cup / **Quaker** — 109
Corn Chex: 1 cup — 110
Corn flakes
    General Mills Country: 1 cup — 110
    Kellogg's: 1 cup — 110
    Post Toasties: 1 cup — 110
    Ralston: 1 cup — 110
    Safeway: 1 cup — 110
Corn germ cereal: 1 cup / **Nutri-Dyne Ener-G** — 490
Corn, puffed: ½ oz / **Arrowhead Mills** — 50
Corn Total: 1 cup — 110
Count Chocula: 1 cup — 110
Cracklin' Oat Bran: ½ cup — 120
Crispix: ¾ cup — 110
Crispy Oatmeal & Raisin Chex: ¾ cup — 140
Crispy rice
    Malt-O-Meal: 1 cup — 110
    Ralston: 1 cup — 110
    Safeway: 1 cup — 110
Crispy Wheat 'n Raisins: ¾ cup — 110
C. W. Post: ¼ cup — 130
C. W. Post w raisins: ¼ cup — 120
Dairy Crisp: ¼ cup — 20
Donkey Kong: 1 cup — 110
Donkey Kong Junior: 1 cup — 110
E. T.: ¾ cup — 130
Familia: ¼ cup — 127
Fiber One: ½ cup — 60
FrankenBerry: 1 cup — 110
Froot Loops: 1 cup — 110
Frosted Flakes: ¾ cup / **Kellogg's** — 110
Frosted Flakes, banana: ⅔ cup / **Kellogg's** — 110
Frosted Krispies: ¾ cup — 110
Frosted Mini-Wheats, sugar or apple flavored:
4 biscuits (1 oz) — 110
Fruit & Fibre, apples and cinnamon: ½ cup — 90
Fruit & Fibre, dates, raisins and walnuts: ½ cup — 90
Fruitful Bran: ⅔ cup — 120
Fruit Rings: 1 cup / **Ralston** — 110

CALORIES

Golden Grahams: ¾ cup — 110
Granola
    Apple amaranth: 1 oz / **Arrowhead Mills** — 113
    Cinnamon and raisin: ⅓ cup / **Nature Valley** — 130
    Coconut and honey: ⅓ cup / **Nature Valley** — 150
    Fruit and nut: ⅓ cup / **Nature Valley** — 130
    Maple nut: 2 oz / **Arrowhead Mills** — 260
    Toasted oat mixture: ⅓ cup / **Nature Valley** — 130
Grape-Nuts: ¼ cup — 100
Grape-Nuts, raisin: 1¼ cup — 100
Grape-Nuts Flakes: ⅞ cup — 100
Heartland, all varieties: ¼ cup — 130
Hearts O'Bran: 1 oz / **Health Valley** — 110
Hearts O'Bran w apples and cinnamon: 1 oz /
    Health Valley — 110
Hearts O'Bran w raisins and spice: 1 oz /
    Health Valley — 110
Honeycomb: 1⅓ cup — 110
Honeycomb, strawberry: 1⅓ cup — 120
Honey and nut corn flakes: ¾ cup / **Kellogg's** — 110
Honey nut crunch, raisin bran: 1 oz / **Post** — 90
Honey Smacks: ¾ cup — 110
Kaboom: 1 cup — 110
King Vitamin: 1¼ cup — 113
Kix: 1½ cup — 110
Life: ⅔ cup — 105
Lites, brown rice: ½ cup / **Health Valley** — 50
Lites, golden corn: ½ cup / **Health Valley** — 50
Lites, golden wheat: ½ cup / **Health Valley** — 50
Lucky Charms: 1 cup — 110
Marshmallow Krispies: 1¼ cup — 140
Millet, whole grain, puffed: ½ oz /
    Arrowhead Mills — 50
Nature O's: 1 oz / **Arrowhead Mills** — 110
Nutri-Grain, corn: ½ cup — 110
Nutri-Grain, wheat: ⅔ cup — 110
Nutri-Grain, wheat and raisins: ⅔ cup — 140
Oat bran: 1 oz / **Arrowhead Mills** — 110
Oat flakes, fortified: ⅔ cup / **Post** — 100
Orangeola w almonds and dates: 1 oz /
    Health Valley — 125

Orangeola w bananas and coconut: 1 oz / **Health Valley**	125
Pac-Man: 1 cup	110
Pebbles, cocoa: ⅞ cup	110
Pebbles, fruity: ⅞ cup	110
Product 19: ¾ cup	110
Quaker 100% Natural: ¼ cup	138
Quaker 100% Natural w apples and cinnamon: ¼ cup	135
Quaker 100% Natural w raisins and dates: ¼ cup	134
Quisp: 1⅙ cup	121
Raisin bran	
Health Valley: 1 oz	110
Kellogg's: ¾ cup	110
Post: ½ cup	90
Ralston: ¾ cup	120
Safeway: 1 oz	100
Raisins, Rice & Rye: ¾ cup	140
REAL Almond Crunch: 1 oz / **Health Valley**	120
REAL Apple Cinnamon: 1 oz / **Health Valley**	120
REAL Hawaiian Fruit: 1 oz / **Health Valley**	120
REAL Maple Nut: 1 oz / **Health Valley**	120
REAL Raisin Nut: 1 oz / **Health Valley**	120
Rice Chex: 1¼ cup	110
Rice Krispies: 1 cup	110
Rice, puffed: ½ oz / **Arrowhead Mills**	50
Rice, puffed / **Malt-O-Meal:** 1 cup	50
Rice, puffed / **Quaker:** 1 cup	55
Rice and Shine: ¼ cup / **Arrowhead Mills**	160
7-Grain Crunchy: 1 oz / **Loma Linda**	110
7-Grain, no sugar: 1 oz / **Loma Linda**	110
Seven Grain Cereal: 1 oz / **Arrowhead Mills**	100
Smurf-Berry Crunch: 1 oz	110
Special K: 1 cup	110
Sprouts 7 w banana: 1 oz / **Health Valley**	105
Sprouts 7 w raisins: 1 oz / **Health Valley**	100
Strawberry Krispies: ¾ cup	110
Strawberry Shortcake: 1 cup	110
Sugar Corn Pops: 1 cup	110
Sugar Frosted Flakes: ¾ cup / **Ralston**	110
Sugar Frosted Rice: 1 cup / **Ralston**	110

CALORIES

Sugar Puffs: ⅞ cup / **Malt-O-Meal**	110
Super Sugar Crisp: ⅞ cup	110
Tasteeos: 1¼ cup	110
Toasty O's: 1¼ cup	110
Total: 1 cup	110
Trix: 1 cup	110
Wheat Chex: ⅔ cup	100
Wheat flakes: 1 oz / **Health Valley**	110
Wheat, puffed: ½ oz / **Arrowhead Mills**	50
Wheat, puffed: 1 cup / **Malt-O-Meal**	50
Wheat, puffed: 1 cup / **Quaker**	54
Wheat & Raisin Chex: ¾ cup	130
Wheat, shredded: 1 biscuit / **Sunshine**	85
Wheat, shredded: 2 biscuits / **Quaker**	104
Wheaties: 1 cup	110

TO BE COOKED

Dry, uncooked, unless noted

Barley, pearled: ¼ cup uncooked (¾ cup cooked) / **Quaker** Scotch Brand Quick	172
Barley, pearled: ¼ cup uncooked (1 cup cooked) / **Quaker** Scotch Brand Regular	172
Bear Mush: 1 oz / **Arrowhead Mills**	100
Complete Cereal: ¼ cup / **Elam's**	110
Cracked wheat: 2 oz / **Arrowhead Mills**	180
Cracked wheat: ¼ cup / **Elam's**	130
Farina: ⅔ cup cooked / **Pillsbury**	80
4-Grain Cereal + Flax: 2 oz / **Arrowhead Mills**	94
Grits	
Bulgur-soy: 2 oz / **Arrowhead Mills**	200
Corn: 2 oz / **Arrowhead Mills**	200
Hominy: 3 tbsp / **Aunt Jemima** Quick	101
Hominy: 3 tbsp / **Aunt Jemima** Regular	101
Hominy: 3 tbsp / **Quaker** Quick	101
Hominy: 3 tbsp / **Quaker** Regular	101
Hominy Quick: ¼ cup dry / **Albers**	150
Instant: 1 pkt / **Quaker** Instant Grits Product	79
Instant w artificial cheese flavor: 1 pkt / **Quaker** Instant Grits Product	104

Instant w imitation bacon bits: 1 pkt /
    Quaker Instant Grits Product   101
Instant w imitation ham bits: 1 pkt /
    Quaker Instant Grits Product   99
Malt-O-Meal, chocolate flavored: 1 oz dry
  (¾ cup cooked)   100
Malt-O-Meal, quick: 1 oz dry (¾ cup cooked)   100
Oats and oatmeal
    Quaker Old Fashioned: ⅔ cup cooked   109
    Quaker Quick: ⅔ cup cooked   109
    Regular and Quick / **Ralston** ⅓ cup uncooked   110
    3-Minute Brand Old-Fashioned: 1 oz   110
    3-Minute Brand Quick: 1 oz   110
    Scotch style: ¼ cup dry / **Elam's**   110
    Steel-cut: ¼ cup dry / **Elam's**   180
    Stone-ground: ¼ cup dry / **Elam's**   110
Oatmeal, instant: 1 pkt
    Harvest Brand   110
    Quaker Regular   105
    w apples and cinnamon / **Harvest Brand**   140
    w apples and cinnamon / **Quaker**   134
    w bran and raisins / **Quaker**   153
    w cinnamon and spice / **Harvest Brand**   180
    w cinnamon and spice / **Quaker**   176
    w honey and graham / **Quaker**   136
    w maple and brown sugar / **Harvest Brand**   170
    w maple and brown sugar / **Quaker**   163
    w peaches and cream / **Harvest Brand**   140
    w raisins, dates and walnuts / **Quaker**   130
    w raisins and spice / **Quaker**   159
    w strawberries and cream / **Quaker**   140
Ralston Instant and Regular: ¼ dry   90
Wheat and oatmeal: ¼ cup / **Elam's**   100
Wheat and soya: ¼ cup dry / **Fearn** Soy-O   140
  ¼ cup prepared with milk   220
Whole wheat: ⅔ cup cooked / **Quaker**
  Pettijohns   106

Cheese

CALORIES

Non-brand name
1 oz unless noted

Blue	100
Brick	105
Brie	95
Camembert, domestic	85
Caraway	107
Cheddar	115
Cheshire	110
Colby	112
Cottage, cream: ½ cup	108
Cottage, dry: ½ cup	62
Cream	99
Edam	101
Feta	75
Fontina	110
Gjetost	132
Gouda	100
Limburger	93
Monterey	105
Mozzarella, part skim	72
Mozzarella, whole milk	80
Muenster	104
Neufchatel	74
Parmesan	111
Port de salut	100
Provolone	100
Ricotta, part skim: ½ cup	170
Ricotta, whole milk: ½ cup	215
Romano	110
Roquefort	105
Swiss	107
Tilsit	96

Brand name

1 oz unless noted

American
Borden	110
Kraft	110
Land O Lakes	110
Slices / **Kraft**	110
Sharp / **Kraft** Old English	110
Sharp slices / **Kraft** Old English	110
Sharp / **Land O Lakes**	110
Blue / **Kraft**	100
Blue / **Land O Lakes**	100
Brick / **Kraft**	110
Brick / **Land O Lakes**	110
Brie / **Kolb-Lena Delico**	85
Camembert / **Kolb-Lena Delico**	85
Caraway / **Kraft**	100
Caraway Jack / **Health Valley**	105
Cheddar / **Land O Lakes**	110
Cheddar, mild / **Kraft**	110
Cheddar, sharp / **Kraft**	110
Cheddar, imitation, mild / **Kraft** Golden Image	110
Colby / **Health Valley**	110
Colby / **Kraft**	110
Colby / **Land O Lakes**	110
Colby, imitation / **Kraft** Golden Image	110
Edam / **Kraft**	100
Feta / **Kolb-Lena Delico**	96
Farmer: ½ cup / **Friendship**	160
Fondue / **Swiss Knight**	60
Gouda / **Kraft**	100
Gouda / **Land O Lakes**	100
Hoop: ½ cup / **Friendship**	84
Jalapeno Jack / **Health Valley**	108
Limburger / **Mohawk Valley** Little Gem Size	100
Longhorn / **Health Valley**	100
Monterey Jack / **Health Valley**	100
Monterey Jack / **Kraft**	110
Monterey Jack / **Land O Lakes**	110
Mozzarella / **Kraft** Casino	80

CALORIES

Mozzarella / **Land O Lakes**	80
Muenster / **Health Valley**	105
Muenster / **Kraft**	110
Muenster / **Land O Lakes**	100
Part-skim milk, natural / **Weight Watchers**	80
Pimento, process / **Kraft**	110
Parmesan / **Kraft**	110
Provolone / **Kraft**	90
Provolone / **Land O Lakes**	100
Romano / **Kraft** Casino	100
Scamorze, low-moisture, part-skim / **Kraft**	80
Swiss	
Kolb-Lena Delico Swiss-Lo	102
Kraft, aged	100
Kraft, chunk	110
Land O Lakes	110
Processed / **Borden**	100
Slices / **Kraft**	110
Processed slices / **Kraft** Deluxe	90

COTTAGE CHEESE

½ cup unless noted

Creamed	
Borden	120
Friendship California Style	120
Land O Lakes	120
Lucerne	120
Meadow Gold	120
w chives / **Lucerne**	120
w fruit salad / **Lucerne**	150
w pineapple / **Friendship**	140
w pineapple / **Lucerne**	150
Dry: **Lucerne**	80
Low-fat	
Friendship	90
Friendship Pot Style	100
Liteline	90
Lucerne	100
Meadow Gold Viva Lowfat	100
Weight Watchers	60

CREAM AND NEUFCHATEL CHEESE

1 oz

Cream cheese
Kraft Philadelphia Brand	100
Land O Lakes	100
Friendship	103
w chives / **Kraft Philadelphia** Brand	100
w pimentos / **Kraft Philadelphia** Brand	100

Cream cheese, whipped
Kraft Philadelphia Brand	100
w bacon and horseradish / **Kraft Philadelphia** Brand	90
w blue cheese / **Kraft Philadelphia** Brand	100
w chives / **Kraft Philadelphia** Brand	90
w onions / **Kraft Philadelphia** Brand	90
w pimentos / **Kraft Philadelphia** Brand	90
w smoked salmon / **Kraft Philadelphia** Brand	100

GRATED AND SHREDDED CHEESE

1 oz (= about ⅓ cup or 5½ tbsp)

Parmesan, grated / **Kraft**	130
Parmesan grated / **Land O Lakes**	130
Romano, grated / **Kraft**	130
Romano, grated / **Land O Lakes**	130

CHEESE FOODS

1 oz unless noted

American
Borden	90
Kraft Light n' Lively	70
Kraft Singles	90
Slices, cheese product / **Lite-Line**	50

Cheddar
Wispride Cold Pack	90
Sharp / **Land O Lakes** Cold Pack	90
Sharp, cheese product / **Lite-Line**	50

CALORIES

Sharp w wine / **Land O Lakes** Cold Pack	90
Sharp flavor / **Weight Watchers** Cold Pack	70
Colby, cheese product / **Lite-Line**	50
Hot pepper / **Land O Lakes**	90
Monterey Jack, cheese product / **Lite-Line**	50
Muenster, cheese product / **Lite-Line**	50
Onion-flavor / **Weight Watchers**	70
Port wine / **Wispride** Cold Pack	100
Process / **Land O Lakes**	90
Process cheese product: 2 slices / **Weight Watchers**	100
Smoked / **Wispride** Cold Pack	90
Smoked flavor / **Weight Watchers** Cold Pack	70
Substitute, processed / **Lite-Line**	90
Swiss: 1 slice (1 oz) / **Weight Watchers**	50
Swiss flavor, cheese product / **Lite-Line**	50

CHEESE SPREADS

1 oz

American / **Nabisco** Snack Mate	80
Cheddar / **Nabisco** Snack Mate	80
Cheese and bacon / **Nabisco** Snack Mate	80
Cheez Whiz	80
Creamed / **Weight Watchers**	80
Jalapeno / **Kraft**	80
Olive and pimento / **Kraft**	60
Pimento / **Kraft**	70
Pimento / **Price's**	80
Pineapple / **Kraft**	70
Relish / **Kraft**	70
Snack Mate, all flavors / **Nabisco**	80
Velveeta / **Kraft**	80
Velveeta, pimento / **Kraft**	80
Velveeta slices / **Kraft**	90

SOUFFLÉ

Cheese soufflé: 6 oz / **Stouffer's**	355

WELSH RAREBIT

Canned: ½ cup / **Snow's**	170
Frozen: 5 oz / **Stouffer's**	355

Chewing Gum

1 stick or piece	CALORIES
Adams Sour	9
Beech-Nut	9
Beechies	6
Big Red	10
Bubble Yum	27
Bubble Yum, sugarless	19
Bubblicious	25
Care Free, all flavors	8
Chiclets	6
Clorets	6
Dentyne	5
Doublemint / **Wrigley's**	10
Estee, all flavors	3
Freedent / **Wrigley's**	10
Fruit Stripe	9
Juicy Fruit / **Wrigley's**	10
Hubba Bubba, all flavors	23
Orbit, sugar free	8
Replay	17
Spearmint / **Wrigley's**	10
Trident	5

Chinese Foods

CALORIES

See also Dinners

	CALORIES
Almond chicken, frozen: 11 oz / **Van de Kamp's**	430
Bamboo shoots, canned: 4¼ oz / **Chun King**	20

CALORIES

Bamboo shoots, canned: ¼ cup / **La Choy**	6
Bean sprouts, canned: ½ cup / **Chun King**	20
Bean sprouts, canned: ⅔ cup / **La Choy**	8
Beef Oriental, frozen: 8⅝ oz / **Stouffer's** Lean Cuisine	280
Beef Oriental, frozen: 10 oz / **Weight Watchers**	260
Beef pepper, frozen: 6 oz / **Chun King** Pouch	80
Beef Teriyaki, frozen: 10 oz / **Stouffer's**	365
Beef and vegetables Szechwan: 11 oz / **Van de Kamp's**	370
Chicken, Oriental, frozen: 9½ oz / **Weight Watchers**	240
Chicken, sweet and sour, frozen: 9 oz / **Weight Watchers**	210
Chop suey beef, frozen: 12 oz / **Stouffer's**	355
Chop suey vegetables, canned: ½ cup / **La Choy**	10
Chow mein, canned	
Beef: 10½ oz / **Chun King** Divider Pak	80
Beef: 12 oz / **Chun King** 24-oz size	90
Beef: ¾ cup / **La Choy**	70
Beef: ¾ cup prepared / **La Choy** Bi-Pack	60
Beef pepper: ¾ cup / **La Choy**	90
Beef pepper: ¾ cup prepared / **La Choy** Bi-Pack	70
Chicken: 10½ oz / **Chun King** Divider Pak	80
Chicken: 12 oz / **Chun King** 24-oz size	90
Chicken: ¾ cup / **La Choy**	80
Chicken: ¾ cup prepared / **La Choy** Bi-Pack	70
Meatless: ¾ cup / **La Choy** vegetable	35
Meatless: ¾ cup prepared / **La Choy** Bi-Pack	60
Pork: 10½ oz / **Chun King** Divider Pak	110
Pork: ¾ cup prepared / **La Choy** Bi-Pack	90
Shrimp: 10½ oz / **Chun King**	70
Shrimp: ¾ cup / **La Choy**	60
Shrimp: ¾ cup prepared / **La Choy** Bi-Pack	70
Vegetables: ½ cup / **Chun King**	20
Chow mein, frozen	
Beef mandarin: 11 oz / **Van de Kamp's**	370
Beef pepper: 12 oz / **La Choy**	250
Beef: 10 oz / **Green Giant** Entrée	240
Chicken: 6 oz / **Chun King** Pouch	90

CALORIES

Chicken: 12 oz / **La Choy**	260
Chicken: 9 oz / **Green Giant** Entrée	220
Chicken wo noodles: 8 oz / **Stouffer's**	145
Chicken: 11¼ oz / **Stouffer's** Lean Cuisine	250
Chicken Mandarin: 11 oz / **Van de Kamp's**	380
Shrimp: 6 oz / **Chun King** Pouch	80
Shrimp: 12 oz / **La Choy**	220
Egg rolls, frozen	
Health Valley: 1 roll	45
Van de Kamp's: 5¼ oz	280
Chicken: 1 roll / **Chun King**	90
Chicken: 1 roll / **La Choy**	30
Lobster: 1 roll / **Health Valley**	170
Lobster: 1 roll / **La Choy**	27
Meat and shrimp: 1 roll /	
Chun King 2-roll pkg	130
Meat and shrimp: 1 roll /	
Chun King 12-roll pkg	33
Meat and shrimp: 7½ oz pkg: 1 roll / **La Choy**	16
Meat and shrimp: 6½ oz pkg: 1 roll / **La Choy**	26
Nut: 1 roll / **Health Valley**	300
Shrimp: 1 roll / **Chun King**	30
Shrimp: 1 roll / **Health Valley**	145
Shrimp: 6½ oz pkg: 1 roll / **La Choy**	26
Shrimp: 6 oz pkg: 1 roll / **La Choy**	160
Teriyaki: 1 roll / **Health Valley**	215
Fried rice, canned: ¾ cup / **La Choy**	190
Fried rice w pork, frozen: ¾ cup / **La Choy**	140
Noodles, canned, Chinatown style: ¾ oz /	
Chun King	100
Noodles, canned, chow mein: ⅝ oz / **Chun King**	100
Noodles, canned, chow mein: ½ cup / **La Choy**	150
Noodles, canned, rice: ½ cup / **La Choy**	130
Pea pods, frozen: ½ pkg (3 oz) / **La Choy**	35
Pepper Oriental, canned: 10½ oz /	
Chun King Divider Pak	70
Stir fry dishes	
Chicken and vegetables, frozen: 10 oz / **Green**	
Giant	250
Chicken, cashew, frozen: 10 oz / **Green Giant**	340

CALORIES

Chicken, sweet and sour, frozen: 10 oz / **Green Giant**	300
Sesame ginger, frozen: 11½ oz / **Legume**	260
Shrimp and fried rice: 10 oz / **Green Giant** Entrée	300
Szechwan beef, frozen: 10 oz / **Green Giant** Entrée	290
Teriyaki, beef, frozen: 10 oz / **Green Giant** Entrée	320
Sukiyaki, canned: ¾ cup prepared / **La Choy** Bi-Pack	70
Sweet and sour	
Chicken, canned: ¾ cup / **La Choy** Oriental	240
Chicken, frozen: ⅔ cup / **La Choy**	190
Pork, canned: ¾ cup / **La Choy** Oriental	260
Pork, frozen: 6 oz / **Chun King** Pouch	200
Pork, frozen: ⅔ cup / **La Choy**	180
Pork, frozen: 11 oz / **Van de Kamp's**	460
Vegetables, Chinese, canned: ½ cup / **La Choy**	12
Vegetables, Chinese style, frozen: ½ cup / **La Choy**	25
Water chestnuts, canned: 4¼ oz / **Chun King**	70
Water chestnuts, canned: ¼ cup / **La Choy**	16
Won ton soup: ½ pkg / **La Choy**	50

Chips, Crisps Bars and Similar Snacks

CALORIES

Breakfast Bars: 1 bar	
All flavors / **Figurines**	138
Chocolate / **Milk Break**	230
Chocolate chip / **Carnation** Breakfast Bar	200
Chocolate chip / **Carnation** Slender	135
Chocolate crunch / **Carnation** Breakfast Bar	190
Chocolate mint / **Milk Break**	230

CALORIES

Chocolate peanut / **Carnation** Slender	135
Honey nut / **Carnation** Breakfast Bar	190
Natural flavor / **Milk Break**	230
Peanut butter / **Milk Break**	230
Peanut butter w chocolate chips / **Carnation** Breakfast Bar	200
Peanut butter crunch / **Carnation** Breakfast Bar	200
Vanilla / **Carnation** Slender	135

Granola bars: 1 bar

Almond / **Nature Valley**	120
Apple / **Nature Valley** Chewy	130
Chocolate chip / **Hershey's** New Trail	200
Chocolate chip / **Nature Valley** Chewy	150
Chocolate chip / **Quaker** Chewy	129
Cinnamon / **Nature Valley**	110
Coconut / **Nature Valley**	120
Honey and oats / **Quaker** Chewy	125
Honey graham / **Hershey's** New Trail	200
Oats and honey / **Nature Valley**	110
Peanut / **Nature Valley**	120
Peanut butter / **Hershey's** New Trail	200
Peanut butter / **Nature Valley**	120
Peanut butter / **Nature Valley** Chewy	140
Peanut butter / **Quaker** Chewy	129
Peanut butter, chocolate chip / **Hershey's** New Trail	200
Raisin / **Nature Valley** Chewy	130
Raisin and cinnamon / **Quaker Chewy**	129

1 oz unless noted

Bugles	150
Bugles, nacho cheese	160
Cheddar sticks / **Flavor Tree**	160
Cheese balls, baked / **Guy's**	160
Cheese 'n Crunch	160
Cheese puffs: 1⅛ oz / **Laura Scudder's**	162
Cheese snacks / **Lite-Line** Puffed Cheese Curls	130
Chee.tos, crunch / **Frito-Lay**	160
Chee.tos, puffs / **Frito-Lay**	160

CALORIES

Chee.tos, puffed balls / **Frito-Lay**	160
Chee.tos, cheddar flavored / **Frito-Lay**	150
Cheez Balls / **Planters**	160
Cheez Curls / **Planters**	160
Cheez Doodles, crunchy	160
Cheez Doodles, puffed	160
Cheez Waffies / **Wise**	140
Cheez Waffies / **Old London**	140
Chipsters / **Nabisco**	130
Corn chips	
Bar-B-Q	150
Flavor Tree	150
Fritos	150
Fritos, king size	150
Granny Goose	157
Laura Scudder's: 1½ oz	237
Planters	170
Corn Crunchies / **Wise**	160
Corn Diggers / **Nabisco**	150
Corn & Sesame Chips / **Nabisco**	160
Corn sticks / **Flavor Tree**	160
Crispy Chinese TV Snacks / **Mother's**	140
Crunch 'N Munch: 1¼ oz / **Franklin**	200
Doo Dads / **Nabisco**	140
Fiesta Chips / **Granny Goose**	147
Flings / **Nabisco**	160
Granola nuts / **Flavor Tree**	170
Jalapeno Corn Toots / **Granny Goose**	161
Korkers / **Nabisco**	160
Mini-Tacos: 7 oz / **Laura Scudder's**	927
Party Mix / **Flavor Tree**	160
Potato chips	
Charles	160
Granny Goose	161
Laura Scudder's	150
Lay's	150
O'Grady's	150
Planter's Stackable	150
Pringle's	170
Pringle's Cheez-ums	170
Pringle's Light	150

Pringle's Rippled	170
Ruffles	150
Wise	160
Au Gratin flavored / **O'Grady's**	150
Bacon & cheddar flavored, waffle / **Charles**	140
Bacon and sour cream / **Ruffles**	150
Barbecue / **Granny Goose**	159
Barbecue / **Laura Scudder's**	146
Barbecue / **Lay's**	150
Barbecue / **Morton's** Ridgies	150
Barbecue / **Ruffles**	150
Green onion / **Granny Goose**	160
Ketchup and french fry flavor / **Buckeye**	160
Salt 'N Vinegar / **Lay's**	150
Sour cream and onion / **Lay's**	150
Sour cream and onion / **Ruffles**	150
Unsalted / **Lay's**	160
Unsalted / **Wise**	150
Potato sticks: 1½ oz / **O&C**	231
Pork rinds, fried / **Granny Goose**	152
Sesame chips / **Flavor Tree**	150
Sesame nuts / **Flavor Tree**	180
Sesame sticks / **Flavor Tree**	150
Sesame sticks w bran / **Flavor Tree**	160
Sesame sticks, unsalted / **Flavor Tree**	160
Sour cream and onion sticks / **Flavor Tree**	150
Tortilla chips	
Doritos	140
Doritos, nacho cheese	140
Doritos, taco flavor	140
Granny Goose	139
Laura Scudder's	137
Nabisco	150
Old El Paso Nachips: 10 chips	169
Tostitos	140
Tostitos, nacho cheese flavor	150
Nacho / **Planters**	130
Nacho cheese flavored / **Lite-Line**	130
Nacho cheese flavored / **Nabisco** Buenos	150
Nacho cheese flavored / **Wise** Bravos	150
Sour cream and onion / **Nabisco** Buenos	150

CALORIES

Taco / **Planters**	130
Wheat nuts / **Flavor Tree**	190
Wheat Snax / **Estee**	110

Chocolate and Chips

CALORIES

For baking: 1 oz unless noted

Chips	
Butterscotch / **Nestlé's** Morsels	150
Chocolate, milk: ¼ cup / **Hershey's**	220
Chocolate, milk / **Nestlé's** Morsels	150
Chocolate, semi-sweet / **Borden**	150
Chocolate, semi-sweet / **Ghirardelli**	153
Chocolate, semi-sweet: ¼ cup / **Hershey's**	220
Chocolate, semi-sweet: ¼ cup /	
Hershey's Mini	220
Chocolate, semi-sweet / **Nestlé's** Morsels	150
Choco-Bake / **Nestlé's**	170
Chocolate, ground: **Ghirardelli**	120
Chocolate, solid	
Hershey's	190
German sweet / **Baker's**	140
Semi-sweet / **Baker's**	130
Unswt / **Baker's**	140

Cocktails

ALCOHOLIC

CALORIES

Canned: 2 fl oz

Apricot Sour / **Party Tyme**	66
Banana Daiquiri / **Party Tyme**	66

CALORIES

Daiquiri / **Party Tyme**	65
Gimlet / **Party Tyme**	82
Gin and Tonic / **Party Tyme**	55
Mai Tai / **Party Tyme**	65
Manhattan / **Party Tyme**	74
Margarita / **Party Tyme**	66
Martini / **Party Tyme**	82
Piña Colada / **Party Tyme**	63
Rum and Cola / **Party Tyme**	55
Scotch Sour / **Party Tyme**	65
Screwdriver / **Party Tyme**	69
Tom Collins / **Party Tyme**	58
Vodka Martini / **Party Tyme**	72
Vodka Tonic / **Party Tyme**	55

NONALCOHOLIC MIXES

Dry: 1 packet

Alexander / **Holland House**	69
Banana Daiquiri / **Holland House**	66
Bloody Mary / **Holland House**	56
Collins: 1 env prepared / **Bar-Tender's**	177
Daiquiri: 1 env prepared / **Bar-Tender's**	177
Daiquiri / **Holland House**	69
Gimlet / **Holland House**	69
Grasshopper / **Holland House**	69
Lite: 1 env prepared / **Bar-Tender's**	72
Mai Tai / **Holland House**	69
Margarita / **Holland House**	69
Mint Julep / **Holland House**	67
Piña Colada / **Holland House**	66
Pink Squirrel / **Holland House**	69
Pussycat: 1 env prepared / **Bar-Tender's**	177
Screwdriver / **Holland House**	69
Slightly Sour: 1 env prepared / **Bar-Tender's**	177
Strawberry Margarita / **Holland House**	62
Strawberry Sting / **Holland House**	74
Tequila Sunrise / **Holland House**	63
Tom Collins / **Holland House**	69
Vodka Sour / **Holland House**	65

CALORIES

Wallbanger / **Holland House**	65
Whiskey Sour: 1 env prepared / **Bar Tender's**	177
Whiskey Sour / **Holland House**	69

Liquid: 1 fl oz unless noted

Amaretto / **Holland House**	79
Apricot Sour / **Holland House**	48
Black Russian / **Holland House**	92
Blackberry Sour / **Holland House**	50
Bloody Mary / **Holland House**	10
Cocktail Host / **Holland House**	47
Cream of Coconut / **Holland House** Coco Casa	117
Daiquiri / **Holland House**	51
Dry Martini / **Holland House**	10
Gimlet / **Holland House**	40
Mai Tai / **Holland House**	33
Manhattan / **Holland House**	29
Margarita / **Holland House**	39
Old Fashioned / **Holland House**	36
Piña Colada / **Holland House**	60
Strawberry Sting / **Holland House**	35
Sweet Sour Mix: 6 fl oz / **Sunkist**	115
Tom Collins / **Holland House**	67
Whiskey Sour / **Holland House**	55
Whiskey Sour / **Holland House** Low Calorie	9

Cocoa

CALORIES

Cocoa: ⅓ cup / **Hershey's**	120

Mix:

Estee: 6 oz prepared	50
Hershey's: 1 oz	120
Nestlé's: 1 oz	110
Instant: 1 env / **Alba**	60

CALORIES

Instant: 1 oz / **Carnation**	110
Instant: 3 tbsp prepared w 8 oz milk / **Hershey's**	240
Instant: 1 pkt / **Ovaltine**	50
Instant: 1 pkt / **Ovaltine** Hot 'n Rich	120
Instant: 1 env / **Superman** instant	70
Instant, chocolate marshmallow: 1 env / **Alba**	60
Instant, chocolate and mini-marshmallows: 1 oz / **Carnation**	110
Instant, mocha: 1 env / **Alba**	60
Instant, rich chocolate: 1 oz / **Carnation**	110
Instant, rich chocolate: 1 pkt / **Carnation** 70-calorie	70
Instant, sugar free: 1 pkt / **Carnation**	50
Instant, sugar free: 1 pkt / **Ovaltine**	40
Instant, sugar-free mint: 1 pkt / **Ovaltine**	40
Instant, w marshmallows: 1 oz / **Nestlé's**	110

Coconut

FRESH

	CALORIES
In shell: 1 coconut	1375
Meat: 1 piece (2 × 2 × ½ in)	155
Meat, shredded or grated: 1 cup	275
Cream (liquid from grated meat): 1 cup	815
Milk (liquid from mixture of grated meat and water): 1 cup	600
Water (liquid from coconuts): 1 cup	55

CANNED OR PACKAGED

¼ cup unless noted

Plain / **Baker's** Angel Flake	90
Plain / **Baker's** Premium Shred	100
Plain / **Baker's** Southern Style	90
Plain, shredded / **Durkee**	70

CALORIES

Plain, shredded or flaked: 1 oz / **Town House**	165
Cookie-coconut / **Baker's**	140

Coffee

All regular coffee has about:
  2 calories per cup for ground roasted
  4 calories per cup for instant and
    instant freeze-dried

CALORIES

Flavored coffee instant mixes, prepared: 6 fl oz	
Cafe Amaretto / **General Foods** International	50
Cafe Francais / **General Foods** International	60
Cafe Vienna / **General Foods** International	60
Irish Mocha Mint / **General Foods** International	50
Orange Cappuccino / **General Foods** International	60
Suisse Mocha / **General Foods** International	60
Postum (cereal beverage), instant: 6 fl oz	3

Condiments

See also Sauces *and* Seasonings

CALORIES

Catsup	
Del Monte: ¼ cup	60
Del Monte No Salt: ¼ cup	60
Dia-Mel: 1 tbsp	6
Heinz: 1 tbsp	18
Heinz Hot: 1 tbsp	18
Heinz Lite: 1 tbsp	8

CALORIES

Heinz Low Sodium Lite: 1 tbsp	8
Hunt's: 1 tbsp	16
Hunt's No Salt: 1 tbsp	20
Chili sauce: 1 tbsp / **Heinz**	17
Chutney: 1 tbsp / **Major Grey's**	53
Durkee Famous Sauce: 1 tbsp	69
Horseradish, cream style: 1 tbsp / **Vita**	10
Horseradish, prepared: 1 tbsp / **Vita**	10
Hot sauce: ½ tsp / **Frank's**	1
Mint sauce: 1 tbsp / **Crosse & Blackwell**	16
Mustard	
Diablo: ¼ oz / **Gulden's**	8
Dijon: 1 tbsp / **Grey Poupon**	18
Dijon: ¼ oz / **Gulden's**	10
French's Bold 'n Spicy: 1 tbsp	16
French's Medford: 1 tbsp	16
French's Yellow: 1 tbsp	10
Gulden's Spicy: ¼ oz	8
Gulden's Creamy Mild: ¼ oz	6
Heinz Brown: 1 tsp	8
Mr. Mustard: 1 tsp	11
w horseradish: 1 tbsp / **French's**	16
w onion: 1 tbsp / **French's**	25
Sauce Diable: 1 tbsp / **Escoffier**	20
Sauce Robert: 1 tbsp	20
Seafood cocktail: 1 tbsp / **Crosse & Blackwell**	22
Seafood cocktail: ½ oz / **Nutri-Dyne Elwood**	5
Seafood cocktail: 1 tbsp / **Vita**	12
Soy sauce: 1 oz / **Health Valley** Tamari-Ya	22
Steak sauce	
A.1. Sauce: 1 tbsp	12
Crosse & Blackwell: 1 tbsp	21
Lea & Perrins: 1 fl oz	40
Mrs. Dash: 1 tbsp	17
Steak Supreme: 1 tbsp	20
Taco sauce: 1 tbsp / **Ortega**	22
Tartar sauce: 1 tbsp / **Hellmann's**	70
Tartar sauce: 1 tbsp / **Vita**	34
Vinegar	
Apple cider: 1 fl oz / **Lucky Leaf**	4
Apple cider: 1 fl oz / **Musselman's**	4

CALORIES

Red wine: 1 fl oz / **Lucky Leaf**	4
Red wine: 1 fl oz / **Musselman's**	4
Red wine: 1 fl oz / **Regina**	4
Red wine and garlic: 1 fl oz / **Regina**	4
White distilled: 1 fl oz / **Lucky Leaf**	4
White distilled: 1 fl oz / **Musselman's**	4
White wine: 1 fl oz / **Regina**	4

Wine, cooking
Burgundy: ¼ cup / **Regina**	2
Sauterne: ¼ cup / **Regina**	2
Sherry: 1 oz / **Great Western**	38
Sherry: ¼ cup / **Regina**	20
Sherry: 1 oz / **Taylor**	37
Sherry: 1 oz / **Taylor Light**	33

Worcestershire
Crosse & Blackwell: 1 tbsp	15
French's Regular: 1 tbsp	10
French's Smoky: 1 tbsp	10
Lea & Perrins: 1 tsp	5
Nutri-Dyne Elwood: ½ oz	12

Cookies

CALORIES

1 piece unless noted

Almond fudge, chocolate chip / **Duncan Hines**	55
Almond supreme / **Pepperidge Farm**	70
Almond toast / **Stella D'Oro**	56
Almond windmills / **Nabisco**	47
Angel bars / **Stella D'Oro**	69
Angelica Goodies / **Stella D'Oro**	104
Angel wings / **Stella D'Oro·**	75
Anginetti / **Stella D'Oro**	32

Animal crackers
Barnum's Animals: 11 pieces	130
Ralston Purina: 15 pieces (1 oz)	130
Sunshine: 1 piece	11

	CALORIES
Animal snaps, cinnamon / **Health Valley**	15
Animal snaps, vanilla / **Health Valley**	15
Anisette sponge / **Stella D'Oro**	52
Anisette toast / **Stella D'Oro**	46
Anisette toast, large / **Stella D'Oro**	138
Apple / **Pepperidge Farm**	50
Apple crisp / **Nabisco**	50
Apple spice / **Pepperidge Farm**	53
Applesauce raisin, iced / **Nabisco** Almost Home	70
Apricot-raspberry / **Pepperidge Farm**	50
Apricot raspberry snack bar / **Pepperidge Farm**	170
Arrowroot biscuit / **National**	22
Biscos / **Nabisco**	47
Blueberry / **Pepperidge Farm**	57
Blueberry snack bar / **Pepperidge Farm**	170
Bordeaux / **Pepperidge Farm**	110
Breakfast Treat / **Stella D'Oro**	120
Brown Edge sandwich / **Nabisco**	80
Brown Edge wafers / **Nabisco**	28
Brownie chocolate nut / **Pepperidge Farm**	57
Brownie nut snack bar / **Pepperidge Farm**	190
Brussels / **Pepperidge Farm**	53
Brussels mint / **Pepperidge Farm**	67
Butter / **Pepperidge Farm**	37
Butter-flavored / **Nabisco**	23
Butter-flavored / **Sunshine**	28
Butterscotch / **Nutri-Dyne Aproten**	70
Butterscotch chocolate chip / **Duncan Hines**	55
Cappuccino / **Pepperidge Farm**	53
Capri / **Pepperidge Farm**	80
Carob snaps / **Health Valley**	14
Champagne / **Pepperidge Farm**	33
Chessman / **Pepperidge Farm**	43
Chinese Dessert / **Stella D'Oro**	178
Chip-A-Roos / **Sunshine**	52
Chips Ahoy!	53
Chocolate chip	
Duncan Hines	55
Keebler Chips Deluxe	90
Keebler Rich 'n Chips	80
Nabisco Almost Home	65

CALORIES

Nabisco Cookie Little: 20 pieces	140
Nutri-Dyne Aproten	80
Pepperidge Farm	50
Snaps	20
Sunshine Chocolate Nuggets	20
Tastykake	61
Chocolate chip macaroon snack bar / **Pepperidge Farm**	210
Chocolate chocolate chip / **Nabisco**	53
Chocolate chocolate chip / **Pepperidge Farm**	53
Chocolate chunk pecan / **Pepperidge Farm**	65
Chocolate peanut bars / **Nabisco**	95
Chocolate snaps / **Nabisco**	16
Chocolate wafers / **Nabisco**	28
Cinnamon chip / **Pepperidge Farm**	50
Cinnamon honey jumbo / **Health Valley**	60
Cinnamon raisin / **Nabisco** Almost Home	70
Cinnamon sugar / **Pepperidge Farm**	53
Cinnamon treats: .9 oz / **Nabisco**	110
Cocoa chocolate chip / **Archway**	77
Coconut, dietetic / **Stella D'Oro**	50
Cocoanut bars / **Nabisco**	43
Cocoanut chocolate chip / **Nabisco**	75
Cocoanut macaroon, soft / **Nabisco**	95
Coconut chocolate chip / **Archway**	81
Coconut granola / **Pepperidge Farm**	57
Coconut macaroon snack bar / **Pepperidge Farm**	210
Coconut snaps / **Health Valley**	12
Coconut squares / **Archway**	117
Como delights / **Stella D'Oro**	138
Cookie Break, mixed / **Nabisco**	53
Cookie Break, vanilla / **Nabisco**	50
Creme wafer sticks / **Nabisco**	47
Date nut granola / **Pepperidge Farm**	53
Date nut snack bar / **Pepperidge Farm**	190
Date pecan / **Health Valley**	40
Date pecan / **Pepperidge Farm**	53
Dietetic / **Estee**	25
Dixie Vanilla / **Sunshine**	58
Duplex / **Estee**	40

CALORIES

Egg biscuits	
Stella D'Oro	44
Stella D'Oro dietetic	40
Anise-rum / **Stella D'Oro**	125
Brandy-vanilla / **Stella D'Oro**	125
Sugared / **Stella D'Oro**	75
Egg jumbo / **Stella D'Oro**	46
Fig bars / **Sunshine**	45
Fig bars, whole wheat / **Nabisco** Fig Wheats	60
Fig Newtons / **Nabisco**	60
Frosty lemon / **Archway**	122
Fruit crescent / **Stella D'Oro**	55
Fruit sticks, all flavors / **Nabisco** Almost Home	70
Fudge bar / **Tastykake**	266
Fudge chocolate chip / **Nabisco** Almost Home	65
Fudge stripes / **Keebler**	50
Geneva / **Pepperidge Farm**	57
Gingerman / **Pepperidge Farm**	33
Ginger snaps / **Health Valley**	15
Ginger snaps / **Nabisco**	30
Ginger snaps / **Sunshine**	16
Golden bars / **Stella D'Oro**	109
Golden fruit / **Sunshine**	60
Graham crackers	
Honey Maid	30
Nabisco	30
Nabisco Fancy Dip	65
Nabisco Party	70
I. Rokeach	15
Chocolate / **Nabisco**	57
Cinnamon / **Keebler**	18
Cinnamon / **Sunshine**	17
Fudge-covered / **Keebler**	40
Honey: 1 oz / **Health Valley**	125
Honey / **Keebler**	18
Sugar honey / **Ralston**	15
Sugar honey / **Sunshine**	15
Hazelnut / **Pepperidge Farm**	57
HeyDay / **Nabisco**	120
Hostess assortment / **Stella D'Oro**	37
Hydrox, chocolate	49

CALORIES

Hydrox, vanilla	51
Irish oatmeal / **Pepperidge Farm**	47
Kettle cookies / **Nabisco**	35
Kichel, dietetic / **Stella D'Oro**	8
Lady Stella assortment / **Stella D'Oro**	39
Lemon coconut / **Archway**	78
Lemon coolers / **Sunshine**	29
Lemon nut crunch / **Pepperidge Farm**	57
Lemon snaps / **Health Valley**	10
Lido / **Pepperidge Farm**	95
Lorna Doones	40
Love cookies, dietetic / **Stella D'Oro**	110
Mallomars	60
MalloPuffs / Sunshine	62
Margherite chocolate / **Stella D'Oro**	72
Margherite vanilla / **Stella D'Oro**	75
Marseilles assortment / **Pepperidge Farm**	45
Marshmallow puffs / **Nabisco**	85
Marshmallow twirls / **Nabisco**	130
Milano / **Pepperidge Farm**	60
Mint chocolate chip / **Duncan Hines**	55
Mint Milano / **Pepperidge Farm**	77
Molasses / **Nabisco** Pantry	60
Molasses crisps / **Pepperidge Farm**	33
Mystic Mints / **Nabisco**	90
Nassau / **Pepperidge Farm**	85
Nilla Wafers / **Nabisco**	18
Nutter Butter	70
Nutter Butter, chocolate	57
Oatmeal	
Archway	116
Drake's	63
Health Valley	40
Keebler	80
Nabisco Bakers Bonus	80
Nabisco Cookie Little	6
Sunshine	61
Date filled / **Archway**	106
Creme / **Nabisco** Almost Home	140
Honey / **Health Valley** Jumbo	60
Iced / **Nabisco** Almost Home	65

Raisin / **Nabisco** Almost Home	65
Raisin / **Pepperidge Farm**	57
Raisin bar / **Tastykake**	239
Oatmeal and nut / **Archway**	71
Old fashion molasses / **Archway**	120
Orange / **Pepperidge Farm**	57
Orange Milano / **Pepperidge Farm**	77
Oreo	50
Oreo, Double Stuff	70
Orleans / **Pepperidge Farm**	30
Orleans sandwich / **Pepperidge Farm**	60
Peanut brittle cookies / **Nabisco**	50
Peanut butter	
Health Valley	40
Nabisco Almost Home	70
Chip / **Archway**	80
Chip / **Pepperidge Farm**	53
Fudge / **Nabisco**	50
Fudge / **Nabisco** Almost Home	70
Fudge and chocolate chip / **Duncan Hines**	55
Honey / **Health Valley** Jumbo	60
Peanut creme patties / **Nabisco**	35
Pecan crunch / **Archway**	85
Pecan sandies / **Keebler**	80
Pecan shortbread / **Nabisco**	80
Pfeffernusse / **Stella D'Oro**	37
Piccolo crepe / **Nabisco**	22
Pirouettes, original / **Pepperidge Farm**	37
Pirouettes, chocolate-laced / **Pepperidge Farm**	37
Pitter Patter / **Keebler**	90
Pretzel, coated / **Tastykake**	108
Pretzel, coated, mini / **Tastykake**	24
Raisin bran / **Health Valley**	35
Raisin bran / **Pepperidge Farm**	53
Raisin fruit biscuit / **Nabisco**	60
Raisin spice snack bar / **Pepperidge Farm**	180
Royal Nuggets, dietetic / **Stella D'Oro**	1
Sandwich, creme	
Nabisco Baronet	53
Nabisco Cameo	70
Nabisco Mayfair	65

CALORIES

Nabisco Mayfair Tea Rose	53
Nabisco Mayfair Crown	53
Nabisco Swiss	50
Chocolate fudge / **Sunshine**	70
Coconut / **Sunshine** Coconut Cremers	51
Fudge / **Keebler** Fudge Cremers	60
Fudge / **Nabisco**	53
Fudge / **Nabisco** Gaiety	53
Fudge and chocolate / **Nabisco** Almost Home	140
Oatmeal / **Keebler**	80
Oatmeal peanut / **Sunshine**	82
Peanut butter / **Nabisco** Almost Home	140
Vanilla / **Sunshine** Cup Custard	65
Sandwich, malted milk peanut butter / **Nabisco**	38
Sesame / **Stella D'Oro**	48
Sesame, dietetic / **Stella D'Oro**	43
Seville / **Pepperidge Farm**	55
Shortbread / **Pepperidge Farm**	75
Shortcake / **Nabisco** Cookie Little	6
Shortcake / **Nabisco** Melt-a-Way	70
Social Tea Biscuit / **Nabisco**	22
Southport assortment / **Pepperidge Farm**	75
Spiced wafers / **Nabisco**	32
Sprinkles / **Sunshine**	59
Strawberry / **Pepperidge Farm**	50
Striped shortbread / **Nabisco**	50
Sugar / **Pepperidge Farm**	50
Sugar rings / **Nabisco**	70
Sugar wafers / **Nabisco** Biscos	19
Swiss fudge / **Stella D'Oro**	67
Tahiti / **Pepperidge Farm**	85
Tea Time Biscuit / **Nabisco** Mayfair	25
Toy cookies / **Sunshine**	13
Twiddle Sticks / **Nabisco**	53
Vanilla shortbread cookie tub / **Tastykake**	49
Vienna fingers / **Sunshine**	69
Wafers	
Creme-filled, assorted / **Estee**	30
Creme-filled, chocolate / **Estee**	20
Creme-filled, vanilla / **Estee**	20
Peanut butter / **Sunshine**	39

Snack, chocolate, strawberry, vanilla / **Estee**	80
Snack, chocolate-coated / **Estee**	120
Sugar / **Sunshine**	42
Vanilla / **Keebler**	60
Vanilla / **Sunshine**	14
Waffle Cremes / **Nabisco** Biscos	43
Yum Yums / **Sunshine**	83

COOKIE MIXES

Prepared according to package directions

Brownies	
Betty Crocker Family Size: 1/24 pkg	130
Betty Crocker Supreme Fudge: 1/24 pkg	120
Betty Crocker Supreme Golden: 1/24 pkg	130
Duncan Hines Double Fudge: 1/24 pkg	130
Estee: 2-in square	45
Pillsbury: 2-in square	150
Pillsbury Family Size: 2-in square	150
Walnut / **Betty Crocker** Family Size: 1/24 pkg	130
Walnut / **Betty Crocker** Regular: 1/16 pkg	160
Walnut / **Pillsbury** Family Size: 2-in square	160
Chocolate chip	
Betty Crocker Big Batch: 1/18 pkg (2 cookies)	120
Duncan Hines: 2 cookies	150
Duncan Hines Double: 2 cookies	140
Pillsbury: 3 cookies	170
Quaker: 8/10 oz dry	92
Coconut macaroon: 1/14 pkg / Betty Crocker	80
Date bar: 1/32 pkg / **Betty Crocker**	60
Double chocolate: 3 cookies / **Pillsbury**	150
Fudge: 1 bar	
Brown sugar and oatmeal / **Pillsbury** Fudge Jumbles	100
Chocolate chip and oatmeal / **Pillsbury** Fudge Jumbles	100
Coconut and oatmeal / **Pillsbury** Fudge Jumbles	100
Peanut butter and oatmeal / **Pillsbury** Fudge Jumbles	100

CALORIES

Oatmeal: 1/18 (2 cookies) / **Betty Crocker** Big Batch	130
Oatmeal raisin: 2 cookies / **Duncan Hines**	130
Peanut butter: 2 cookies / **Duncan Hines**	140
Peanut butter: 3 cookies / **Pillsbury**	150
Sugar: 1/18 (2 cookies) / **Betty Crocker** Big Batch	120
Sugar: 2 cookies / **Duncan Hines** Golden	130
Sugar: 3 cookies / **Pillsbury**	170
Vienna Dream Bar: 1/14 pkg / **Betty Crocker**	90

REFRIGERATED DOUGH

1 cookie

Chocolate chip / **Merico**	55
Chocolate chip w pecan / **Merico**	55
Chocolate chip: 1/36 pkg / **Pillsbury**	53
Fudge brownie: 1/16 pkg / **Pillsbury**	110
Peanut butter / **Merico**	55
Peanut butter: 1/36 pkg / **Pillsbury**	53
Sugar / **Merico**	55
Sugar: 1/36 pkg / **Pillsbury**	63

Crackers

CALORIES

1 cracker unless noted

Amaranth / **Health Valley**	22
Bacon 'n Dip / **Nabisco**	9
Banquet Wafers / **Sunshine**	14
Buttery Flavored Sesame / **Nabisco**	16
Cheddar: 1 oz / **Charles**	130
Cheddar Snacks / **Ralston**	7
Cheddar Triangles / **Nabisco**	9
Cheddar 'n Sesame / **Nabisco** Country	9
Cheese Nips / **Nabisco**	5
Cheese Peanut Butter Sandwich / **Nabisco**	35
Cheese Sandwich / **Nabisco**	28

CALORIES

Cheese Snacks / **Ralston**	6
Cheese Tid-Bit / **Nabisco**	5
Cheese Wheels: 1 oz / **Health Valley**	140
Cheez-It / **Sunshine**	6
Chicken in a Biskit / **Nabisco**	11
Chippers / **Nabisco**	15
Club: smallest piece when broken on score line / **Keebler**	15
Cracked Wheat / **Pepperidge Farm**	28
Crown Pilot / **Nabisco**	75
Dip in a Chip / **Nabisco**	10
Dixies / **Nabisco**	8
English Water Biscuit / **Pepperidge Farm**	18
Escort / **Nabisco**	21
French Onion / **Nabisco**	13
Goldfish: 1 piece has about 3 calories	
Cheddar Cheese: 45 pieces / **Pepperidge Farm**	140
Parmesan Cheese: 45 pieces / **Pepperidge Farm**	140
Pizza Flavored: 45 pieces / **Pepperidge Farm**	140
Pretzel: 40 pieces / **Pepperidge Farm**	120
Salted: 45 pieces / **Pepperidge Farm**	140
Harvest Wheats / **Keebler**	23
Hearty Wheat / **Pepperidge Farm**	25
Herb: 1 oz / **Health Valley**	140
Herb: 1 oz / **Health Valley** No Salt	137
Hi Ho / **Sunshine**	19
Holland Rusk / **Nabisco**	40
Matzos: 1 sheet or 1 cracker	
American / **Manischewitz**	115
Egg 'n Onion / **Manischewitz**	112
Egg Passover / **Manischewitz**	132
Matzo crackers / **Manischewitz**	9
Passover / **Manischewitz**	129
Thins / **Manischewitz**	91
Thin Salted / **Manischewitz**	95
Thin Tea / **Manischewitz**	103
Thin Tea Passover / **Manischewitz**	103
Unsalted / **Manischewitz**	112
Whole Wheat w bran / **Manischewitz**	110
Whole Wheat Passover / **Manischewitz**	118
Meal Mates / **Nabisco**	22

CALORIES

Melba Toast: 1 piece	
Old London	17
Bacon / **Old London** Bacon Rounds	12
Cheese / **Old London** Cheese Rounds	12
Garlic / **Old London** Garlic Rounds	10
Onion / **Old London** Onion Rounds	10
Pumpernickel / **Old London**	17
Rye / **Old London**	17
Salty Rye / **Old London** Salty-Rye Rounds	10
Sesame / **Old London** Sesame Rounds	12
Unsalted / **Old London**	17
Whole Grain / **Old London**	20
Milk Crackers / **Nabisco** Royal Lunch	55
Oyster / **Ralston**	2
Oyster / **Sunshine**	4
Rich & Crisp / **Ralston**	16
Ritz / **Nabisco**	17
Rye	
Wasa Golden	37
Wasa Hearty	54
Wasa Lite	30
Wasa Sport	43
Wasa Fiber Plus	30
Rye Snacks / **Ralston**	9
Ry Krisp, Natural	25
Ry Krisp, Seasoned	25
Ry Krisp, Sesame	25
Saltines and soda crackers	
Krispy / **Sunshine**	12
Krispy, unsalted / **Sunshine**	13
Premium / **Nabisco**	12
Premium, unsalted tops / **Nabisco**	12
Ralston	12
Rokeach Kosher	12
Zesta / **Keebler**	12
Sea Rounds / **Nabisco**	45
Sesame: 1 oz / **Health Valley**	130
Sesame: 1 oz / **Health Valley** No Salt	140
Sesame / **Pepperidge Farm**	20
Sesame Wheats! / **Nabisco**	17
7-Grain: 1 oz / **Health Valley**	140

CALORIES

7-Grain: 1 oz / **Health Valley** No Salt	150
Snack / **Rokeach**	14
Snackers / **Ralston**	18
Snacks Ahoy / **Nabisco**	9
Snack sticks	
Cheese / **Pepperidge Farm**	18
Original / **Pepperidge Farm**	16
Pumpernickel / **Pepperidge Farm**	16
Rye / **Pepperidge Farm**	16
Sesame / **Pepperidge Farm**	16
Sociables / **Nabisco**	11
Soup and Oyster: 40 pieces / **Nabisco** Dandy	120
Soup and Oyster: 36 pieces / **Nabisco** Oysterettes	120
Swiss Cheese Flavor / **Nabisco**	10
Tams, garlic / **Manischewitz**	15
Tams, onion / **Manischewitz**	15
Tams, wheat / **Manischewitz**	15
Tam Tams / **Manischewitz**	15
Tam Tams, no salt / **Manischewitz**	14
Thins	
Bacon Flavored / **Nabisco**	11
Butter Flavored / **Pepperidge Farm**	20
Cheese / **Pepperidge Farm**	18
Salted / **Pepperidge Farm**	15
Vegetable / **Nabisco**	12
Wheat / **Nabisco**	9
Wheat / **Pepperidge Farm**	15
Toasted Rye / **Keebler**	16
Toasted Sesame / **Keebler**	16
Toasted Wheat / **Keebler**	16
Town House / **Keebler**	16
Triscuit / **Nabisco**	20
Tuc / **Keebler**	23
Twigs / **Nabisco**	14
Uneeda Biscuit / **Nabisco**	22
Unsalted crackers / **Estee**	15
Unsalted top / **Ralston**	12
Waverly Wafers / **Nabisco**	18
Wheat	
Estee 6 Calorie Wheat Wafers	6
Manischewitz	9

CALORIES

Wasa Poppyseed	54
Wasa Sesame	54
Wheat Snacks / **Ralston**	9
Wheat, stoned: 1 oz / **Health Valley**	130
Wheat, stoned: 1 oz / **Health Valley** No Salt	140
Wheat, stoneground	
Hain Rich	16
Cheese / **Hain** Rich	12
Cheese & Garlic / **Hain** Rich	13
Onion / **Hain**	12
Sesame / **Hain**	13
Sour Cream & Chive / **Hain**	12
Sourdough / **Hain**	12
Vegetable / **Hain**	12
Wheat & Rye / **Hain**	11
Wheat & Sweet Rye: 1 oz / **Health Valley**	140
Wheat & Sweet Rye: 1 oz / **Health Valley** No Salt	140
Wheat Wafers / **Sunshine**	9
Wheatsworth / **Nabisco**	14
Yogurt & Green Onion: 1 oz / **Health Valley**	140
Yogurt & Green Onion: 1 oz / **Health Valley** No Salt	140
Zwieback / **Nabisco**	30

Cream

CALORIES

Half and half (cream and milk, 11.7% fat)	
1 cup	325
1 tbsp	20
Light, coffee or table (20.6% fat)	
1 cup	506
1 tbsp	32
Light whipping (31.3% fat)	
1 cup (about 2 cups whipped)	715
1 tbsp	45

Heavy whipping (37.6% fat)
    1 cup (about 2 cups whipped)   840
    1 tbsp   53

NONDAIRY CREAMERS

Dry
    Coffee-mate
        1 pkt   17
        1 tsp   11
        1 fl oz   27
    Coffee Tone: 1 tsp / **Lucerne**   10
    Cremora: 1 tsp   12
Liquid
    Coffee Tone, freezer pack: ½ fl oz (1 tbsp) /
        Lucerne   20
    Lucerne Cereal Blend: 1 fl oz   30

SOUR CREAM

Sour cream
    1 tbsp   25
    1 cup   490
Sour cream, half and half
    1 tbsp   20
    1 cup   390
Imitation sour cream: 1 tbsp / **Pet**   25

Dinners

	CALORIES
1 dinner	
Beans and franks: 10¼ oz / **Banquet**	500
Beans and franks: 10¾ oz / **Morton**	530
Beans and franks: 12½ oz / **Swanson**	550
Beef	
Banquet: 10 oz	345
Banquet Extra Helping: 16 oz	864
Morton: 10 oz	260
Swanson: 11½ oz	320
Burgundy: 10¼ oz / **Dinner Classics**	330
Chopped: 11 oz / **Banquet**	434
Chopped: 18 oz / **Banquet** Extra Helping	1028
Chopped sirloin: 11½ oz / **Swanson**	370
Chopped sirloin: 12¼ oz / **Le Menu**	420
Chopped sirloin: 9½ oz / **Morton** Steak House	760
Chopped steak: 17¼ oz /	
Swanson Hungry Man	620
Pepper oriental / **Chun King**	310
Pepper steak: 10 oz / **Classic Lite**	290
Short ribs: 10¼ oz / **Dinner Classics**	500
Sirloin tips: 11 oz / **Dinner Classics**	380
Sirloin tips: 11½ oz / **Le Menu**	390
Sliced: 14 oz / **Morton** Country Table	510
Sliced: 16 oz / **Swanson** Hungry Man	490

Sliced: 10¼ oz / **Classic Lite**	290
Steak, sirloin strip: 9½ oz / **Morton** Steak House	760
Steak, rib eye: 9 oz / **Morton** Steak House	820
Stroganoff: 11¼ oz / **Dinner Classics**	360
Tenderloin: 9½ oz / **Morton** Steak House	890
Burrito, Grande: 14¾ oz / **Van de Kamp's**	531
Burrito, bean and beef: 15¾ oz / **Swanson**	720

Chicken

À la king: 10¼ oz / **Le Menu**	320
Boneless: 10 oz / **Morton**	230
Boneless: 17 oz / **Morton** King Size	530
Boneless: 17½ oz / **Swanson** Hungry Man	790
Burgundy: 11¼ oz / **Classic Lite**	240
Fricassee: 11¾ oz / **Dinner Classics**	330
Fried: 11 oz / **Banquet**	359
Fried: 17 oz / **Banquet** Extra Helping	744
Fried: 11 oz / **Morton**	460
Fried: 15 oz / **Morton** Country Table	710
Fried: 17 oz / **Morton** King Size	860
Fried, barbecue: 9½ oz / **Swanson**	520
Fried, breast portion: 10¾ oz / **Swanson**	650
Fried, breast portion: 14 oz / **Swanson** Hungry Man	870
Fried, dark meat: 10¼ oz / **Swanson**	600
Fried, dark portions: 14 oz / **Swanson** Hungry Man	890
Oriental: 10 oz / **Classic Lite**	230
Parmigiana: 20 oz / **Swanson** Hungry Man	820
Parmigiana, breast of chicken / **Le Menu**	410
Sweet and sour: 11 oz / **Dinner Classics**	390
Sweet and sour: 11¼ oz / **Le Menu**	460
w dressing: 19 oz / **Banquet Extra Helping**	808
w dumplings: 19 oz / **Banquet Extra Helping**	883
Chicken Suiza: 14¾ oz / **Van de Kamp's**	552

Chow mein

Chicken / **Chun King**	320
Chicken and sweet and sour pork / **Chun King**	390
Shrimp / **Chun King**	300
Shrimp and beef pepper / **Chun King**	350

CALORIES

Enchilada
   El Charrito — 580
   Beef: 12 oz / **Banquet** — 497
   Beef: 11 oz / **Morton** — 280
   Beef / **Patio** — 550
   Beef: 15 oz / **Swanson** — 510
   Beef: 16 oz / **Swanson** Hungry Man — 660
   Beef: 12 oz / **Van de Kamp's** Holiday — 390
   Beef w rice and corn: 14¾ oz /
      Van de Kamp's — 485
   Beef w chili and beans / **Patio** — 850
   Beef and cheese / **Patio** — 820
   Beef and cheese: 14¾ oz / **Van de Kamp's** — 539
   Cheese: 12 oz / **Banquet** — 543
   Cheese: 21¼ oz / **Banquet** Extra Helping — 777
   Cheese / **El Charrito** — 540
   Cheese / **Patio** — 470
   Cheese: 12 oz / **Van de Kamp's** Holiday — 450
   Cheese w rice and beans: 14¾ oz /
      Van de Kamp's — 623
Fish
   Banquet: 8¾ oz — 553
   Morton: 9 oz — 260
   Van de Kamp's: 12 oz — 300
   and chips: 14 oz / **Banquet** Extra Helping — 769
   and chips: 10½ oz / **Swanson** — 590
   and chips: 14¾ oz / **Swanson** Hungry Man — 850
   Cod almondine: 12 oz / **Dinner Classics** — 350
   Cod divan: 13¼ oz — 290
      9 oz / **Classic Lite** — 180
   Seafood newburg: 10½ oz / **Dinner Classics** — 270
   Seafood natural herbs: 12 oz / **Classic Lite** — 260
Green peppers, stuffed: 12 oz / **Dinner Classics** — 350
Ham: 10 oz / **Banquet** — 532
Ham: 10 oz / **Morton** — 440
Italian style: 12 oz / **Banquet** — 597
Lasagna: 10 oz / **Dinner Classics** — 380
Lasagna: 13 oz / **Swanson** — 420
Lasagna w meat: 18¾ oz / **Swanson** Hungry Man — 680
Macaroni and beef: 10 oz / **Morton** — 260
Macaroni and beef: 12 oz — 370

Macaroni and cheese: 11 oz / **Morton**	320
Macaroni and cheese: 12¾ oz / **Swanson**	380
Meat loaf	
Banquet: 11 oz	437
Banquet Extra Helping: 19 oz	984
Morton: 11 oz	340
Swanson: 11 oz	510
Meatballs, Swedish: 11½ oz / **Dinner Classics**	500
Mexican style	
Banquet: 12 oz	483
Banquet Combination: 12 oz	518
El Charrito	650
Morton: 11 oz	300
Patio	510
Patio Combination	590
Patio Fiesta	510
Swanson: 16 oz	590
Swanson Hungry Man: 22 oz	910
Van de Kamp's Holiday: 11½ oz	421
Noodles and chicken: 10½ oz / **Swanson**	270
Pepper steak: 11½ oz / **Le Menu**	360
Polynesian style: 12 oz / **Swanson**	510
Pork, loin: 11¼ oz / **Swanson**	310
Pork, sweet and sour: 11½ oz / **Dinner Classics**	470
Queso / **El Charrito**	470
Salisbury steak	
Banquet: 11 oz	395
Banquet Extra Helping: 19 oz	1024
Dinner Classics: 11 oz	480
Morton: 11 oz	290
Morton Country Table: 15 oz	500
Morton King Size: 19 oz	780
Swanson: 11 oz	460
Swanson Hungry Man: 16½ oz	710
Saltillo / **El Charrito**	530
Spaghetti and meatballs: 11 oz / **Morton**	360
Spaghetti and meatballs: 12½ oz / **Swanson**	410
Spaghetti in tomato sauce w veal: 8¼ oz / **Swanson**	270
Swiss steak: 10 oz / **Swanson**	360
Tacos, beef / **Patio**	640
Teriyaki, chicken: 10¼ oz / **Dinner Classics**	460

CALORIES

Teriyaki, steak: 10 oz / **Dinner Classics**	360
Turkey	
Banquet: 11 oz	320
Banquet Extra Helping: 19 oz	723
Le Menu: 11¼ oz	470
Morton: 11 oz	340
Morton Country Table: 15 oz	520
Morton King Size: 19 oz	580
Swanson: 11½ oz	340
Swanson Hungry Man: 18½ oz	630
Turkey parmesan: 11 oz / **Classic Lite**	270
Turf and Surf: 10 oz / **Classic Lite**	250
Veal parmigiana	
Banquet: 11 oz	413
Banquet Extra Helping: 20 oz	1092
Dinner Classics: 10¾ oz	370
Morton: 11 oz	250
Morton King Size: 20 oz	600
Swanson: 12¾ oz	480
Swanson Hungry Man: 20 oz	560
Veal pepper steak: 11 oz / **Classic Lite**	280
Western style	
Banquet: 11 oz	513
Morton: 11⅕ oz	400
Swanson: 12¼ oz	430
Swanson Hungry Man: 17½ oz	650
Yankee pot roast: 11 oz / **Le Menu**	360

DINNER MIXES

⅕ prepared dinner unless noted

Beef Noodle / **Hamburger Helper**	320
Beef Romanoff / **Hamburger Helper**	340
Burger 'N Cheese Dinner /	
Creamette Hamburger Mate	310
Cheeseburger Macaroni / **Hamburger Helper**	360
Chili Tomato / **Hamburger Helper**	330
Country Dumplings, Noodles and Tuna /	
Tuna Helper	230
Creamy Noodles and Tuna / **Tuna Helper**	280

CALORIES

Hamburger Hash / **Hamburger Helper**	300
Hamburger Pizza Dish / **Hamburger Helper**	340
Hamburger Stew / **Hamburger Helper**	290
Lasagna / **Hamburger Helper**	320
Noodles, Cheese Sauce and Tuna / **Tuna Helper**	230
Potatoes Au Gratin / **Hamburger Helper**	320
Potato Stroganoff / **Hamburger Helper**	320
Rice Oriental / **Hamburger Helper**	340
Stroganoff: 1 cup prepared dinner / **Durkee**	820
Tamale Pie / **Hamburger Helper**	370
Tuna Tetrazzini / **Tuna Helper**	260

Doughnuts

CALORIES

1 doughnut

Chocolate / **Dolly Madison**	150
Chocolate-coated / **Hostess**	130
Chocolate-coated / **Hostess** Donette	60
Cinnamon / **Hostess**	110
Cinnamon-apple / **Earth Grains**	400
Devil's food / **Earth Grains**	350
Krunch / **Hostess**	110
Old fashioned / **Hostess**	180
Old fashioned, glazed / **Earth Grains**	360
Old fashioned, glazed / **Hostess**	230
Old fashioned, powdered / **Earth Grains**	350
Plain / **Hostess**	110
Powdered / **Hostess** Donette	40
Powdered, sugar / **Dolly Madison**	140
Powdered, sugar / **Hostess**	110

FROZEN

1 doughnut

Bavarian creme / **Morton**	180
Boston creme / **Morton**	210

Eggs and Egg Dishes

EGGS

	CALORIES
Chicken	
Raw, hard cooked or poached	
Extra large	94
Large	82
Medium	72
Raw, white only	
Extra large	19
Large	17
Medium	15
1 cup	124
Raw, yolk only	
Extra large	66
Large	59
Medium	52
Fried	
Extra large	113
Large	99
Medium	86
Scrambled in fat	
Extra large	126
Large	111
Medium	97
Duck, raw: 1 egg	134
Goose, raw: 1 egg	266
Turkey, raw: 1 egg	135

EGG DISHES, FROZEN

Omelet w cheese sauce and ham: 7 oz / **Swanson**	400
Omelet, Spanish style: 8 oz / **Swanson**	250
Scrambled eggs, Canadian bacon and cheese in pastry: 1 piece / **Pepperidge Farm** Deli's	290

EGG MIXES AND SEASONINGS

Egg, imitation	
Country Morning: 1 fl oz	170
Morningstar Farm Scramblers: ¼ cup	60
Scramblend: 1 fl oz	140
Omelet mix, Western: 1 pkg dry / **Durkee**	170
Quiche filling: 4⅓ oz / **Land O Lakes** Pour-A-Quiche	240
Scrambled, mix: 1 pkg dry / **Durkee**	124
Scrambled, mix w bacon: 1 pkg dry / **Durkee**	181

Fish and Seafood

FRESH

	CALORIES 3½ oz unless noted	1 oz unless noted
Abalone, cooked	160	45
Barracuda, cooked, baked or broiled	176	50
Barracuda, fried, floured	236	67
Bass, fillet, breaded, fried	228	65
Bass, fillet, broiled	168	48
Bass, striped, raw: 4 oz	120	30
Bluefish, broiled or baked	182	51
Bluefish, fillet, fried	239	68
Carp, smoked	173	49
Catfish, breaded, fried	254	72
Catfish, raw, meat only	103	29
Caviar, sturgeon, granular: 1 tbsp	42	
Caviar, sturgeon, pressed: 1 tbsp	54	
Clams, raw: 1 clam	12	
Clams, raw	76	22
Clams, 4 cherrystone or 5 littleneck clams	56	
Clams, smoked in oil	181	51
Clams, soft, raw, meat only: 1 pint (1 lb)	345	
Cod, broiled	141	40
Cod, dried, salted	127	36

CALORIES

Cod, fillet, breaded, fried	219	62
Cod, raw: 4 oz	90	22
Cod, smoked	96	27
Crab, Chesapeake Bay, steamed	88	25
Crab, cooked, flaked: 1 cup	116	
Crab, cooked pieces: 1 cup	144	
Crab, King, meat, steamed	101	29
Crab, soft shell, fried	326	93
Crappie, breaded, fried	257	73
Crayfish, stewed: 1 cup	139	
Crayfish, stewed	99	28
Crayfish tails, breaded, fried	86	24
Croaker, breaded, fried	255	72
Cusk, cooked	141	40
Cuttlefish, raw	74	21
Dogfish, cooked, broiled, baked	227	64
Eel, smoked	330	94
Flounder fillet, breaded, fried	203	58
Flounder, fillet, broiled	138	39
Flounder, raw	80	23
Frog legs, cooked	200	57
Frog legs, raw, meat only	73	21
Grouper, steak, broiled w bone	160	45
Haddock, breaded, fried	219	62
Haddock, broiled	141	40
Haddock, raw: 4 oz	90	22
Haddock, smoked	96	27
Hake, fillet, broiled	141	40
Hake, fried	200	57
Halibut fillet, fried	164	47
Halibut, raw: 4 oz	115	29
Halibut, smoked	218	62
Halibut steak, broiled w bone	138	39
Herring, pickled	218	62
Herring, smoked, kippered	205	58
Lobster meat, cooked pieces: 1 cup	138	
Lobster meat, steamed, broiled	90	26
Lobster meat in 1 lb. lobster	105	
Lobster tail in shell, cooked	90	26
1 small tail	43	
1 medium tail	94	

CALORIES

1 large tail	171	
Mackerel, dried	300	85
Mackerel, fillet, broiled	230	65
Mackerel, pickled	222	63
Mackerel, raw: 4 oz	220	55
Mackerel, salted	300	85
Mackerel, smoked	238	68
Mahimahi (dolphin), fillet, broiled	157	45
Mullet, fillet, fried	218	62
Mullet, raw	140	40
Mussels, cooked: 1 small mussel	11	
Mussels, cooked: ½ cup	118	
Octopus, cooked	179	51
Octopus, smoked	300	85
Oysters, raw	66	19
Eastern: 1 cup (13–19 Selects or		
27–44 Standards)	158	
Pacific and Western: 1 cup (about 4–6		
medium or 6–9 small)	218	
Oysters, breaded, fried, 4 select	108	
Oysters, smoked	102	29
Perch, fillet, broiled	148	42
Perch w bone, breaded, fried	257	73
Pickerel, fillet, breaded, fried	212	60
Pike, fillet, breaded, fried	212	60
Pike, northern, raw, meat only	88	25
Pompano w bone, broiled	160	45
Pompano w bone, fried	287	82
Redfish, breaded, fried	185	53
Redfish, fillet, broiled	148	42
Rockfish, fillet, broiled	148	42
Roe, herring	130	37
Roe, shad, baked: ½ pair	297	
Sable, smoked	219	62
Sable steak w bone, broiled	239	68
Salmon, broiled	143	41
Salmon, smoked	170	48
Salmon steak w bone, broiled	196	56
Salmon steak w bone, breaded, fried	224	64
Salmon, raw		
Atlantic: 4 oz	245	61

CALORIES

Chinook: 4 oz	251	63
Pink	134	34
Scallops, bay and sea, raw: 4 oz	92	23
Scallops, breaded, fried	210	60
Scallops, broiled	183	52
Scallops, steamed	120	34
Scrod, fillet, breaded, broiled	224	64
Scrod, fillet, broiled	141	40
Shad, w bone, baked	241	68
Shad, raw: 4 oz	192	48
Shark, fillet, cooked	227	64
Shrimp, breaded, fried	230	65
Shrimp, broiled	131	37
Shrimp, raw, peeled: 4 oz	103	26
Shrimp, steamed	110	31
Shrimp w shell, cooked	110	31
Skate w bone, baked	180	51
Smelts w bone, breaded, fried	250	71
Smelts w bone, broiled	201	57
Snails, cooked (escargots)	152	43
1 snail	8	
Spot, w bone, breaded, fried	255	72
Snapper, fillet, broiled	153	43
Snapper, fillet, breaded, fried	215	61
Sole, fillet, breaded, fried	203	58
Sole, fillet, broiled	138	39
Sole, raw: 4 oz	90	22
Squid, boiled	93	26
Squid, dried	300	85
Squid, fried (calamare): ½ cup	135	
Squid, raw, edible portions only	84	24
Sturgeon, smoked	141	40
Sturgeon, steamed	112	32
Swordfish, w bone, broiled	196	56
Swordfish, raw: 4 oz	135	34
Trout, fillet, batter-fried	161	46
Trout, fillet, breaded, baked	156	44
Trout, fillet, broiled	196	56
Trout, smoked	120	34
Trout w bone, breaded, fried	224	64
Trout w bone, fried	186	53

CALORIES

Turbot, fillet, broiled	138	39
Turbot, fillet, fried	203	58
Turbot, raw: 4 oz	165	41
Tuna, fillet, broiled	230	65
Tuna, raw	132	37
Tuna, smoked	238	67
Turtle, baked	153	43
Walleye w bone, breaded, fried	257	73
Whitefish, fillet, batter-fried	161	46
Whitefish, raw: 4 oz	175	50
Whitefish, smoked	155	44
Whitefish w bone, broiled	196	56
Whiting, fillet, baked	141	40
Whiting, fillet, fried	158	45
Yellowtail, raw	161	46
Yellowtail w bone, broiled	160	45

CANNED AND FROZEN

Catfish fillets, frozen: 1 fillet / **Mrs. Paul's**	215
Catfish fingers, frozen: 4 oz / **Mrs. Paul's**	250
Clams	
Minced, canned: 6½ oz / **Snow's**	100
Fried, frozen: 5 oz / **Howard Johnson's**	395
Fried, frozen: 2½ oz / **Mrs. Paul's**	230
Juice: 8 fl oz / **Doxsee**	20
Juice: 3 fl oz / **Snow's**	14
Cod, frozen: 4 oz / **Van de Kamp's** Today's Catch	80
Cod, frozen, breaded: 5 oz / **Van de Kamp's**	290
Crab	
Deviled, frozen: 1 pc (3 oz) / **Mrs. Paul's**	170
Deviled, frozen: 3½ oz / **Mrs. Paul's**	
Miniatures	220
King, frozen: 3 oz / **Wakefield**	60
Snow, frozen: 3 oz / **Wakefield**	60
and shrimp, frozen: 3 oz / **Wakefield**	60
Fancy Gems, frozen: 3 oz / **Wakefield**	80
Fish, frozen	
Cakes: 2 cakes (4 oz) / **Mrs. Paul's**	220
Cakes: 2 cakes (5 oz) / **Mrs. Paul's** Thins	300
Fillet: 8 oz / **Wakefield**	230

CALORIES

Fillets: 2 oz / **Van de Kamp's** Light & Krispy	180
Fillets: 4 oz / **Van de Kamp's** Today's Catch	90
Fillets, batter-fried: 2 fillets (6 oz) / **Mrs. Paul's**	360
Fillets, batter-fried: 2 fillets (4½ oz) / **Mrs. Paul's** Crunchy Light	310
Fillets, batter-fried: 1 fillet (3⅝ oz) / **Mrs. Paul's** Supreme Light	220
Fillets, batter-fried: 3 oz / **Van de Kamp's**	190
Fillets, breaded, fried: 2 fillets (4¼ oz) / **Mrs. Paul's** Crispy Crunchy	290
Fillets, breaded, fried: 1 fillet (6 oz) / **Mrs. Paul's** Light & Natural	290
Fillets, buttered: 2 fillets (5 oz) / **Mrs. Paul's**	210
Fillets, country seasoned: 2 oz / **Van de Kamp's**	195
Nuggets: 2 oz / **Van de Kamp's** Light & Crispy	130
Portions, batter-fried: 3 oz / **Van de Kamp's**	190
Sticks, Alaskan: 3½ oz / **Health Valley**	180
Sticks, batter-fried: 4 sticks (3½ oz) / **Mrs. Paul's** Crunchy Light	240
Sticks, batter-fried: 4 oz / **Van de Kamp's**	220
Sticks, breaded, fried: 4 sticks (3 oz) / **Mrs. Paul's** Crispy Crunch	200
Sticks: 3¾ oz / **Van de Kamp's** Light & Crispy	270
Flounder, frozen	
Mrs. Paul's Light & Natural: 1 fillet (6 oz)	320
Van de Kamp's Today's Catch: 4 oz	90
Batter-fried: 2 fillets (4½ oz) / **Mrs. Paul's** Crunchy Light	310
Breaded: 5 oz / **Van de Kamp's**	293
Breaded, fried: 2 fillets (4 oz) / **Mrs. Paul's** Crispy Crunchy	280
Gefilte fish, canned or in jars: 1 piece unless noted	
Manischewitz (4-piece, 12-oz jar)	53
Manischewitz (8-piece, 24-oz jar)	53
Manischewitz (24-piece, 4-lb jar)	48
Manischewitz, sweet (4-piece, 12-oz jar)	65
Manischewitz, sweet (8-piece, 24-oz jar)	65

CALORIES

Manischewitz, sweet (24-piece, 4-lb jar)	59
Manischewitz, homestyle (4-piece, 12-oz jar)	55
Manischewitz, homestyle (8-piece, 24-oz jar)	55
Manischewitz, homestyle (24-piece, 4-lb jar)	50
Mother's in jellied broth	45
Mother's Old Fashioned in liquid broth	70
Mother's Old World, jellied	60
Rokeach, jelled	60
Rokeach, in jellied broth, low sodium	50
Rokeach in natural liquid broth	50
Rokeach Old Vienna in jellied broth	70
Whitefish and pike (4-piece, 12-oz jar) / **Manischewitz**	49
Whitefish and pike (8-piece, 24-oz jar) / **Manischewitz**	49
Whitefish and pike (24-piece, 4-lb jar) / **Manischewitz**	44
Whitefish and pike, sweet (4-piece, 12-oz jar) / **Manischewitz**	64
Whitefish and pike, sweet (8-piece, 24-oz jar) / **Manischewitz**	64
Whitefish and pike, sweet (24-piece, 4-lb jar) / **Manischewitz**	58
Whitefish and pike, jellied / **Mother's**	60
Whitefish and pike, in jellied broth / **Rokeach**	60
Fishlets: 1 piece / **Manischewitz**	8
Haddock, frozen	
Van de Kamp's Today's Catch: 4 oz	90
Fillets, fried: 2 oz / **Van de Kamp's** Light & Crispy	180
Fried: 2 fillets (4 oz) / **Mrs. Paul's** Crispy Crunchy	280
Fried: 1 fillet (6 oz) / **Mrs. Paul's** Light & Natural	320
Fried in batter: 2 fillets (4½ oz) / **Mrs. Paul's** Crunchy Light	320
Fried in batter: 4 oz / **Van de Kamp's**	240
Halibut, frozen: 3½ oz / **Health Valley**	100
Halibut, frozen: 8 oz / **Wakefield**	210
Halibut, frozen, fried: 4 oz / **Van de Kamp's**	260
Herring, pickled in jars: 1 oz	

CALORIES

Lunch herring / **Vita**	41
Party snacks / **Vita**	45
Salad / **Vita**	66
in sour cream / **Vita**	52
Oysters wo shell, canned: ½ cup / **Bumble Bee**	109
Perch, frozen	
Van de Kamp's Today's Catch: 4 oz	110
Fried: 2 fillets (4 oz) /	
Mrs. Paul's Crispy Crunchy	290
Fried: 4 oz / **Van de Kamp's**	270
Fried: 2 oz / **Van de Kamp's** Light & Crispy	170
Salad Gems, frozen: 3 oz / **Wakefield**	70
Salmon, canned	
Keta: ½ cup / **Bumble Bee**	153
Pink: ½ cup / **Bumble Bee**	155
Pink: ½ cup / **Del Monte**	160
Pink: 7¾ oz / **Libby's**	310
Red: ½ cup / **Del Monte**	180
Red sockeye: ½ cup / **Bumble Bee**	188
Red sockeye: 7¾ oz / **Libby's**	380
Salmon, smoked, Nova: 1 oz / **Vita**	24
Salmon steak, frozen: 3½ oz / **Health Valley**	220
Sardines, canned	
in mustard sauce: 1 can (3¾ oz) / **Underwood**	230
in olive oil: 3 oz / **King Oscar**	260
in soy bean oil: 1 can (3¾ oz) / **Underwood**	380
in tomato sauce: ½ cup / **Del Monte**	360
in tomato sauce: 1 can (3¾ oz) / **Underwood**	230
Scallops, frozen: 4 oz / **Wakefield** Scallop Gems	110
Scallops, fried, frozen: 3½ oz / **Mrs. Paul's**	210
Seafood combination, fried, frozen: 9 oz /	
Mrs. Paul's	510
Shrimp, frozen: 3 oz / **Mrs. Paul's**	190
Sole, frozen	
Van de Kamp's Today's Catch: 4 oz	80
Fried: 1 fillet (6 oz) /	
Mrs. Paul's Light & Natural	280
Fried in batter: 4 oz / **Van de Kamp's**	280
Fried, breaded: 5 oz / **Van de Kamp's**	293
Trout, boned, frozen: 3½ oz / **Health Valley**	195
Tuna, canned	

CALORIES

Health Valley Best of Seafood: 6½ oz	180
Health Valley No Salt Dietetic: 7 oz	240
Light, chunk in oil: 2 oz / **A & P**	150
Light, chunk in oil: ½ cup undrained / **Bumble Bee**	265
Light, chunk in oil: 1 cup / **Chicken of the Sea**	550
Light, chunk in water: 2 oz / **A & P**	60
Light, chunk in water: ½ cup undrained / **Bumble Bee**	117
Light, chunk in water: 1 cup / **Chicken of the Sea**	200
Light, solid in oil: 1 cup / **Chicken of the Sea**	460
Light, solid in water: 1 cup / **Chicken of the Sea**	240
White, chunk in oil: 1 cup / **Chicken of the Sea**	500
White, chunk in water: 2 oz / **A & P**	100
White, chunk in water: 1 cup / **Chicken of the Sea** Dietetic Pack, Low Sodium	220
White, solid in oil: 2 oz / **A & P**	150
White, solid in oil: ½ cup undrained / **Bumble Bee**	285
White, solid in oil: 1 cup / **Chicken of the Sea**	450
White, solid in water: 2 oz / **A & P**	70
White, solid in water: ½ cup undrained / **Bumble Bee**	126

FISH AND SEAFOOD ENTRÉES, FROZEN

Fish and chips: 7 oz / **Van de Kamp's**	440
Fish Dijon: 8½ oz / **Mrs. Paul's**	210
Fish Divan: 12⅜ oz / **Stouffer's** Lean Cuisine	270
Fish Florentine: 9 oz / **Mrs. Paul's**	200
Fish Florentine: 9 oz / **Stouffer's** Lean Cuisine	240
Fish Kabobs: 4 oz / **Van de Kamp's**	240
Fish Mornay: 10 oz / **Mrs. Paul's**	230
Fish Parmesan: 5 oz / **Mrs. Paul's**	220
Haddock, au gratin: 10 oz / **Howard Johnson's**	318
Lobster Newburg: 6½ oz / **Stouffer's**	350
Scallops: 10 oz / **Light and Elegant**	210

CALORIES

Scallops Mediterranean: 11 oz / **Mrs. Paul's**	250
Scallops Oriental: 11 oz / **Stouffer's Lean Cuisine**	220
Scallops and Shrimp Mariner: 10¼ oz / **Stouffer's**	400
Seafood Newburg: 8½ oz / **Mrs. Paul's**	310
Seafood Potato: 3 oz / **Wakefield**	110
Shrimp Creole: 10 oz / **Light and Elegant**	200
Shrimp Croquettes: 6 oz / **Howard Johnson's**	239
Shrimp Marinara: 11 oz / **Buitoni**	210
Shrimp Oriental: 11 oz / **Mrs. Paul's**	230
Shrimp Primavera: 11 oz / **Mrs. Paul's**	310
Sole Florentine: 8 oz / **Wakefield**	250
Sole w stuffing: 8 oz / **Wakefield**	295
Tuna noodle casserole: 5¾ oz / **Stouffer's**	200

Flavorings, Sweet

CALORIES

1 tsp

Almond extract, pure / **Durkee**	13
Almond extract, pure / **Ehlers**	5
Anise extract, pure / **Durkee**	16
Anise extract, pure / **Ehlers**	12
Banana flavoring, imitation / **Durkee**	15
Banana flavoring, imitation / **Ehlers**	7
Black walnut flavoring, imitation / **Durkee**	4
Brandy flavoring, imitation / **Durkee**	15
Brandy flavoring, imitation / **Ehlers**	18
Butter flavoring, imitation / **Durkee**	3
Chocolate flavoring / **Durkee**	7
Coconut flavoring, imitation / **Durkee**	8
Coconut flavoring, imitation / **Ehlers**	13
Lemon extract, imitation / **Durkee**	17
Lemon extract, pure / **Ehlers**	14
Maple extract, imitation / **Durkee**	6
Maple extract, imitation / **Ehlers**	9
Orange extract, imitation / **Durkee**	14
Orange extract, pure / **Ehlers**	14

	CALORIES
Peppermint extract, imitation / **Durkee**	15
Peppermint extract, pure / **Ehlers**	12
Pineapple flavoring, imitation / **Durkee**	6
Pineapple extract, pure / **Ehlers**	13
Raspberry extract, imitation / **Ehlers**	10
Rum flavoring, imitation / **Durkee**	14
Rum flavoring, imitation / **Ehlers**	11
Strawberry extract, imitation / **Durkee**	12
Strawberry extract, imitation / **Ehlers**	13
Vanilla extract, pure / **Durkee**	8
Vanilla flavoring, imitation / **Durkee**	3

Flour and Meal

FLOUR

CALORIES
1 cup unless noted

	CALORIES
Biscuit mix / **Bisquick**	480
Buckwheat, dark, sifted	326
Buckwheat, light, sifted	340
Carob	250
Lima bean, sifted	432
Peanut, defatted	224
Rye	
Light	314
Medium / **Pillsbury's** Best	400
Dark	420
and wheat / **Pillsbury's** Best Bohemian Style	400
Tortilla, corn / **Quaker** Masa Harina	410
Tortilla, wheat / **Quaker** Masa Trigo	445
White	
Aunt Jemima Self-Rising: ¼ cup	109
Ballard All-Purpose	400
Drifted Snow: 4 oz	400
Gold Medal All-Purpose	400

CALORIES

Gold Medal Self-Rising: 4 oz	380
Gold Medal Unbleached	400
Pillsbury's Best All-Purpose	400
Pillsbury's Best Bread	400
Pillsbury's Self-Rising	380
Pillsbury's Best Unbleached	400
Red Band Plain	400
Red Band Self-Rising	380
Red Band Unbleached	400
Softasilk: 4 oz	100
Wondra	400
High protein / **Gold Medal** Better for Bread	400
Thickening: 2 tbsp / **Pillsbury's** Best Sauce 'n Gravy	50

Wheat

All-purpose	500
Bread	500
Cake or pastry	430
Gluten	530
Self-rising	440
Whole wheat	400
Whole wheat: 4 oz / **Gold Medal**	390
Pillsbury's Best	400

MEAL

Note: 1 ounce equals about 4 tablespoons

Almond, partially defatted: 1 oz	116

Corn

White: 1 oz / **Albers**	100
White: 1 oz / **Aunt Jemima** Enriched	102
White: 1 oz / **Quaker** Enriched	102
White: ⅙ cup / **Aunt Jemima**	99
White: ⅙ cup / **Aunt Jemima** Self-Rising	99
Yellow: 1 oz / **Albers**	100
Yellow: 1 oz / **Aunt Jemima** Enriched	102
Yellow: 1 oz / **Quaker** Enriched	102
Matzo meal: 1 oz / **Manischewitz**	108
Passover cake meal: 1 cup / **Manischewitz**	571

Frostings

READY TO SPREAD

CALORIES

¹⁄₁₂ can unless noted

Butter pecan / **Betty Crocker**	160
Cake and cookie decorator, all colors: 1 tbsp / **Pillsbury**	70
Caramel pecan / **Pillsbury**	160
Cherry / **Betty Crocker**	160
Chocolate / **Betty Crocker**	170
Chocolate chocolate chip / **Betty Crocker**	160
Chocolate chip / **Betty Crocker**	170
Chocolate fudge / **Pillsbury**	150
Chocolate mint / **Pillsbury**	150
Chocolate nut / **Betty Crocker**	160
Coconut almond / **Pillsbury**	150
Coconut pecan / **Betty Crocker**	170
Coconut pecan / **Pillsbury**	160
Cream cheese / **Betty Crocker**	160
Cream cheese / **Pillsbury**	160
Dark Dutch fudge / **Betty Crocker**	160
Double Dutch / **Pillsbury**	150
Lemon / **Betty Crocker**	160
Lemon / **Pillsbury**	160
Milk chocolate / **Betty Crocker**	160
Milk chocolate / **Pillsbury**	150
Orange / **Betty Crocker**	160
Sour cream chocolate / **Betty Crocker**	170
Sour cream vanilla / **Pillsbury**	160
Sour cream white / **Betty Crocker**	160
Strawberry / **Pillsbury**	160
Vanilla / **Betty Crocker**	160
Vanilla / **Pillsbury**	160

MIXES

¹/₁₂ pkg, prepared

Banana / **Betty Crocker**	170
Butter brickle / **Betty Crocker**	170
Butter pecan / **Betty Crocker**	170
Caramel / **Pillsbury** Rich 'n Easy	140
Cherry, creamy / **Betty Crocker**	170
Chocolate / **Duncan Hines**	160
Chocolate almond fudge / **Betty Crocker**	180
Chocolate fudge / **Betty Crocker**	170
Chocolate fudge / **Pillsbury** Rich 'n Easy	150
Coconut almond / **Betty Crocker**	140
Coconut almond / **Pillsbury**	160
Coconut pecan / **Betty Crocker**	140
Coconut pecan / **Pillsbury**	150
Cream cheese and nuts / **Betty Crocker**	150
Dark chocolate fudge / **Betty Crocker**	170
Dark Dutch fudge / **Duncan Hines**	160
Double Dutch / **Pillsbury** Rich 'n Easy	150
Lemon / **Betty Crocker**	170
Lemon / **Pillsbury** Rich 'n Easy	140
Milk chocolate / **Betty Crocker**	170
Milk chocolate / **Duncan Hines**	160
Milk chocolate / **Pillsbury**	150
Sour cream chocolate fudge / **Betty Crocker**	170
Sour cream white / **Betty Crocker**	170
Strawberry / **Pillsbury** Rich 'n Easy	140
Vanilla / **Duncan Hines**	160
Vanilla / **Pillsbury** Rich 'n Easy	150
White / **Betty Crocker** Creamy	180
White / **Betty Crocker** Fluffy	60
White / **Pillsbury** Fluffy	60

Fruit

FRESH

	CALORIES
Acerola cherries: 10 fruits	23
Apples	
w skin: 1 small (about 4 per lb)	61
w skin: 1 medium (about 3 per lb)	80
w skin: 1 large (about 2 per lb)	123
Peeled: 1 small (about 4 per lb)	53
Peeled: 1 medium (about 3 per lb)	70
Peeled: 1 large (about 2 per lb)	107
Apricots	
Raw, halves: 1 cup	79
Raw, halves: 1 lb	231
Raw, whole: 3 apricots	55
Raw, whole (12 per lb): 1 lb	217
Avocados	
California: ½ average	185
California, cubed: 1 cup	257
California, puree: 1 cup	393
Florida: ½ average	196
Florida, cubed: 1 cup	192
Florida, puree: 1 cup	294
Bananas	
1 small (7¾ in)	81
1 medium (8¾ in)	101
1 large (9¾ in)	116
Mashed: 1 cup	191
Red, 7¼ in: 1 banana	118
Red, sliced: 1 cup	135
Sliced: 1 cup	128
Dehydrated or flakes: 1 tbsp	21
Dehydrated or flakes: 1 cup	340
Blackberries (including dewberries, boysenberries, youngberries) raw: 1 cup	84

CALORIES

Blueberries, raw: 1 cup	90
Blueberries, raw: 1 lb	281
Cherries	
Raw, sour, red: 1 cup	60
Raw, sour, red: 1 lb	237
Raw, sweet: 1 cup	82
Raw, sweet: 1 lb	286
Cranberries, raw, chopped: 1 cup	51
Cranberries, raw, whole: 1 cup	44
Figs, raw, whole: 1 small	32
Figs, raw, whole: 1 medium	40
Figs, raw, whole: 1 large	52
Gooseberries, raw: 1 cup	59
Grapefruit, 3½-in diam: half	40
Grapefruit sections: 1 cup	94
Grapes	
Concord, Delaware, Niagara, Catawba,	
Scuppernong: 10 grapes	18
Flame Tokay, Emperor: 10 grapes	38
Ribier: 10 grapes	45
Thompson Seedless, Malaga, Muscat: 10 grapes	34
Lemons, wedge: 1 from large lemon	7
Lemons, whole fruit: 1 large	29
Limes, raw: 1 lime	19
Loganberries, raw: 1 cup	89
Loquats, raw: 10 fruits	59
Lychees, raw: 10 fruits	58
Mangoes, raw, whole: 1 fruit	152
Muskmelons	
Cantaloupes, cubed, diced or balls: 1 cup	48
Cantaloupes, 5-in diam: half	82
Casaba, cubed, diced or balls: 1 cup	46
Honeydew, cubed, diced or balls: 1 cup	56
Honeydew, ⅒ melon	45
Nectarines, raw, 2½-in diam: 1 nectarine	88
Oranges	
California navels (winter): 1 small	45
California navels (winter): 1 medium	71
California navels (winter): 1 large	87
California navels, sections: 1 cup	77
Valencias (summer): 1 small	50

CALORIES

Valencias (summer): 1 medium	62
Valencias (summer): 1 large	96
Valencias, sections: 1 cup	92
Florida: 1 small	57
Florida: 1 medium	71
Florida: 1 large	89
Florida, sections: 1 cup	87
Papaws, raw, whole: 1 pawpaw	83
Papayas, raw, cubed, ½-in pieces: 1 cup	55
Papayas, raw, whole (about 1 lb): 1 papaya	119

Peaches

Raw, peeled, sliced: 1 cup	65
Raw, whole, peeled: 1 small (about 4 per lb)	38
Raw, whole, peeled: 1 large (about 2½ per lb)	58
Raw, whole, peeled: 1 lb	150

Pears

Raw, sliced or cubed: 1 cup	100
Raw, whole, Bartlett: 1 pear (about 2½ per lb)	100
Raw, whole, Bosc: 1 pear (about 3 per lb)	86
Raw, whole, D'Anjou: 1 pear (about 2 per lb)	122
Persimmons, raw, Japanese or kaki: 1 persimmon	129
Persimmons, raw, native: 1 persimmon	31
Pineapple, raw, diced pieces: 1 cup	81
Pineapple, raw, sliced, ¾-in thick: 1 slice	44

Plums

Raw, whole, Damson, 1-in diam: 10 plums	66
Raw, whole, Damson: 1 lb	272
Raw, Japanese and hybrid, 2⅛ in diam: 1 plum	32
Raw, Japanese and hybrid: 1 lb	299
Prune type, raw, 1½ in diam: 1 plum	21
Prune type, raw: 1 lb	320
Pomegranate, 3⅜ in diam: 1 pomegranate	97
Raspberries, raw, black: 1 cup	98
Raspberries, red: 1 cup	70
Rhubarb, raw, diced: 1 cup	20
Rhubarb, cooked w sugar: 1 cup	381
Strawberries, raw, whole: 1 cup	55
Tangerines, raw, whole: 1 large (2½ in diam)	46

Watermelon

Raw: 1 lb	118

CALORIES

Raw, diced, pieces: 1 cup	42
Raw, slice: 10 in diam × 1 in thick	111
Raw, wedge: 4 in × 8 in radius	111

CANNED AND FROZEN

Apples, canned
  Sliced

Lucky Leaf chipped: 4 oz	50
Lucky Leaf diced: 4 oz	50
Lucky Leaf syrup pack: 4 oz	50
Lucky Leaf water pack: 4 oz	50
Musselman's chipped: 4 oz	50
Musselman's diced: 4 oz	50
Musselman's syrup pack: 4 oz	50
Musselman's water pack: 4 oz	50
Dessert: 4 oz / **Lucky Leaf**	70
Dessert: 4 oz / **Musselman's**	70
Fried: 8 oz / **Luck's**	100
Unpeeled: 4 oz / **Lucky Leaf**	90
Unpeeled: 4 oz / **Musselman's**	90

  Whole

Lucky Leaf: 1 apple	90
Musselman's: 1 apple	90
Baked: 1 apple / **Lucky Leaf**	110
Baked: 1 apple / **Musselman's**	110
Apples, frozen, escalloped: 4 oz / **Stouffer's**	140
Apples, frozen, sliced: 4 oz / **Lucky Leaf**	105
Apples, frozen, sliced: 4 oz / **Musselman's**	105
Apple rings, sliced, canned: 4 oz / **Lucky Leaf**	100
Apple rings, spiced, canned: 4 oz / **Musselman's**	100

Applesauce in cans or jars

A & P: ½ cup	110
A & P Natural Style: ½ cup	50
Del Monte: ½ cup	90
Del Monte Lite: ½ cup	50
Lucky Leaf Chunky: 4 oz	80
Lucky Leaf juice pack: 4 oz	50

CALORIES

Lucky Leaf sweetened: 4 oz	80
Lucky Leaf unsweetened: 4 oz	50
Lucky Leaf w Cranberry: 4 oz	80
Mott's: 8 oz	230
Mott's Natural Style: 8 oz	100
Musselman's chunky: 4 oz	80
Musselman's juice pack: 4 oz	50
Musselman's sweetened: 4 oz	80
Musselman's unsweetened: 4 oz	50
Seneca: ½ cup	90
Seneca Cinnamon: ½ cup	90
Seneca Golden Delicious: ½ cup	90
Seneca Macintosh: ½ cup	90
Seneca Natural: ½ cup	50
Apricots, canned: ½ cup	
Halves / **Del Monte**	100
Halves / **Del Monte** Lite	60
Halves, unpeeled / **Scotch Buy**	80
Halves, unpeeled / **Town House**	110
Unpeeled, in heavy syrup / **A & P**	110
Whole / **Del Monte**	100
Whole peeled / **Town House**	100
Blueberries, canned: 4 oz /	
Lucky Leaf Water Pack	40
Blueberries, canned: 4 oz /	
Musselman's Water Pack	40
Blueberries, canned, in heavy syrup:	
½ cup / **A & P**	110
Cherries, canned	
Dark, sweet w pits: ½ cup / **Del Monte**	90
Dark, sweet, pitted: ½ cup / **Del Monte**	90
Light, sweet w pits: ½ cup / **Del Monte**	100
Red tart: ½ cup / **A & P**	50
Red tart, pitted: 4 oz / **Lucky Leaf**	50
Red tart, pitted: 4 oz / **Musselmans**	50
Cherries, frozen: 4 oz / **Lucky Leaf**	130
Cherries, frozen: 4 oz / **Musselman's**	130
Crabapples, spiced, canned: 4 oz / **Lucky Leaf**	110
Crabapples, spiced, canned: 4 oz / **Musselman's**	110
Cranberry orange, crushed: 2 oz / **Ocean Spray**	100
Cranberry orange relish: 2 oz / **Ocean Spray**	100

Cranberry sauce, canned: ¼ cup / **A & P**	100
Cranberry sauce, canned: ½ oz / **Nutri-Dyne Elwood**	3
Cranberry sauce, jellied: 2 oz / **Ocean Spray**	90
Cranberry sauce, whole: 2 oz / **Ocean Spray**	90
Figs, canned: ½ cup / **Del Monte**	100
Figs, canned, in heavy syrup: 1 cup / **Town House**	200
Fruit cocktail, canned: ½ cup	
A & P, in heavy syrup	90
A & P, in pear juice	50
Del Monte	80
Del Monte Lite	50
Town House	90
Weight Watchers	60
Fruit compote, canned: 4 oz / **Rokeach**	120
Fruits for salad, canned: ½ cup / **Del Monte**	90
Fruit salad, canned: ½ cup / **Del Monte** Tropical	90
Mixed, canned	
A & P Fruit Mix: ½ cup	75
Del Monte Chunky: ½ cup	80
Del Monte Chunky Lite: ½ cup	50
Del Monte Fruit Cup: 5 oz	100
Mother's: 4 oz	120
Scotch Buy Fruit Mix: ½ cup	80
Mixed, frozen: 5 oz / **Birds Eye** Quick Thaw	100
Oranges, Mandarin, canned: ½ cup / **A & P**	80
Oranges, Mandarin, canned: 5½ oz / **Del Monte**	100
Peaches, canned: ½ cup unless noted	
Weight Watchers	60
Cling / **Del Monte**	80
Cling, 5 oz / **Del Monte** Fruit Cup	110
Cling, halves, in heavy syrup / **A & P**	100
Cling, halves or slices / **Del Monte** Lite	50
Cling, halves, in light syrup / **Scotch Buy**	70
Cling, halves, in light syrup / **Town House**	100
Cling, halves, in pear juice / **A & P**	50
Cling, slices, in heavy syrup / **A & P**	100
Cling, slices, in light syrup / **Scotch Buy**	70
Cling, sliced, in light syrup / **Town House**	100
Cling, sliced, in pear juice / **A & P**	50
Freestone / **Del Monte** Lite	60

CALORIES

Freestone, halves or slices / **Del Monte**	90
Freestone, halves / **Town House**	100
Freestone, pieces, in light syrup / **Scotch Buy**	70
Freestone, slices, in light syrup / **Town House**	100
Spiced, w pits: 3½ oz / **Del Monte**	80
Pears, canned: ½ cup unless noted	
Weight Watchers: 2 halves + 2 tbsp juice	60
Bartlett, halves or slices / **Del Monte**	80
Bartlett, halves or slices / **Del Monte** Lite	50
Halves, in heavy syrup / **A & P**	95
Halves, in light syrup / **A & P**	70
Halves, in pear juice / **A & P**	60
Slices, in heavy syrup / **A & P**	95
Slices, in light syrup / **A & P**	70
Slices, in pear juice / **A & P**	60
Pineapple, canned	
All cuts, in juice: ½ cup	
Del Monte	70
Dole	70
Libby's	70
All cuts, in syrup: ½ cup	
Del Monte	90
Dole	95
Libby's	95
Chunks, in heavy syrup: ½ cup w syrup / **A & P**	90
Chunks, in heavy syrup: ½ cup / **Town House**	90
Chunks, in juice, unsweetened: ½ cup / **A & P**	70
Chunks, in juice, unsweetened: ½ cup / **Town House**	70
Crushed, in heavy syrup: ½ cup w syrup / **A & P**	90
Crushed, in heavy syrup: ½ cup / **Town House**	90
Crushed, in juice, unsweetened: ½ cup / **A & P**	70
Crushed, in juice, unsweetened: ½ cup / **Town House**	70
Slices, in heavy syrup: 2 slices w syrup / **A & P**	90

CALORIES

Slices, in heavy syrup: ½ cup / **Town House**	90
Slices, in juice, unsweetened: 2 slices w juice / **A & P**	70
Slices, in juice, unsweetened: ½ cup / **Town House**	70
Spears, in juice: 2 spears / **Del Monte**	50
Prunes, canned, stewed: ½ cup / **Rokeach**	90
Raspberries, red, frozen: 5 oz / **Birds Eye** Quick Thaw	100
Strawberries, frozen, halves in lite syrup: 5 oz / **Birds Eye** Quick Thaw	60
Strawberries, frozen, halves in syrup: 5 oz / **Birds Eye** Quick Thaw	120
Strawberries, frozen, whole, in lite syrup: 4 oz / **Birds Eye**	60

DRIED, UNCOOKED

Apples: 2 oz / **Del Monte**	140
Apples: 2 oz / **Sun-Maid**	150
Apples: 1 pkg / **Weight Watchers** Fruit Snacks	50
Apricots: 2 oz / **Del Monte**	140
Apricots: 2 oz / **Sun-Maid**	140
Apricots: 2 oz / **Sunsweet**	140
Currants, Zante: ½ cup / **Del Monte**	200
Dates, chopped: ½ cup / **Dromedary**	130
Dates, pitted: 5 dates / **Dromedary**	100
Figs, California Mission: ½ cup / **Blue Ribbon**	210
Figs, California Mission: ½ cup / **Sun-Maid**	210
Figs, Calimyrna: ½ cup / **Blue Ribbon**	250
Figs, Calimyrna: ½ cup / **Sun-Maid**	250
Mixed	
Carnation All Fruit Mix: 1 pouch	80
Del Monte: 2 oz	130
Sun-Maid: 2 oz	150
Sun-Maid Fruit Bits: 2 oz	150
Sunsweet: 2 oz	150
Weight Watchers Fruit Snacks: 1 pkg	50
Weight Watchers Tropical Snacks: 1 pkg	50
Peaches: 2 oz / **Del Monte**	140
Peaches: 2 oz / **Sun-Maid**	140

CALORIES

Peaches: 2 oz / **Sunsweet**	140
Prunes: 2 oz	
Del Monte Moist-Pak	120
Sunsweet	120
Town House	140
w pits / **Del Monte**	120
pitted / **Del Monte**	140
pitted / **Sunsweet**	140
Raisins	
Town House: 1½ oz	130
Golden / **Del Monte:** 3 oz	260
Natural / **Del Monte:** 3 oz	250
Seedless / **Sun-Maid:** ½ cup	290
Fruit rolls: 1 roll	
All flavors / **Sunkist**	45
Apple / **Betty Crocker** Fruit Roll-Ups	50
Apple / **Flavor Tree**	90
Apricot / **Betty Crocker** Fruit Roll-Ups	50
Apricot / **Flavor Tree**	100
Cherry / **Betty Crocker** Fruit Roll-Ups	50
Cherry / **Flavor Tree**	90
Fruit Punch / **Flavor Tree**	90
Grape / **Betty Crocker** Fruit Roll-Ups	50
Grape / **Flavor Tree**	90
Orange / **Flavor Tree**	90
Peach / **Flavor Tree**	90
Plum / **Flavor Tree**	90
Raspberry / **Flavor Tree**	90
Strawberry / **Betty Crocker** Fruit Roll-Ups	50
Strawberry / **Flavor Tree**	90

CANDIED

Cherry: 1	12
Citron: 1 oz	90
Lemon peel: 1 oz	90
Orange peel: 1 oz	90
Pineapple slice: 1 slice	180

Fruit Drinks and Fruit-Flavored Beverages

CALORIES

**In bottles, cans, cartons, pouches,
frozen or as a packaged mix:**

6 fl ounces unless noted

Apple Drinks	
Apple + Plus / **Juicy Juice**	90
CapriSun: 6¾ fl oz	90
Hawaiian Punch*	90
Hi-C	90
Sunkist: 250 ml	133
Mix: 8 fl oz / **Kool-Aid**	100
Mix: 8 fl oz / **Wyler's Crystals**	90
Hot spiced cider, mix / **Boyd's** Today	70
Apple-cherry / **Musselman's BC**	100
Apple-cranberry / **Lucky Leaf**	130
Apple-grape / **Musselman's BC**	110
Banana Frost, mix: 7 fl oz prepared / **Libby**	120
Berry / **Hawaiian Punch** Very Berry*	90
Black cherry, mix, unswt: 8 fl oz / **Wyler's**	2
Cherry	
Hawaiian Punch*	90
Hi-C	90
Mix, prepared: 8 fl oz / **Kool-Aid**	90
Mix, prepared: 8 fl oz / **Kool-Aid** sugar free	4
Mix, prepared: 8 fl oz / **Safeway**	90
Cranberry juice cocktail	
A & P	100
Ocean Spray	110

*For both frozen concentrate and shelf.

CALORIES

Ocean Spray Low Calorie	35
Ocean Spray, frozen, reconstituted	110
P & Q	100
Town House	110
Sunkist, in carton	77
Welch's, frozen, reconstituted	100
Cranberry: 4 fl oz / **Sunkist,** in portion cup	80
Cranberry-apple	
A & P	130
Ocean Spray Cranapple	130
Ocean Spray Low Calorie	30
P & Q	130
Town House	130
Frozen, reconstituted /	
Ocean Spray Cranapple	120
Frozen, reconstituted / **Welch's**	120
Cranberry-apricot / **Ocean Spray** Cranicot	110
Cranberry-grape / **Ocean Spray** Cran-Grape	110
Cranberry-grape, frozen, reconstituted / **Welch's**	110
Cranberry-orange / **Ocean Spray** Cranorange	100
Fruit / **Hawaiian Punch** Island,	
Juicy Red and Tropical	90
Funny Face, mix, swt: 8 fl oz	88
Funny Face, swt w aspartame: 8 fl oz	4
Golden Good / **Juicy Juice**	98
Grape / **Welchade**	90
Grape	
CapriSun: 6¾ fl oz	104
Hawaiian Punch*	90
Hi-C	100
Sunkist	79
Texsun in "brik-pak"	100
Welch's, frozen, reconstituted	90
Welch's Concord Juice Cocktail	110
Welch's Grape Juice Drink	110
Frozen / **A & P**	100
Mix: 8 fl oz / **Kool-Aid**	90
Mix, prepared / **Kool-Aid** Sugar Free: 8 fl oz	4
Mix, prepared / **Tang**	90

*For both frozen concentrate and shelf.

CALORIES

Mix, prepared / **Safeway**	90
Grape and apple / **Welch's**	
Concord 'N Apple Juice Cocktail	110
Grapefruit, mix, prepared / **Tang**	90
Lemonade	
CapriSun: 6¾ fl oz	92
Sunkist	88
Frozen, reconstituted: 8 fl oz / **A & P**	110
Frozen, reconstituted: 8 fl oz / **Minute Maid**	75
Mix, prepared: 8 fl oz / **Country Time**	90
Mix, prepared: 8 fl oz /	
Country Time Sugar Free	4
Mix, prepared: 8 fl oz /	
Crystal Light Sugar Free	4
Mix, prepared / **Elam's** Sweetened	130
Mix, prepared / **Elam's** Unsweetened	12
Mix, prepared: 8 fl oz / **Kool-Aid**	90
Mix, prepared: 8 fl oz / **Kool-Aid** Sugar Free	4
Mix, prepared: 8 fl oz / **Safeway**	90
Mix, prepared: 8 fl oz / **Wyler's** Crystals	90
Mix, prepared: 8 fl oz / **Wyler's** Sugar Free	6
Lemon-lime	
Gatorade: 8 fl oz	50
Mix, prepared: 8 fl oz / **Country Time**	90
Mix, prepared: 8 fl oz / **Gatorade**	60
Mix, prepared: 8 fl oz / **Crystal Light**	
Sugar Free	4
Orange	
Awake, frozen, reconstituted / **Birds Eye**	80
Bama	90
CapriSun: 6¾ fl oz	103
Gatorade: 8 fl oz	50
Hawaiian Punch*	100
Hi-C	100
Orange Plus, frozen, reconstituted	100
Sunkist, in carton: 250 ml	133
Texsun, in "brik-pak"	90
Mix, prepared: 4 fl oz /	
Borden Instant Breakfast Drink	60

*For both frozen concentrate and shelf.

CALORIES

Mix, prepared: 8 fl oz / **Crystal Light
  Sugar Free** 4
Mix, prepared: 8 fl oz / **Gatorade** 60
Mix, prepared: 8 fl oz / **Kool-Aid** 90
Mix, prepared: 8 fl oz / **Libby** Orange Frost 120
Mix, prepared: 8 fl oz / **Safeway** 90
Mix, prepared / **Tang** 90
Mix, prepared, unswt: 8 fl oz / **Wyler's** 2
Orange-apricot / **Musselman's BC** 90
Orange-pineapple / **Musselman's BC** 90
Pineapple, mix, prepared / **Libby** Pineapple Frost 110
Pineapple-grapefruit / **Del Monte** 90
Pineapple-orange / **Del Monte** 90
Pineapple–pink grapefruit / **Del Monte** 90
Pineapple–pink grapefruit / **Dole** 101
Punch
  Bama 90
  CapriSun: 6¾ fl oz 102
  Hawaiian Punch Low Sugar* 30
  Hi-C Florida 100
  Sunkist 103
  Sunkist, in portion cup: 4 fl oz 60
  Texsun, in "brik-pak" 90
  Mix, prepared / **Crystal Light** Sugar Free 4
  Mix, prepared: 8 fl oz / **Kool-Aid** Rainbow 100
  Mix, prepared: 8 fl oz / **Kool Aid** Sunshine 100
  Mix, prepared: 8 fl oz / **Kool-Aid** Tropical 100
  Mix, prepared: 8 fl oz / **Kool-Aid** Sugar Free 4
  Mix, prepared: 8 fl oz / **Safeway** 90
  Mix, prepared: 8 fl oz /
    Wyler's Crystals Tropical 90
  Mix, prepared: 8 fl oz /
    Wyler's Tropical Sugar Free 4
Pure Purple / **Juicy Juice** 103
Raspberry, mix: 8 fl oz / **Kool-Aid** 90
Raspberry-cranberry / **A & P** 110
Real Red / **Juicy Juice** 103
Strawberry, mix, prepared: 8 fl oz / **Kool-Aid** 90
Strawberry, mix, prepared: 8 fl oz / **Safeway** 90

*For both frozen concentrate and shelf.

CALORIES

Strawberry, mix, prepared: 8 fl oz / **Libby** Strawberry Frost	120
Wild berry / **Hi-C**	90
Wild cherry, mix: 8 fl oz / **Wyler's** Crystals	90
Wild cherry, mix: 8 fl oz / **Wyler's** Sugar Free	4
Wild fruit / **Hawaiian Punch***	90
Wild grape, mix: 8 fl oz / **Wyler's** Crystals	90
Wild grape, mix: 8 fl oz / **Wyler's** Sugar Free	4

Fruit Juices

FRESH

CALORIES

1 cup unless noted

Acerola cherry	56
Grapefruit	96
Lemon	61
Lemon: 1 tbsp	4
Lime: 1 tbsp	4
Orange	
California navels	120
Florida	106
Valencias	117
Tangerine	106

BOTTLED, CANNED AND FROZEN

6 fl oz unless noted

Apple	
A & P, frozen	90
Mott's	80
Mott's Natural Style	80
Seneca	90

*For both frozen concentrate and shelf.

	CALORIES
Seneca Natural	90
Lucky Leaf	90
Musselman's	90
Sunkist, in carton	88
Sunkist, in portion cup: 4 fl oz	78
Texsun, in "brik-pak"	90
Town House	90
Apple cider / **Lucky Leaf**	90
Apple cider, sparkling / **Lucky Leaf**	80
Apple cider / **Musselman's**	90
Apple-grape / **Welch's**	90
Apricot nectar	
Del Monte	100
Libby's	110
Sunkist, in portion cup: 4 fl oz	68
Town House	100
Banana nectar / **Libby's**	60
Blend / **Welch's** Frozen Harvest	90
Cranberry / **Lucky Leaf**	110
Grape	
A & P	200
Lucky Leaf	130
Minute Maid	100
Seneca, bottled, canned	115
Seneca, frozen, reconstituted	100
Sunkist, in portion cup: 4 fl oz	64
Welch's, red and white, bottled, canned	120
Welch's, frozen, reconstituted	100
Welch's Orchard, frozen, reconstituted	120
Sparkling, red or white / **Welch's**	120
Grapefruit	
A & P, frozen, reconstituted	80
Del Monte	70
Libby's, unswt	75
Minute Maid, frozen, reconstituted	75
Ocean Spray	60
Ocean Spray, frozen reconstituted	70
Sunkist, in portion cup: 6 fl oz	75
Texsun, in "brik-pak"	77
pink / **Texsun**	77
Guava nectar / **Libby's**	70

CALORIES

Lemon
    A & P: 2 tbsp   6
    Lucky Leaf   30
    Minute Maid, frozen, reconstituted   40
    Realemon: 2 tbsp   6
    Seneca: 2 tbsp   6
    Sunkist   42
Mango nectar / **Libby's**   60
Mixed: ⅓ cup / **Weight Watchers**
  Fruit Juice Medley   45
Orange
    A & P, frozen, reconstituted   80
    Citrus Hill   90
    Del Monte, unswt   80
    Libby's, swt   100
    Libby's, unswt   90
    Minute Maid, frozen, reconstituted   90
    Minute Maid, in carton   85
    Sunkist, in carton   83
    Sunkist, in portion cup   83
    Texsun   83
    Texsun, in "brik-pak"   83
Orange-grapefruit, unswt / **Libby's**   80
Orange-grapefruit, in portion cup: 4 fl oz / **Sunkist**   43
Orange-pineapple / **Texsun**   89
Orange-pineapple, in portion cup: 4 fl oz / **Sunkist**   43
Peach nectar / **Libby's**   90
Pear nectar / **Libby's**   100
Pear-passion fruit nectar / **Libby's**   60
Pineapple
    Del Monte   100
    Dole   103
    Texsun   97
    Sunkist, in portion cup: 4 fl oz   60
Pineapple-grapefruit / **Texsun**   91
Prune
    Del Monte   120
    Lucky Leaf   150
    Mott's   120
    Sunkist, in portion cup: 4 fl oz   92
    Sunsweet   130
Strawberry / **Libby's**   60

Gelatin

	CALORIES
All flavors, mix, prepared: ½ cup / **D-Zerta**	8
All flavors, mix, prepared: ½ cup / **Dia-Mel**	8
All flavors, mix, prepared: ½ cup / **Estee**	8
All flavors, mix, prepared: ½ cup / **Jell-O**	80
All flavors, mix, prepared: ½ cup / **Nutri-Dyne Elwood**	8
All flavors, mix, prepared: 2.7 oz / **Nutri-Dyne** Prono Gelled Dessert	55
All flavors, mix, prepared: ½ cup / **Safeway**	80
Gel-a-thin: ½ cup / **Dia-Mel**	2
Orange flavor: 1 env / **Knox**	70
Unflavored: 1 env / **Knox**	25

Gravies

	CALORIES
½ cup unless noted	
Au jus	
Canned / **Franco-American**	5
Mix, prepared / **Durkee**	8
Mix, prepared / **French's**	8
Mix w roasting bag: 1 pkg /	

CALORIES

Durkee Roastin' Bag	64
Beef, canned / **Franco-American**	25
Brown	
Mix, prepared / **Durkee**	15
Mix, prepared / **French's**	20
Mix, prepared: ¼ pkg / **McCormick**	22
Mix, prepared / **Pillsbury**	15
Mix, prepared / **Spatini** Family Style	16
Mix, prepared / **Weight Watchers**	8
w mushrooms, mix, prepared / **Durkee**	15
w mushrooms, mix, prepared /	
Weight Watchers	12
w onions, canned / **Franco-American**	25
w onions, mix, prepared / **Durkee**	17
w onions, mix, prepared / **Weight Watchers**	13
Brown beef / **Howard Johnson's**	25
Chicken	
Canned / **Franco-American**	50
Mix, prepared / **Durkee**	23
Mix, prepared / **McCormick**	20
Mix, prepared / **Pillsbury**	25
Mix, prepared / **Weight Watchers**	10
Mix w roasting bag: 1 pkg /	
Durkee Roastin' Bag	122
Creamy, mix, prepared / **Durkee**	39
Creamy, mix w roasting bag: 1 pkg /	
Durkee Roastin' Bag	242
Giblet, canned / **Franco-American**	30
Italian style, mix w roasting bag: 1 pkg /	
Durkee Roastin' Bag	144
for chicken, mix, prepared / **French's**	25
Homestyle, mix, prepared / **Durkee**	18
Homestyle, mix, prepared / **French's**	25
Homestyle, mix, prepared / **Pillsbury**	15
Meatloaf, mix w roasting bag: 1 pkg /	
Durkee Roastin' Bag	129
Mushroom, canned / **Franco-American**	25
Mushroom, mix, prepared / **Durkee**	15
Mushroom, mix, prepared / **French's**	20
Onion, mix, prepared / **Durkee**	21
Onion, mix, prepared / **French's**	25

CALORIES

Onion, mix, prepared / **McCormick**	18
Pork	
Canned / **Franco-American**	40
Mix, prepared / **Durkee**	18
Mix w roasting bag: 1 pkg /	
Durkee Roastin' Bag	130
for pork, mix, prepared / **French's**	20
Pot roast and stew, mix w roasting bag: 1 pkg /	
Durkee Roastin' Bag	125
Pot roast, onion, mix w roasting bag: 1 pkg /	
Durkee Roastin' Bag	124
Swiss steak, mix, prepared / **Durkee**	11
Swiss steak, mix w roasting bag: 1 pkg /	
Durkee Roastin' Bag	115
Turkey	
Canned / **Franco-American**	30
Mix, prepared / **Durkee**	22
For turkey, mix, prepared / **French's**	25
Giblet / **Howard Johnson's**	27

Health and "Natural" Foods

Flour, Grains, Meal, Rice, Yeast

Amaranth, whole grain: 2 oz / **Arrowhead Mills**	200
Baking Mix	
Brown rice: ½ cup dry / **Fearn**	215
Brown rice: 1 cup dry / **Nutri-Dyne** Ener-G	655
Low protein: 3½ oz dry / **Nutri-Dyne** Aproten	400
White rice: ½ cup dry / **Fearn**	251
White rice: 1 cup dry / **Nutri-Dyne** Ener-G	830
Barley, pearled: 2 oz / **Arrowhead Mills**	200
Barley, hulled: 2 oz / **Arrowhead Mills**	200
Buckwheat groats, brown or white: 2 oz / **Arrowhead Mills**	190
Corn: 2 oz / **Arrowhead Mills**	210
Corn bran: 1 cup / **Nutri-Dyne** Ener-G	43
Corn germ: ¼ cup / **Fearn** Naturfresh	140
Flax seeds: 2 oz / **Arrowhead Mills**	140
Flour	
Barley: 2 oz / **Arrowhead Mills**	200
Brown rice: 2 oz / **Arrowhead Mills**	200
Brown rice: ¼ cup / **Elam's**	120
Brown rice: 1 cup / **Nutri-Dyne** Ener-G	500
Buckwheat: 2 oz / **Arrowhead Mills**	190
Buckwheat: ½ cup / **Elam's**	250
Durum: 2 oz / **Arrowhead Mills**	190
Graham: 2 oz / **Arrowhead Mills**	200
Millet: 2 oz / **Arrowhead Mills**	185

CALORIES

Oat: 2 oz / **Arrowhead Mills**	200
Pastry: 2 oz / **Arrowhead Mills**	180
Rye: 2 oz / **Arrowhead Mills**	190
Rye: ½ cup / **Elam's**	240
Soy: 2 oz / **Arrowhead Mills**	250
Soy: ¼ cup / **Elam's**	110
Tapioca: 1 cup / **Nutri-Dyne** Ener-G	391
Triticale: 2 oz / **Arrowhead Mills**	190
White, unbleached: 2 oz / **Arrowhead Mills**	200
White w wheat germ: ½ cup / **Elam's**	200
White rice: 1 cup / **Nutri-Dyne** Ener-G	430
Whole wheat: 2 oz / **Arrowhead Mills**	200
Whole wheat: ½ cup / **Elam's**	230
Whole wheat pastry: ¼ cup / **Elam's**	120
Grain side dishes: ½ cup prepared	
Herb / **Hain**	90
Italian / **Hain**	140
Spanish / **Hain**	90
Meal, corn: 2 oz / **Arrowhead Mills**	210
Meal, corn: ¼ cup / **Elam's**	130
Millet, hulled: 2 oz / **Arrowhead Mills**	90
Oats, hulled: 2 oz / **Arrowhead Mills**	220
Oats, steel cut: 2 oz / **Arrowhead Mills**	220
Rice bran: 1 cup / **Nutri-Dyne** Ener-G	224
Rice mix: 1 cup / **Nutri-Dyne** Ener-G	490
Rye, whole grain: 2 oz / **Arrowhead Mills**	190
Sesame seeds: 2 oz / **Arrowhead Mills**	160
Triticale, whole grain: 2 oz / **Arrowhead Mills**	190

Seasonings and Gravy

Catch-Up: 1 tbsp / **Health Valley**	10
Catsup: ½ oz / **Nutri-Dyne** Elwood	5
Chef Seasoning: 1 tsp / **Nutri-Dyne** Chef Otto	6
Chicken, mix: 1 oz dry / **Nutri-Dyne**	
Chef Otto	111
Mustard: ½ oz / **Nutri-Dyne** Elwood	10
Savorex: 1 oz / **Loma Linda**	65

Soy Milk and Beverage Mixes

80% Protein Mix: ¼ cup / **Fearn**	60

CALORIES

Liquid soya lecithin: 1 tbsp / **Fearn**	120
Liquid soya lecithin, mint: 1 tbsp / **Fearn**	113
Nutquick-almond milk powder: 8½ oz prepared / **Nutri-Dyne**	84
Soy milk, powder: 8 oz prepared / **Nutri-Dyne** Soyquick	60
Soy Moo, dry: 1 cup / **Health Valley**	130
Soy Moo, dry, carob: 1 cup / **Health Valley**	150
Soya granules: ¼ cup / **Fearn**	130
Soya powder: ½ cup / **Fearn**	100
Soyamel, powder: 1 oz dry / **Worthington**	130
Soya protein isolate: 4 tbsp / **Fearn**	50

Soybeans and Legumes

Beans

Adzuki: 2 oz dry / **Arrowhead Mills**	190
Black turtle: 2 oz dry / **Arrowhead Mills**	190
Boston baked: 4 oz / **Health Valley**	130
Boston baked, no salt: 4 oz / **Health Valley**	120
Great Northern: 2 oz dry / **Arrowhead Mills**	190
Kidney: 2 oz dry / **Arrowhead Mills**	190
Navy: 2 oz dry / **Arrowhead Mills**	190
Pinto: 2 oz dry / **Arrowhead Mills**	200
Soybeans: 2 oz dry / **Arrowhead Mills**	230
Soybeans, canned: 7½ oz / **Hain**	190
Soybeans, chili, canned: ½ cup / **Hain**	110
Tri-bean casserole, mix: 1.9 oz dry / **Fearn**	179
Vegetarian w miso: 4 oz / **Health Valley**	110
Chickpeas: 2 oz dry / **Arrowhead Mills**	200
Lentils, red: 2 oz dry / **Arrowhead Mills**	195
Lentils, green: 2 oz dry / **Arrowhead Mills**	190
Peas, split: 2 oz dry / **Arrowhead Mills**	200

Spreads and Sandwich Fillings: 2 tbsp unless noted

Almond butter, raw / **Hain**	190
Almond butter, toasted / **Hain**	210
Cashew butter, raw / **Hain**	190
Cashew butter, toasted / **Hain**	190

CALORIES

Peanut butter

Creamy old-fashioned / **Hain**	210
Creamy toasted / **Hain**	190
Creamy / **Health Valley**	166
Chunky / **Health Valley**	166
Crunchy / **Health Valley**	166
Crunchy old-fashioned / **Hain**	210
Unsalted, raw / **Hain**	180
Unsalted, toasted / **Hain**	190
Unsalted / **Health Valley**	166
w wheat germ / **Elam's**	180
Peanut-sesame butter / **Hain**	200
Sandwich spread: 3 tbsp / **Loma Linda**	70
Sesame butter / **Hain**	180
Sesame tahini / **Sahadi**	190
Sunflower butter / **Hain**	180

Sweets, Nuts and Snacks—1 oz unless noted

Almonds, dry roast, smoke-flavored / **Laura Scudder's**	178
Apple Bakes: 1 bar / **Health Valley**	90
Apple date fruit and nut mix / **Harmony**	110
Apricot bars, whole wheat / **Harmony**	90
Banana chips / **Harmony**	160
Carob almonds / **Harmony**	150
Carob cashews / **Harmony**	140
Carob coconut clusters / **Harmony**	140
Carob drops / **Harmony**	130
Carob fruit and nut clusters / **Harmony**	140
Carob granola clusters / **Harmony**	140
Carob maltballs / **Harmony**	130
Carob peanuts / **Harmony**	150
Carob peanut clusters / **Harmony**	150
Carob raisins / **Harmony**	120
Carob walnuts / **Harmony**	150
Cashews, dry roasted / **Laura Scudder's**	168
Cashews, oil roasted: ¾ oz / **Laura Scudder's**	119
Cheddar Lites, regular or no salt / **Health Valley**	140
Corn chips / **Health Valley**	160

CALORIES

Corn chips w cheese / **Health Valley**	160
Corn chips w cheese, no salt / **Health Valley**	160
Corn snacks party mix / **Harmony**	160
Country chips / **Health Valley**	160
Country Ripples / **Health Valley**	160
Crunchy raisins / **Harmony**	120
Date Bakes: 1 bar / **Health Valley**	85
Deluxe super trail mix / **Harmony**	130
Deluxe tamari nut mix / **Harmony**	140
Dip chips / **Health Valley**	160
Fig bars, whole wheat / **Harmony**	90
Golden Hawaiian / **Health Valley**	150
Granola Snack: 1 pouch	
Cinnamon / **Nature Valley**	130
Honey nut / **Nature Valley**	140
Oats and honey / **Nature Valley**	130
Peanut butter / **Nature Valley**	200
Raspberry glaze / **Nature Valley**	190
Vanilla glaze / **Nature Valley**	190
Halvah / **Sahadi**	150
Hot Stuff / **Harmony**	150
Mint yogurt raisins / **Harmony**	120
Mixed munchies / **Harmony**	120
Oat bran snack bar: 1 bar / **Elam's**	150
Oriental party mix / **Harmony**	150
Peanuts: 1 oz unless noted	
Arrowhead Mills	160
Dry roast / **Laura Scudder's** Snackin'	173
Roasted in shell: 1¾ oz /	
Laura Scudder's Goober	193
Spanish, oil roasted / **Laura Scudder's**	179
Virginia, oil roasted: 1¼ oz /	
Laura Scudder's	228
Pistachios, roasted in shell: 1¼ oz /	
Laura Scudder's	105
Potato chips: 1 oz / **Health Valley**	150
Pretzels, mini: 1 oz / **Health Valley**	112
Pretzels, mini, whole wheat: 1 oz /	
Health Valley	120
Pretzels, sesame whole wheat: 1 oz /	
Health Valley	130

CALORIES

Raisin Bakes: 1 bar / **Health Valley**	85
Raisins and nuts: 1 pouch / **Carnation**	130
Rice thins: 4 / **Nutri-Dyne** Hol-Grain	30
Rice thins, unsalted: 4 / **Nutri-Dyne** Hol-Grain	40
Ruskets biscuits / **Loma Linda**	105
Rusks / **Nutri-Dyne** Aproten	12
Seeds, sunflower	
Arrowhead Mills	80
Laura Scudder's, dry roasted	140
Laura Scudder's oil roasted	190
Roasted in shell: 1¼ oz / **Laura Scudder's**	107
Sesame sticks / **Harmony**	150
Sesame walnut mix / **Harmony**	160
Tamari roasted almonds / **Harmony**	160
Trail mix: 1 pouch / **Carnation Deluxe**	130
Trail mix, raw / **Harmony**	130
Tortilla chips / **Health Valley**	150
Tortilla chips, nacho cheese and chili /	
Health Valley	150
Tropical Fruit & Nuts: 1 pouch / **Carnation**	100
Tropical Trail Mix / **Harmony**	110
Yogurt almonds / **Harmony**	150
Yogurt coconut clusters / **Harmony**	140
Yogurt fruit and nut clusters / **Harmony**	150
Yogurt granola clusters / **Harmony**	140
Yogurt maltballs / **Harmony**	140
Yogurt peanuts / **Harmony**	150
Yogurt raisins / **Harmony**	130
Yogurt raisin fruit and nut mix / **Harmony**	140
Yogurt raspberry clusters / **Harmony**	150

Tofu and Tofu Dishes

Tofu, hard: 4 oz / **Health Valley** Tofu-Ya	110
Tofu, soft: 4 oz / **Health Valley** Tofu-Ya	60
Cannelloni Florentine: 11 oz / **Legume**	270
Lasagna, vegetable: 12 oz / **Legume**	260
Sesame ginger, stir-fry: 11½ oz / **Legume**	260
Stuffed shells Provencale: 11 oz / **Legume**	270
Tofu Bourguignon: 11¼ oz / **Legume**	250
Tofu Lasagna: 8 oz / **Legume**	280

CALORIES

Tofu Manicotti: 8 oz / **Legume**	240
Tofu Tetrazzini: 10¼ oz / **Legume**	280

Vegetarian Meat Substitutes

Beef style	
Hain: ½ cup prepared	30
Frozen / **Worthington:** 1 slice	60
Frozen, smoked: 1 slice / **Worthington**	17
Bologna, meatless, frozen: 2 slices /	
Loma Linda	150
Bolono, frozen: 2 slices / **Worthington**	70
Brazil nut burger mix: ¼ cup dry / **Fearn**	110
Breakfast patty mix: ¼ cup dry / **Fearn**	118
Chicken style	
Hain: ½ cup prepared	110
Loma Linda Chicken Supreme:	
¼ cup dry	50
1 slice prepared	120
fried, canned: 2 pieces / **Loma Linda**	140
fried, frozen: 1 piece / **Loma Linda**	180
frozen: 1 slice / **Worthington**	70
frozen: 1 oz / **Worthington** Chic-Ketts	60
frozen: 1 piece / **Worthington** Chik Stiks	120
Chili, canned: ½ cup / **Worthington**	190
Choplets, canned: 1 piece / **Worthington**	50
Corned beef style, frozen: 1 slice /	
Worthington	40
Corn dogs, frozen: 1 corn dog / **Loma Linda**	200
Cutlets, canned: 1½ slices / **Worthington**	90
Dinner cuts, canned: 2 cuts / **Loma Linda**	110
Dinner roast, frozen: 2 oz / **Worthington**	140
Falafel mix: .8 oz dry / **Fearn**	85
Fillets, frozen: 2 pieces / **Worthington**	230
Frankfurters, canned: 1 frank /	
Loma Linda Big Franks	100
Frankfurters: 2 franks /	
Loma Linda Sizzle Franks	170
Fri Chik, canned: 1 piece / **Worthington**	95
Fri Pats, frozen: 1 patty / **Worthington**	180
Gran Burger: 1 oz dry / **Worthington**	105

CALORIES

Griddle Steaks, frozen: 1 steak / **Loma Linda**	190
Linketts, canned: 2 links / **Loma Linda**	150
Little Links, canned: 2 links / **Loma Linda**	80
Nuteena (peanut butter base), canned: ½-in slice / **Loma Linda**	160
Nonmeat balls, canned: 1 piece / **Worthington**	40
Numete, canned: ½-in slice / **Worthington**	160
Ocean fillets, frozen: 1 fillet / **Loma Linda**	160
Ocean platter, canned / **Loma Linda:**	
¼ cup dry	50
1 slice prepared	120
Patty mix, canned / **Loma Linda:**	
¼ cup dry	50
1 patty prepared	130
Prime Stakes, canned w gravy: 1 piece / **Worthington**	160
Prosage links, frozen: 1 link / **Worthington**	60
Prosage patties, frozen: 1 patty / **Worthington**	100
Prosage roll, frozen: ⅜-in slice / **Worthington**	85
Proteena (gluten–peanut butter base), canned: ½-in slice / **Loma Linda**	140
Redi-Burger, canned: ½-in slice / **Loma Linda**	130
Salami, meatless, frozen: 2 slices / **Worthington**	100
Saucettes, canned: 1 link / **Worthington**	65
Savory dinner loaf, canned / **Loma Linda:**	
¼ cup dry	50
1 slice prepared	110
Sesame burger mix / **Fearn:** ¼ cup dry	120
Sizzle burger, frozen: 1 burger / **Loma Linda**	210
Scallops, vegetable, canned: ½ cup / **Worthington**	70
Stakelets, frozen: 1 piece / **Worthington**	180
Stripples, frozen: 1 slice / **Worthington**	25
Sunflower burger, mix: ¼ cup dry / **Fearn**	130
Super-Links, canned: 1 link / **Worthington**	120
Swedish meatballs, frozen: 8 pieces / **Loma Linda**	190
Swiss steak, canned: 1 steak / **Loma Linda**	140
Tastee Cuts, canned: 2 cuts / **Loma Linda**	70
Tender Bits, canned: 4 pieces / **Loma Linda**	80

CALORIES

Tender Rounds, canned: 6 pieces / **Loma Linda**	120
Tuno, frozen: 2 oz / **Worthington**	90
Turkey style, frozen: 1 slice / **Worthington**	50
Vege-Burger, canned: ½ cup / **Loma Linda**	110
Vegelona, canned: ½-in slice / **Loma Linda**	100
Vege-Scallops, canned: 6 pieces / **Loma Linda**	70
Vegetable steaks, canned: 2½ pieces / **Worthington**	100
Vegetarian burger, canned: ⅓ cup / **Worthington**	150
Veja-Bits, canned: 4.3 oz / **Worthington**	67
Veja-Links, canned: 1 link / **Worthington**	65
Vita-Burger, canned: 3 tbsp / **Loma Linda**	70
Wham, frozen: 1 slice / **Worthington**	47

Wheat and Wheat Germ

Bran, unprocessed: 1 oz	90
Bulgur, club wheat: 1 cup dry	628
Bulgur, hard red winter wheat: 1 cup dry	600
Bulgur, white wheat: 1 cup dry	550
Bulgur: 2 oz dry / **Arrowhead Mills**	200
Wheat, hard red winter or soft pastry: 2 oz / **Arrowhead Mills**	190
Wheat bran: 2 oz / **Arrowhead Mills**	200
Wheat bran: 2 tbsp / **Elam's** Miller's Bran	16
Wheat germ: 2 oz / **Arrowhead Mills**	210
Wheat germ: 2 tbsp / **Elam's**	60
Wheat germ: ¼ cup / **Fearn**	110
Wheat germ, toasted: ¼ cup / **Kretschmer**	110
Wheat germ, toasted w brown sugar and honey: ¼ cup / **Kretschmer**	110
Wheat germ w almonds and dates: 1 oz / **Health Valley**	110
Wheat germ w bananas: 1 oz / **Health Valley**	100
Wheat starch: 1 oz / **Nutri-Dyne** Aproten	100

Ice Cream and Similar Frozen Products

FROZEN DESSERT

	CALORIES
Chocolate supreme: ½ cup / **Toffuti**	210
Frozen dessert: 5 fl oz / **Weight Watchers**	100
Frosted treat / Frappe: ¾ cup / **Weight Watchers**	120
Maple walnut: ½ cup / **Toffuti**	230
Mountain coffee: ½ cup (1 scoop) / **Baskin-Robbins**	90
Snack cups: 1 Snack Cup (5 fl oz) / **Weight Watchers**	100
Sundae cone: 1 cone / **Weight Watchers**	150
Sunny orange: ½ cup (1 scoop) / **Baskin-Robbins**	90
Wild strawberry: ½ cup (1 scoop) / **Baskin-Robbins**	90
Wildberry supreme: ½ cup / **Toffuti**	210

ICE CREAM

Black raspberry: ½ cup / **Breyer's**	130
Butter almond: ½ cup / **Sealtest**	160
Butter almond chocolate: ½ cup / **Breyer's**	160
Butter brickle: ½ cup / **Sealtest**	150
Butter pecan: 1 scoop / **Baskin-Robbins**	136
Butter pecan: ½ cup / **Haagen-Dazs**	316
Butter pecan: ½ cup / **Lady Borden**	180
Butter pecan: ½ cup / **Lucerne**	160
Butter pecan: ½ cup / **Sealtest**	160
Caramel pecan crunch: ½ cup / **Breyer's**	160

CALORIES

Carob: ½ cup / **Haagen-Dazs**	256
Cherry nugget: ½ cup / **Sealtest**	140
Cherry-vanilla: ½ cup / **Breyer's**	140
Cherry-vanilla: ½ cup / **Sealtest**	130
Chocolate	
Baskin-Robbins: 1 scoop	165
Breyer's: ½ cup	161
Haagen-Dazs: ½ cup	280
Howard Johnson's: ½ cup	221
Lady Borden: ½ cup	160
Lucerne: ½ cup	140
Meadow Gold: ½ cup	140
Meadow Gold Olde Fashioned: ½ cup	140
Chocolate almond: ½ cup / **Breyer's**	180
Chocolate almond: ½ cup / **Sealtest**	160
Chocolate chip: ½ cup / **Haagen-Dazs**	312
Chocolate chip: ½ cup / **Lucerne**	150
Chocolate chip: ½ cup / **Sealtest**	150
Chocolate chip, mint: ½ cup / **Breyer's**	170
Chocolate cups: 3 fl oz / **A & P**	90
Chocolate fudge: 1 scoop / **Baskin-Robbins**	178
Chocolate marble: ½ cup / **Lucerne**	140
Chocolate marshmallow marble: ½ cup / **Lucerne**	140
Chocolate mint: 1 scoop / **Baskin-Robbins**	162
Chocolate mousse royale: 1 scoop / **Baskin-Robbins**	183
Coffee: ½ cup / **Breyer's**	140
Coffee: ½ cup / **Sealtest**	140
Coffee: ½ cup / **Haagen-Dazs**	272
Cookies & cream: ½ cup / **Haagen-Dazs**	272
Dutch chocolate: ½ cup / **Borden**	130
Dutch chocolate almond: 1.2 cups /	
Borden All Natural	160
French vanilla	
Baskin-Robbins: 1 scoop	181
Borden All Natural: ½ cup	150
Lady Borden: ½ cup	170
Lucerne: ½ cup	150
Honey: ½ cup / **Haagen-Dazs**	256
Jamoca: 1 scoop / **Baskin-Robbins**	146
Macadamia nut: ½ cup / **Haagen-Dazs**	260
Maple nut: ½ cup / **Lucerne**	150

Maple walnut: ½ cup / **Haagen-Dazs**	320
Maple walnut: ½ cup / **Sealtest**	160
Mint chocolate chip: ½ cup / **Lucerne**	150
Mocha chip: ½ cup / **Haagen-Dazs**	272
Neapolitan: ½ cup / **Lucerne**	140
Peach: ½ cup / **Haagen-Dazs**	252
Peach: ½ cup / **Sealtest**	130
Pralines 'n cream: 1 scoop / **Baskin-Robbins**	177
Rocky road: 1 scoop / **Baskin-Robbins**	182
Rocky road: ½ cup / **Lucerne**	150
Rum raisin: ½ cup / **Haagen-Dazs**	264
Strawberry	
Baskin-Robbins: 1 scoop	141
Borden: ½ cup	120
Breyer's: ½ cup	130
Haagen-Dazs: ½ cup	268
Howard Johnson's: ½ cup	187
Lucerne: ½ cup	130
Meadow Gold: ½ cup	140
Sealtest: ½ cup	130
Strawberry cheesecake: ½ cup / **Lucerne**	140
Swiss chocolate almond: ½ cup / **Haagen-Dazs**	292
Vanilla	
Baskin-Robbins: 1 scoop	147
Borden: ½ cup	130
Borden All Natural: ½ cup	140
Breyer's: ½ cup	150
Haagen-Dazs: ½ cup	268
Howard Johnson's: ½ cup	210
Land O Lakes: ½ cup	140
Lucerne: ½ cup	140
Meadow Gold: ½ cup	140
Sealtest: ½ cup	140
Vanilla ice cream and orange sherbet: ½ cup / **Lucerne**	130
Vanilla slices: 1 slice / **Good Humor**	110
Vanilla slices: 1 slice / **Good Humor** Cal-Control	60
Vanilla swiss almond: ½ cup / **Haagen-Dazs**	344

ICE MILK

Banana-strawberry twirl: ½ cup / **Sealtest** Light N' Lively	110

CALORIES

Chocolate: ½ cup / **Borden** All Natural	110
Chocolate: ½ cup / **Sealtest** Light N' Lively	100
Coffee: ½ cup / **Sealtest** Light N' Lively	100
Fudge twirl: ½ cup / **Sealtest** Light N' Lively	100
Strawberry: ½ cup / **Borden** All Natural	110
Vanilla: ½ cup / **Borden** All Natural	100
Vanilla: ½ cup / **Land O Lakes**	90
Vanilla: ½ cup / **Sealtest** Light N' Lively	100

SHERBET AND ICES

All flavors: ½ cup / **Land O Lakes**	130
Cantaloupe: ½ cup / **Le Sorbet**	72
Cassis: ½ cup / **Le Sorbet**	80
Daiquiri ice: 1 scoop / **Baskin-Robbins**	84
Lemon ice: ½ cup / **Haagen-Dazs**	140
Lemon: ½ cup / **Borden**	110
Lemon: ½ cup / **Le Sorbet**	96
Orange	
Baskin-Robbins: 1 scoop	99
Borden: ½ cup	110
Howard Johnson's: ½ cup	132
Haagen-Dazs: ½ cup	140
Mango: ½ cup / **Le Sorbet**	98
Passion fruit: ½ cup / **Le Sorbet**	80
Pineapple: 1 scoop / **Baskin-Robbins**	94
Raspberry: ½ cup / **Le Sorbet**	78
Strawberry: ½ cup / **Le Sorbet**	86

ICE CREAM AND FROZEN BARS

1 bar or piece

Almond toasted / **Good Humor**	190
Bon Bon, ice cream nugget, chocolate	34
Bon Bon, ice cream nugget, vanilla	33
Caramel toasted / **Good Humor**	170
Chip crunch / **Good Humor**	200
Chocolate: 2½ oz bar / **Fudgsicle**	102
Chocolate dip / **Weight Watchers**	100
Chocolate eclair / **Good Humor**	180
Chocolate fudge: 2 oz bar / **Ann Page**	80

CALORIES

Chocolate fudge: 2½ oz bar / **Ann Page**	110
Chocolate fudge cake / **Good Humor**	260
Chocolate malt / **Good Humor**	190
Chocolate mint treat / **Weight Watchers**	100
Chocolate treat / **Weight Watchers**	100
Cookie sandwich: 2.7 oz / **Good Humor** ice milk	290
Cookie sandwich: 4 oz / **Good Humor** ice milk	400
Creamsickle: 2½ oz bar	78
Dreamsickle: 2½ oz bar	70
Drumstick, ice cream	181
Drumstick, ice milk	163
Fat Frog / **Good Humor** ice milk	140
Heart / **Good Humor** ice milk	200
Heath toffee	130
Lemonade bar / **Sunkist**	70
Orange juice bar / **Sunkist**	70
Orange vanilla treat / **Weight Watchers**	100
Pops / **Ann Page**	50
Pudding Pops, all flavors / **Jello-O**	90
Pudding sticks / **Good Humor**	90
Sandwich / **Ann Page**	160
Sandwich, mint / **Weight Watchers**	130
Sandwich, vanilla / **Good Humor**	170
Sandwich, vanilla / **Weight Watchers**	130
Shark / **Good Humor** ice milk	70
Strawberry vanilla treat / **Weight Watchers**	100
Twin pops / **Ann Page**	70
Vanilla / **Ann Page**	160
Vanilla / **Ann Page** ice milk	140
Vanilla / **Good Humor**	170
Whammy / **Good Humor** ice milk	90

CONES

1 cone (alone)

Cones / Comet	20
Cake cones / **Baskin-Robbins**	19
Sugar cones / **Baskin-Robbins**	57
Sugar cones / **Comet**	40

CALORIES

ICE CONES

Snow cones and slurps: 1 cup	150

Italian Foods

See also Dinners, Pizza and Spaghetti

	CALORIES
Cannelloni, canned: 7½ oz / **Chef Boy-ar-dee**	230
Cannelloni, canned: 7½ oz / **Ezo**	240
Cannelloni, beef and pork, frozen: 9⅝ oz / **Stouffer's Lean Cuisine**	260
Cannelloni, cheese, frozen: 9⅛ oz / **Stouffer's Lean Cuisine**	270
Cannelloni Florentine, frozen: 11 oz / **Legume**	270
Chicken cacciatore, frozen: 11¼ oz / **Stouffer's**	310
Chicken cacciatore, frozen: 10 oz / **Weight Watchers**	290
Chicken parmigiana, frozen: 9½ oz / **Weight Watchers**	240
Eggplant parmigiana, frozen: 12 oz / **Buitoni**	430
Fettucine Alfredo: 2.85 oz dry / **Pasta Suprema**	290
Fettucine Alfredo, frozen: 10 oz / **Buitoni**	440
Fettucine Alfredo, frozen: 5 oz / **Stouffer's**	270
Fettucine Alfredo, mix: ¼ pkg / **Betty Crocker**	220
Fettucine carbonara, frozen: 10 oz / **Buitoni**	440
Fettucine primavera, frozen: 10 oz / **Buitoni**	440
Lasagna	
Canned: 7½ oz / **Chef Boy-ar-dee**	220
Canned: 8 oz / **Chef Boy-ar-dee**, 40 oz can	240
Canned: 6 oz / **Chef Boy-ar-dee**	290
Canned: 7 oz / **Ezo**	220
Frozen: 9½ oz / **Green Giant**	290
Frozen: 12 oz / **Legume** (tofu)	260
Frozen: 10½ oz / **Stouffer's**	385
Frozen: 11 oz / **Van de Kamp's**	430
Frozen: 11 oz pkg / **Weight Watchers**	350

CALORIES

Frozen, chicken: 12 oz / **Green Giant**	640
Frozen, deep-dish: 11 oz / **Buitoni**	390
Frozen, deep-dish w meat sauce: 10½ oz / **Buitoni**	400
Frozen, Florentine: 9½ oz / **Buitoni**	480
Frozen, Florentine: 11¼ oz / **Light and Elegant**	280
Frozen w meat: 8 oz / **Banquet** Buffet Supper	372
Frozen w meat sauce: 12¾ oz / **Swanson** Hungry Man	480
Frozen w meat sauce: 13¼ oz / **Swanson** Main Course	480
Frozen w meat sauce: 14 oz / **Buitoni**	540
Frozen w meat sauce: 10½ oz / **Green Giant**	430
Frozen w meat sauce: 12 oz / **Green Giant** Single Serve	490
Frozen w meat sauce and cheese: 12 oz pkg / **Weight Watchers**	360
Frozen w sausage: 11 oz / **Van de Kamp's**	440
Frozen, spinach: 12 oz / **Green Giant**	540
Frozen, spinach: 9 oz / **Health Valley**	370
Frozen, spinach: 11 oz / **Van de Kamp's**	400
Frozen, zucchini: 11 oz / **Stouffer's** Lean Cuisine	260
Linguini w clam sauce, frozen: 10½ oz / **Stouffer's**	285
Manicotti, frozen: 5⅓ oz / **Banquet** Buffet Supper	232
Manicotti, frozen: 6 oz / **Buitoni**	270
Manicotti w sauce: 13 oz / **Buitoni**	420
Mostaccioli, frozen: 8 oz / **Banquet** Buffet Supper	251
Pizza style pastry, cheese filling in pastry w tomato sauce: 1 pastry / **Pepperidge Farm** Deli's	300

Ravioli

Beef, canned: ½ can / **Chef Boy-ar-dee** Mini 15-oz can	210
Beef, canned: ⅕ can (8 oz) / **Chef Boy-ar-dee** Mini 40-oz can	220
Beef, canned: 8 oz / **Dia-Mel**	260
Beef, canned: 7 oz / **Ezo**	180
Beef, canned: 7½ oz / **Ezo** Chef's Special	180
Beef, canned: 7½ oz / **Franco American**	230
Beef, canned: 7½ oz / **Lido Club**	190

CALORIES

Beef, canned in sauce: 8 oz / **Chef Boy-ar-dee**	220
Beef, canned in tomato-meat sauce: ½ can (7½ oz) / **Chef Boy-ar-dee**	200
Cheese, canned in beef-tomato sauce: ½ can (7½ oz) / **Chef Boy-ar-dee**	200
Cheese, canned in tomato sauce: ½ can (7½ oz) / **Chef Boy-ar-dee**	200
Cheese, canned in tomato sauce: 7½ oz / **Ezo**	210
Cheese, frozen: 3¾ oz / **Buitoni**	260
Cheese, frozen, parmesan: 12 oz / **Buitoni**	440
Cheese, frozen, round: 5½ oz / **Buitoni**	310
Chicken, canned: ½ can (7½ oz) / **Chef Boy-ar-dee**	180
Chicken, canned: ½ can (7½ oz) / **Chef Boy-ar-dee**	220
Meat, frozen: 3¾ oz / **Buitoni**	265
Meat, frozen, parmesan: 12 oz / **Buitoni**	520
Meat, frozen, round: 5½ oz / **Buitoni**	340
Sausage, canned: ½ can (7½ oz) / **Chef Boy-ar-dee**	210
RavioliOs, canned: 7½ oz / **Franco American**	210

Shells

Frozen w sauce: 10½ oz / **Buitoni**	320
Stuffed, frozen w sauce: 10 oz / **Buitoni**	350
Stuffed, frozen: 11 oz / **Legume** Provencale (tofu)	270
Stuffed, frozen w sauce: 9 oz / **Stouffer's**	290
Stuffed w broccoli, frozen: 5 oz / **Buitoni**	150
Stuffed w cheese, frozen: 9 oz / **Stouffer's**	320
Stuffed w chicken, frozen: 9 oz / **Stouffer's**	400
Stuffed w spinach, frozen: 5½ oz / **Buitoni**	160
Tortellini, frozen: 10 oz / **Buitoni**	380
Veal parmigian, frozen: 6⅖ oz / **Banquet** Buffet Supper	277
Veal parmigian, frozen: 5 oz / **Banquet** Cookin' Bag	293
Veal parmigiana, frozen: 5 oz / **Morton** Boil-in-bag	130
Veal parmigiana, frozen: 8 oz / **Morton** Family Meal	300
Ziti, frozen: 10½ oz / **Buitoni**	360
Ziti w meat, frozen: 11¼ oz pkg / **Weight Watchers**	290

Jams, Jellies, Preserves, Butters, Marmalade and Spreads

1 tsp unless noted

Butters
Apple / **Bama**	14
Apple: 1 oz / **Lucky Leaf**	50
Apple: 1 oz / **Musselman's**	50
Apple / **Smucker's**	14
Peach / **Smucker's**	15

Jams
All flavors / **Kraft**	18
All flavors / **Smucker's**	17
All flavors, imitation / **Smucker's** Low Calorie Slenderella	8
All flavors / **Welch's**	17
Red plum / **Bama**	15

Jellies
All flavors: 1 tbsp / **Crosse & Blackwell**	50
All flavors / **Dia-Mel**	2
All flavors / **Kraft**	16
All flavors / **Smucker's**	17
All flavors, imitation / **Smucker's** Low Calorie Slenderella	8
All flavors / **Welch's**	17
Apple: 1 oz / **Lucky Leaf**	80
Apple: 1 oz / **Musselman's**	80
Apple: ½ oz / **Nutri-Dyne** Elwood	2
Apple blackberry: 1 oz / **Musselman's**	80

CALORIES

Apple cherry: 1 oz / **Musselman's**	80
Apple grape: 1 oz / **Musselman's**	80
Apple raspberry: 1 oz / **Musselman's**	80
Apple strawberry: 1 oz / **Musselman's**	80
Black raspberry: ½ oz / **Nutri-Dyne** Elwood	3
Grape / **Bama**	15
Grape: 1 oz / **Musselman's**	80
Grape: ½ oz / **Nutri-Dyne** Elwood	4
Mint flavored apple / **Bama**	15
Strawberry: ½ oz / **Nutri-Dyne** Elwood	4

Marmalade
All flavors: about 1 tbsp / **Crosse & Blackwell**	60
Orange: ½ oz / **Nutri-Dyne** Elwood	3

Preserves
All flavors: about 1 tbsp / **Crosse & Blackwell**	60
All flavors / **Dia-Mel**	2
All flavors / **Kraft**	16
All flavors / **Safeway**	17
All flavors / **Smucker's**	17
Apricot / **Bama**	15

Spreads
All flavors / **Smucker's** Low Sugar	8
All flavors / **Welch's** Lite	10

Liqueurs and Brandies

BRANDIES

CALORIES

1 fl oz

Leroux Deluxe	67
Apricot / **Hiram Walker**	88
Apricot / **Leroux**	92
Blackberry / **Hiram Walker**	88
Blackberry / **Leroux**	91
Blackberry / **Leroux** Polish type	92
Cherry / **Hiram Walker**	88
Cherry / **Leroux**	91
Cherry / **Leroux** Kirschwasser	80
Coffee / **Hiram Walker**	96
Coffee / **Leroux**	91
Ginger / **Leroux**	76
Peach / **Hiram Walker**	88
Peach / **Leroux**	93
Raspberry / **Hiram Walker**	88

LIQUEURS

1 fl oz

Amaretto / **Hiram Walker**	76
Amaretto & Cognac / **Hiram Walker**	62
Anesone / **Leroux**	86

CALORIES

Anisette / **Leroux**	89
Anisette, red and white / **Hiram Walker**	92
Apricot / **Leroux**	85
Apricot Cordial / **Hiram Walker**	79
Aquavit / **Leroux**	75
Banana / **Leroux**	92
B & B	95
Benedictine	110
Blackberry / **Leroux**	78
Blackberry Cordial / **Hiram Walker**	93
Cherry / **Kijafa**	49
Cherry / **Leroux**	80
Cherry / **Leroux** Cherry Karise	71
Cherry Heering	80
Chocolate, cherry / **Cheri-Suisse**	90
Chocolate, minted / **Vandermint**	90
Chocolate, orange / **Sabra**	91
Cidermill Schnapps / **Hiram Walker**	77
Cinnamon Schnapps / **Hiram Walker**	80
Claristine / **Leroux**	114
Coffee / **Pasha** Turkish Coffee	97
Cranberry Cordial / **Hiram Walker**	64
Creme de Banana / **Hiram Walker**	96
Creme de Cacao, brown / **Hiram Walker**	102
Creme de Cacao, brown / **Leroux**	101
Creme de Cacao, white / **Hiram Walker**	96
Creme de Cacao, white / **Leroux**	98
Creme de Cafe / **Leroux**	104
Creme de Cassis / **Hiram Walker**	95
Creme de Cassis / **Leroux**	88
Creme de Menthe, green / **Hiram Walker**	96
Creme de Menthe, green / **Leroux**	110
Creme de Menthe, white / **Hiram Walker**	96
Creme de Menthe, white / **Leroux**	101
Creme de Noya / **Leroux**	108
Creme de Noyaux / **Hiram Walker**	99
Curacao / **Leroux**	88
Drambuie	110
Gold-O-Mint / **Leroux**	110
Grenadine / **Leroux**	81
Haagen-Dazs / **Hiram Walker**	95

CALORIES

Hazelnut Schnapps / **Hiram Walker**	73
Kahlua / **Hiram Walker**	106
Kirschwasser / **Hiram Walker**	74
Kummel / **Hiram Walker**	71
Kummel / **Leroux**	75
Maraschino / **Leroux**	88
Orange Curacao / **Hiram Walker**	95
Orange Schnapps / **Hiram Walker**	79
Peach / **Leroux**	85
Peppermint Schnapps / **Hiram Walker** 60 proof	80
Peppermint Schnapps / **Hiram Walker** 90 proof	105
Peppermint Schnapps / **Leroux**	87
Praline / **Hiram Walker**	98
Raspberry / **Leroux**	74
Rock & Rye / **Hiram Walker**	88
Rock and Rye / **Leroux**	91
Rock and Rye–Irish Moss / **Leroux**	110
Sambuca / **Hiram Walker**	115
Sloe Gin / **Hiram Walker**	66
Sloe Gin / **Leroux**	74
Spearmint Schnapps / **Hiram Walker**	80
Strawberry / **Hiram Walker**	76
Strawberry / **Leroux**	74
Strawberry Schnapps / **Hiram Walker**	76
Swiss Chocolate Almond / **Hiram Walker**	91
Tia Maria / **Hiram Walker**	84
Triple Sec / **Hiram Walker**	90
Triple Sec / **Leroux**	102
Valenciana / **Hiram Walker**	69

Macaroni

Plain, all types, cooked to firm "al dente" stage: 1 cup	190
Plain, all types, cooked to tender stage: 1 cup	155
Macaroni and beef	
Canned: 7½ oz / **Franco American** BeefyOs	220
Canned: 7¼ oz / **Heinz** Mac 'n Beef	200
Frozen: 5¾ oz / **Stouffer's**	190
Macaroni and cheese	
Canned: 7 oz / **Ezo**	180
Canned: 7⅜ oz / **Franco American**	170
Canned: 7½ oz / **Heinz**	190
Frozen: 8 oz / **Banquet** Buffet Supper	336
Frozen: 8 oz / **Banquet** Casserole	344
Frozen: 5 oz / **Banquet** Cookin' Bag	227
Frozen: 9 oz / **Green Giant**	290
Frozen: 10 oz / **Howard Johnson's**	541
Frozen: ⅓ pkg / **Howard Johnson's** 19-oz size	343
Frozen: 8 oz / **Morton** Casserole	270
Frozen: 8 oz / **Morton** Family Meal	260
Frozen: 6 oz / **Stouffer's**	260
Frozen: 12 oz / **Swanson**	440
Mix: 2 oz dry / **Creamette**	220
Mix: ¼ pkg dry / **Golden Grain**	220
Mix: ¾ cup prepared / **Kraft** Dinner	300
Mix: ¾ cup prepared / **Kraft** Dinner Family Size	300

CALORIES

Mix: ¾ cup prepared / **Kraft** Deluxe Dinner	260
Mix: ¾ cup prepared / **Kraft** Dinner Spiral	300
Mix: ½ cup prepared / **Lipton**	210
Macaroni in pizza sauce, canned: 7½ oz / **Franco American** PizzOs	170
Macaroni in tomato sauce, canned: 7½ oz / **Chef Boy-ar-dee**	150

Mayonnaise

CALORIES

1 tbsp

Bama	100
Hellmann's	100
Mrs. Filbert's Real	100
NuMade	100
Nutri-Dyne Elwood: ½ oz	80
Scotch Buy	100
Weight Watchers reduced calorie	29
Imitation	
Dia-Mel	106
Mrs. Filbert's	40
Scotch Buy	60
Hain Naturals (eggless)	110

Meat

FRESH

Note: All figures are for meat that has been trimmed according to ordinary retail practices. "Lean w fat" means you eat both the lean and fat of the cooked meat. "Lean" means you trim off any removable fat and eat only the lean meat. Figures are given in many cases for the cooked yield from a pound of raw meat as purchased. When cooked, meat shrinks in weight by 25 to 40 percent.

Beef, choice grade
  Chuck, boneless, stewed, lean w fat: 10.7 oz
    (1 lb raw beef)   994
  Chuck, boneless, stewed, lean w fat:
    1 cup diced   458
  Chuck, boneless, stewed, lean: 10.7 oz
    (1 lb raw beef)   651
  Chuck, arm, roast or steak, braised, lean w fat:
    9.5 oz (1 lb raw w bone)   780
  Chuck, arm, roast or steak, braised, lean w fat:
    10.7 oz (1 lb raw boneless)   879
  Chuck, arm, roast or steak, braised,
    lean w fat: 3 oz   246
  Chuck, arm, roast or steak, braised, lean:
    8.1 oz (1 lb raw w bone)   444
  Chuck, arm, roast or steak, braised, lean:
    9.1 oz (1 lb raw boneless)   498
  Chuck, arm, roast or steak, braised,
    lean: 3 oz.   164
  Club steak, broiled, lean w fat:
    11.7 oz (1 lb raw boneless)   1503
  Club steak, broiled, lean:
    6.8 oz (1 lb raw boneless)   468
  Corned beef, boneless:
    10.7 oz (1 lb beef raw)   1131
  Flank steak, braised: 3 oz   167
  Ground beef, raw, extra lean,
    10% fat (steak tartar): 1 cup   405
  Ground beef, broiled, extra lean, 10% fat:
    3 oz patty (4 patties per lb raw)   186
  Ground beef, broiled, lean, 21% fat:
    2.9 oz patty (4 patties per lb raw)   235
  Marrow: 1 tbsp   130
  Oxtails, braised: 3½ oz   249
  Neckbones, cooked: 3½ oz   289
  Porterhouse steak, broiled, lean w fat:
    10.6 oz (1 lb raw w bone)   1400
  Porterhouse steak, broiled, lean:
    6.1 oz (1 lb raw w bone)   385
  Rib roast, roasted, lean and fat:
    10¾ oz (1 lb raw beef w bone)   1342

CALORIES

Rib roast, roasted, lean and fat: 3 oz	374
Rib roast, roasted, lean: 6.9 oz	
(1 lb raw beef w bone)	470
Rib roast, roasted, lean: 3 oz	205
Round steak, braised, broiled, sauteed, lean	
and fat: 10.7 oz (1 lb raw beef w bone)	793
Round steak, braised, broiled, sauteed,	
lean and fat: 3 oz.	222
Round steak, braised, broiled, sauteed, lean:	
9.2 oz (1 lb raw beef w bone)	491
Round steak, braised, broiled,	
sauteed, lean: 3 oz	161
Rump roast, roasted, lean and fat:	
11.7 oz (1 lb raw beef boneless)	1149
Rump roast, roasted, lean and fat: 3 oz	295
Rump roast, roasted, lean:	
8.8 oz (1 lb raw beef boneless)	516
Rump roast, roasted, lean: 3 oz	177
Sirloin, broiled, lean w fat:	
10.9 oz (1 lb raw w bone)	1192
Sirloin, broiled, lean w fat: 3 oz	329
Sirloin, broiled, lean: 7.2 oz (1 lb raw w bone)	420
Sirloin, broiled, lean: 3 oz	176
T-bone steak, broiled, lean w fat:	
10.4 oz (1 lb raw w bone)	1395
T-bone steak, broiled, lean:	
5.8 oz (1 lb raw w bone)	368
Brains, all varieties, cooked: 1 oz	35
Goat, boneless, boiled: 3½ oz	266
Heart, cooked: 1 oz	
beef, lean	53
calf	35
lamb	73
Kidney, beef, cooked: 1 oz	70
Lamb	
Chop, loin, broiled, lean w fat, 3.4 oz	
(3 raw chops per lb)	341
Chop, loin, broiled, lean:	
2.3 oz (3 raw chops per lb)	122
Chop, rib, broiled, lean w fat:	
3.1 oz (3 raw chops per lb)	362

Chop, rib, broiled, lean:	
2 oz (3 raw chops per lb)	120
Leg, roasted, lean w fat:	
9.4 oz (1 lb raw lamb w bone)	745
Leg, roasted, lean w fat: 3 oz	237
Leg, roasted, lean:	
7.8 oz (1 lb raw lamb w bone)	411
Leg, roasted, lean: 3 oz	158
Shoulder, roasted, lean w fat:	
9.5 oz (1 lb raw lamb w bone)	913
Shoulder, roasted, lean w fat: 3 oz	287
Shoulder, roasted, lean:	
7 oz (1 lb raw lamb w bone)	410
Shoulder, roasted, lean: 3 oz	174
Liver	
Beef, fried: 3 oz	195
Calf, fried: 3 oz	222
Hog, fried: 3 oz	205
Lamb, broiled: 3 oz	220
Moose, cooked: 3½ oz	176
Mutton, boneless, cooked: 3½ oz	405
Pork	
Chop, loin, broiled, lean w fat: 2.7 oz	
(3 raw chops per lb)	305
Chop, loin, broiled, lean: 2 oz	
(3 raw chops per lb)	151
Ham, cured, baked, lean w fat: 3 oz	246
Ham, cured, baked, lean: 3 oz	159
Ham, cured, baked, ground, lean w fat: 1 cup	318
Ham, cured, baked, ground, lean: 1 cup	206
Ham, fresh, roasted, lean w fat: 9.2 oz	
(1 lb raw pork w bone)	980
Ham, fresh, roasted, lean w fat: 3 oz	318
Ham, fresh, roasted, ground: 1 cup	411
Ham, fresh, roasted, lean: 6.8 oz	
(1 lb raw ham w bone)	421
Ham, fresh, roasted, lean: 3 oz	184
Ham, fresh, roasted, lean, ground: 1 cup	239
Loin, roasted, lean w fat: 8.6 oz	
(1 lb raw loin w bone)	883
Loin, roasted, lean w fat: 3 oz	308

Loin, roasted, lean: 6.9 oz (1 lb raw loin w bone)	495
Loin, roasted, lean: 3 oz	308
Shoulder, Boston butt, roasted, lean w fat: 3 oz	300
Shoulder, Boston butt, roasted, lean: 3 oz	207
Shoulder, picnic, roasted, lean w fat: 3 oz	318
Shoulder, picnic, roasted, lean: 3 oz	180
Spareribs, braised: 6.3 oz (1 lb raw ribs)	792
Steak or cutlet, broiled, lean w fat: 3½ oz	359
Steak or cutlet, broiled, lean: 3½ oz	270
Pork cracklings, cooked: 3½ oz	770
Pork rinds: 1 oz	153
Pigs feet, cooked or pickled: 3½ oz	205
Salt pork or fatback: 1 oz	215
Rabbit, domestic w bone, cooked: 3½ oz	216
1 leg	54
1 thigh	97
Squirrel, cooked: 3½ oz	216
1 hindleg	93
Sweetbreads, calf, cooked: 2 oz	95
Tongue, cooked: 2 oz	
Beef	140
Calf	90
Lamb	145
Tripe, beef, cooked: 1 cup	140
Veal	
Boneless chuck, braised, stewed, medium fat: 10.6 oz (1 lb raw boneless veal)	703
Boneless chuck, braised, stewed, medium fat: 3 oz	200
Breast, roasted, medium fat: 8.3 oz (1 lb raw veal w bone)	718
Breast, roasted, medium fat: 3 oz	260
Cutlet, braised or broiled, medium fat: 3 oz	184
Rib roast, roasted, medium fat: 3 oz	229
Rump roast, braised, medium fat: 3 oz	184
Venison, boneless, roasted: 3½ oz	174

CANNED, CURED, PROCESSED

Bacon, cooked	
Hormel Black Label: 1 slice	35

CALORIES

Hormel Range Brand: 1 slice	45
Hormel Red Label: 1 slice	37
Oscar Mayer: 1 slice	35
Swift: 1 slice	40
Bits: 1 ¼ cup / **Oscar Mayer**	20
Canadian: 1 oz / **Eckrich** Calorie Watcher	35
Canadian: 1 slice **Oscar Mayer**	40
Banquet loaf: 1 slice / **Eckrich** Beef Smorgas Pack	50
Bar-B loaf: 1 slice / **Eckrich** Calorie Watcher	35
Bar-B-Q loaf: 1 slice / **Oscar Mayer**	45
Beef breakfast strips: 1 strip / **Oscar Mayer** Lean 'n Tasty	40
Beef, corned, canned: 3 oz / **Dinty Moore**	190
Beef, corned, canned: 2.3 oz / **Libby's** 7-oz can	160
Beef, corned, canned: 2.4 oz / **Libby's** 12-oz can	160
Beef, corned, chopped: 1 oz / **Safeway**	45
Beef, corn, jellied loaf: 1 slice / **Oscar Mayer**	45
Beef, corned, sliced: 1 oz / **Eckrich** Calorie Watcher	40
Beef, dried, chunked and formed: ¾ oz / **Swift** Premium	35
Beef pastry w bacon sauce: 1 piece / **Pepperidge Farm** Deli's	260
Beef pastry w barbecue sauce: 1 piece / **Pepperidge Farm** Deli's	270
Beef, sliced: 1 oz / **Eckrich** Calorie Watcher	40
Beef, smoked, sliced: 1 oz / **Safeway**	45
Beef steaks, breaded, frozen: 4 oz / **Hormel**	370
Bologna	
Eckrich: 1 slice	90
Eckrich German Brand: 1 slice	80
Eckrich Smorgas Pac (12-oz pkg): 1 slice	70
Eckrich Smorgas Pac (1-lb pkg): 1 slice	90
Hormel: 1 oz	85
Swift Premium: 1 oz	95
Oscar Mayer: 1 slice	75
Beef / **Eckrich:** 1 slice	90
Beef: 1 slice / **Eckrich** Beef Smorgas Pac	70
Beef: 1 oz / **Health Valley**	88
Beef: 1 slice / **Oscar Mayer**	75
Beef, thick sliced: 1 slice / **Eckrich**	140

Beef, thin sliced: 2 slices / **Eckrich**	110
Chicken: 1 oz / **Health Valley**	85
Chub: 1 oz / **Eckrich** German Brand	80
Garlic: 1 slice / **Eckrich**	90
Lunch, chub: 1 oz / **Eckrich**	100
Ring: 1 oz / **Eckrich**	90
Ring, pickled: 1 oz / **Eckrich**	90
Sandwich: 1 slice / **Eckrich**	90
Sliced: 1 slice / **Eckrich** (12-oz pkg)	90
Sliced: 1 slice / **Eckrich** (1-lb pkg)	90
Thick sliced: 1 slice / **Eckrich**	160
Thin sliced: 2 slices / **Eckrich**	110
w cheese: 1 slice / **Eckrich**	90
w cheese: 1 slice / **Oscar Mayer**	75
Braunschweiger: 1 oz / **Oscar Mayer**	95
Braunschweiger, chub: 1 oz / **Eckrich**	70
Breakfast strips, pork: 1 strip / **Oscar Mayer** Lean 'N Tasty	45
Breakfast strips: 1 strip / **Swift** Sizzlean	50
Corn dogs: 1 piece / **Hormel**	230
Corn dogs: 1 piece / **Oscar Mayer**	330
Frankfurters: 1 frankfurter unless noted	
Eckrich	120
Hormel Range Brand Wranglers	180
Hormel Wieners (12-oz pkg)	105
Hormel Wieners (16-oz pkg)	140
Oscar Mayer	145
Beef / **Eckrich**	110
Beef / **Hormel** Wieners (12-oz pkg)	105
Beef / **Hormel** Wieners (16-oz pkg)	140
Beef / **Hormel** Wranglers	160
Beef / **Oscar Mayer**	145
Beef, jumbo / **Eckrich**	190
Cheese / **Eckrich**	
Cheese / **Oscar Mayer**	145
Chicken: 1 oz / **Health Valley**	82
Turkey: 1 oz / **Health Valley**	78
Gourmet loaf: 1 slice / **Eckrich** Beef Smorgas Pac	25
Gourmet loaf: 1 slice / **Eckrich** Calorie Watcher	35
Ham	
Canned: 1 oz / **Oscar Mayer** Jubilee	30

CALORIES

Canned: 3½ oz / **Swift** Premium	220
Canned: 3½ oz / **Swift** Premium Hostess	140
Chopped: 1 slice / **Eckrich** Calorie Watcher	45
Chopped: 1 slice / **Eckrich** Smorgas Pac	35
Chopped: 1 oz / **Hormel**	70
Chopped: 1 slice / **Oscar Mayer**	65
Cooked, sliced: 1 slice / **Eckrich**	30
Cooked, sliced: 1 slice / **Eckrich** Calorie Watcher	30
Cooked, smoked: 1 slice / **Oscar Mayer**	25
Danish: 1 oz / **Eckrich**	25
Loaf: 1 slice / **Eckrich**	70
Patties: 1 patty / **Hormel**	200
Patties: 1 patty / **Swift** Premium Brown 'n Serve	250
Slice: 1 oz / **Oscar Mayer** Jubilee	30
Smoked, boneless: 1 oz / **Oscar Mayer** Jubilee	50
Smoked, sliced: 1 oz / **Eckrich** Calorie Watcher	45
Smoked, sliced: 1 oz / **Safeway**	45
Smoked, sweet: 1 slice / **Eckrich** Calorie Watcher	25
Steaks: 1 slice / **Oscar Mayer** Jubilee	70
and cheese loaf: 1 slice / **Eckrich**	60
and cheese loaf: 1 slice / **Oscar Mayer**	75
Head cheese: 1 slice / **Oscar Mayer**	55
Honey loaf: 1 slice / **Oscar Mayer**	35
Honey style loaf: 1 slice / **Eckrich** Calorie Watcher	40
Honey style loaf: 1 slice / **Eckrich** Smorgas Pac (12-oz pkg)	30
Honey style loaf: 1 slice / **Eckrich** Smorgas Pac (1-lb pkg)	35
Kielbasa: 1 oz / **Eckrich** Polska	95
Kielbasa, links, skinless: 2 links / **Eckrich** Polska	180
Kielbasa, skinless: 1 link / **Eckrich** Polska	180
Knockwurst: 1 oz / **Health Valley**	80
Liver cheese: 1 slice / **Oscar Mayer**	115
Luncheon meat: 1 slice / **Oscar Mayer**	95
Luxury loaf: 1 slice / **Oscar Mayer**	40
Macaroni-cheese loaf: 1 slice / **Eckrich**	70
Old-fashioned loaf: 1 slice / **Eckrich**	70

Old-fashioned loaf: 1 slice / **Eckrich** Smorgas Pac (12-oz pkg)	50
Old-fashioned loaf: 1 slice / **Eckrich** Smorgas Pac (1-lb pkg)	70
Old-fashioned loaf: 1 slice / **Oscar Mayer**	65
Olive loaf: 1 slice / **Eckrich**	80
Olive loaf: 1 slice / **Oscar Mayer**	65
Pastrami, sliced: 1 oz / **Eckrich** Calorie Watcher	40
Pastrami, sliced, smoked: 1 oz / **Safeway**	45
Peppered loaf: 1 slice / **Eckrich** Calorie Watcher	40
Peppered loaf: 1 slice / **Oscar Mayer**	40
Pepperoni, sliced: 1 oz / **Eckrich**	135
Pepperoni, sliced: 1 oz / **Hormel**	140
Pepperoni, sliced: 1 oz / **Swift**	150
Pickle loaf: 1 slice / **Eckrich**	80
Pickle loaf: 1 slice / **Eckrich** Smorgas Pac	90
Pickle loaf, beef: 1 slice / **Eckrich** Beef Smorgas Pac	50
Pickle and pimento loaf: 1 slice / **Oscar Mayer**	65
Picnic loaf: 1 slice / **Oscar Mayer**	65
Pork, slender sliced, smoked: 1 oz / **Eckrich** Calorie Watcher	45
Salami	
Beer, sliced: 1 slice / **Eckrich**	70
Beer: 1 slice / **Oscar Mayer**	55
Beer, beef: 1 slice / **Oscar Mayer**	75
Chub, cooked: 1 oz / **Eckrich**	70
Cotto: 1 slice / **Eckrich**	70
Cotto: 1 slice / **Oscar Mayer**	50
Cotto, beef: 1 slice / **Eckrich**	50
Cotto, beef: 1 slice / **Oscar Mayer**	50
Hard: 1 slice / **Oscar Mayer**	35
Hard, sliced: 1 oz / **Eckrich**	130
Sausage	
Cheese-smoked: 2 oz / **Eckrich**	180
Ham roll: 1 slice / **Oscar Mayer**	35
Honey roll, beef: 1 slice / **Oscar Mayer**	40
Luncheon, pressed: 1 slice / **Oscar Mayer**	35
Luncheon roll: 1 slice / **Oscar Mayer**	35
Luncheon, spiced: 1 oz / **Hormel**	80
Minced roll: 1 slice / **Eckrich**	80

New England Brand: 1 slice / **Eckrich** Calorie Watcher	35
New England Brand: 1 slice / **Oscar Mayer**	35
Patty, fresh: 1 patty / **Eckrich**	240
Patty, pork: 1 patty / **Oscar Mayer** Southern Brand	125
Pork: 2 oz / **Eckrich**	260
Pork: 2 oz / **Jimmy Dean**	227
Pork roll, hot, fresh: 2 oz / **Eckrich**	240
Smoked: 2 oz / **Eckrich**	190
Smoked, beef: 2 oz / **Eckrich**	190
Sausage links	
Eckrich: 1 link	110
Hormel Brown 'n Serve: 1 link	78
Hormel Little Sizzlers: 1 link	67
Hormel Midget Links: 1 link	112
Oscar Mayer Little Friers: 1 link	80
Swift The Original: 1 link	75
Swift Premium Bacon 'n Sausage: 1 link	70
Swift Premium Brown 'n Serve Kountry Kured: 1 link	95
Beef / **Swift** Premium Brown 'n Serve: 1 link	85
Sausage links, smoked	
Eckrich Cheese: 1 link	240
Eckrich Hot: 1 link	240
Eckrich Skinless: 1 link	180
Eckrich Smok-y-Links, beef: 1 link	70
Eckrich Smok-y-Links, ham: 1 link	75
Eckrich Smok-y-Links, maple-flavored: 1 link	75
Eckrich Smok-y-Links, skinless: 1 link	75
Hormel Smokies: 1 link	92
Oscar Mayer Beef Smokies: 1 link	130
Oscar Mayer Cheese Smokies: 1 link	140
Oscar Mayer Smoky Links: 1 link	135
Sausage sticks	
Beef: 1¼ oz / **Slim Jim** Polish Sausage	108
Beef: ⅝ oz / **Cow-Boy-Jo's**	81
Beef, smoked: ¼ oz / **Cow-Boy-Jo's** Smok-O-Roni	42
Beef, smoked: ½ oz / **Slim Jim**	83
Pickled: 1¼ oz / **Lowrey's** Hot Sausage	110

CALORIES

Pickled: ⅝ oz / **Lowrey's** Polish Sausage	50
Spam: 3 oz / **Hormel**	260
Spam w cheese chunks: 3 oz / **Hormel**	260
Summer sausage	
Eckrich Smoky Tang: 1 oz	80
Eckrich Sliced: 1 slice	90
Oscar Mayer: 1 slice	75
Beef: 1 slice / **Oscar Mayer**	70
Swift Premium: 1 oz	90
Vienna sausage, canned / **Hormel:** 1 link	52
Vienna sausage, canned in barbeque sauce: 2½ oz / **Libby's**	180
Vienna sausage, canned in beef broth: 1 link / **Libby's** 5-oz can	46
Vienna sausage, canned in beef broth: 1 link / **Libby's** 9-oz can	46

MEAT ENTRÉES, FROZEN

Beef burgundy: 9 oz / **Green Giant**	280
Beef, chipped, creamed: 4 oz / **Banquet** Cookin' Bag	125
Beef, chipped, creamed: 5 oz / **Morton** Boil-in-Bag	160
Beef, chipped, creamed: 5½ oz / **Stouffer's**	235
Beef julienne: 8½ oz / **Light and Elegant**	260
Beef patty: 5 oz / **Morton** Boil-in-Bag	200
Beef patties: 8 oz / **Morton** Family Meal	300
Beef patties w onion gravy: 8 oz / **Morton** Family Meal	300
Beef shortribs: 5¾ oz / **Stouffer's**	350
Beef shortribs / **Green Giant**	390
Beef, sliced	
Morton Boil-in-Bag: 5 oz	120
Morton Family Meal: 8 oz	210
w barbecue sauce: 4 oz / **Banquet** Cookin' Bag	133
w gravy: 8 oz / **Banquet** Buffet Supper	344
w gravy: 4 oz / **Banquet** Cookin' Bag	136
w gravy: 8 oz / **Swanson**	200
Sirloin: 13 oz / **Weight Watchers**	410
Beef steak in green pepper sauce: 9¾ oz / **Weight Watchers**	320

CALORIES

Beef stroganoff: 9 oz / **Green Giant**	380
Beef stroganoff: 9¾ oz / **Stouffer's**	390
Beef teriyaki: 8 oz / **Light and Elegant**	240
Cabbage rolls stuffed w beef: ½ pkg / **Green Giant**	220
Crepes, ham and asparagus: 6¼ oz / **Stouffer's**	325
Crepes, ham and swiss cheese: 7½ oz / **Stouffer's**	410
Green pepper steak: 10½ oz / **Stouffer's**	350
Green peppers stuffed w beef: 7¾ oz / **Stouffer's**	225
Green peppers stuffed w veal: 11¾ oz /	
Weight Watchers	240
Hash, roast beef: 5¾ oz / **Stouffer's**	265
Meatballs w brown gravy: 8½ oz / **Swanson**	280
Meatballs, Swedish: 11 oz / **Stouffer's**	475
Meatballs, sweet and sour: 9.4 oz / **Green Giant**	370
Meat loaf	
Banquet Buffet Supper: 6 oz	302
Banquet Cookin' Bag: 5 oz	251
w tomato sauce: 8 oz / **Morton** Family Meal	200
w tomato sauce: 9 oz / **Swanson**	310
Salisbury steak	
Banquet Buffet Supper: 5⅓ oz	235
Banquet Cookin' Bag: 5 oz	251
Howard Johnson's: 4½ oz	273
Morton: 10.3 oz	500
Morton Boil-in-Bag: 5 oz	150
Morton Family Meal: 8 oz	240
Swanson: 5½ oz	370
Swanson Main Course: 10 oz	430
Swanson Hungry Man: 11¾ oz	570
w creole sauce: 9 oz / **Green Giant**	410
w gravy: ½ pkg / **Green Giant**	280
w Italian sauce: 9½ oz /	
Stouffer's Lean Cuisine	270
w mashed potatoes: 11 oz / **Green Giant**	450
w onion gravy: 6 oz / **Stouffer's**	250
Sausage and peppers: 10½ oz / **Buitoni**	460
Sloppy Joe: 5 oz / **Morton** Boil-in-Bag	210
Steak w green peppers: 9 oz / **Green Giant**	250
Steak w green peppers: 8½ oz /	
Swanson Main Course	200

Stew, beef
Banquet Buffet Supper: 8 oz	254
Green Giant: 9 oz	180
Morton Family Meal: 8 oz	190
Stouffer's: 10 oz	310
Stew, meatball: 10 oz / **Stouffer's** Lean Cuisine	240
Swiss steak w stuffed potato: 1 pkg / **Green Giant**	350
Veal patty Pomodoro: 10½ oz / **Buitoni**	350

MEAT ENTRÉES, CANNED

Beef, corned w cabbage: 8 oz / **Hormel**	150
Beef goulash: 7½ oz / **Heinz**	240
Beef goulash: 7½ oz / **Hormel** Short Orders	240
Hash, corned beef: 7 oz / **Ezo**	370
Hash, corned beef: 7½ oz / **Libby's** 15 oz	400
Hash, corned beef: 8 oz / **Libby's** 24 oz	420
Hash, corned beef: 7½ oz / **Mary Kitchen**	400
Hash, roast beef: 7½ oz / **Mary Kitchen**	390
Meatballs in gravy: ½ can / **Chef Boy-ar-dee**	290
Sloppy Joe: 7½ oz / **Hormel**	365
Sloppy Joe, beef: ⅓ cup / **Libby's**	110
Sloppy Joe, pork: ⅓ cup / **Libby's**	120

Stew, beef
Dia-Mel: 8 oz	200
Dinty Moore: 7½ oz	180
Ezo: 7 oz	220
Heinz: 7½ oz	210
Libby's 15 oz: 7½ oz	160
Libby's 24 oz: 8 oz	170
Stew, meatball: ⅓ can (8 oz) / **Chef Boy-ar-dee**	330
Stew, Mulligan: 7½ oz / **Dinty Moore**	240

MEAT SUBSTITUTES

Bacon: 1 tbsp / **Bac*Os**	40
Bacon: 1 tsp / **French's** Crumbles	6
Bacon: 3 strips / **Morningstar Farms** Breakfast Strips	110
Hamburger: 1 patty / **Morningstar Farms** Grillers	190
Sausage: 3 links /	
Morningstar Farms Breakfast Links	200

CALORIES

Sausage: 2 patties / **Morningstar Farms** Breakfast Patties	220

Mexican Foods

See also Dinners

CALORIES

Beans	
Chili, canned: 7½ oz / **Dennison's**	180
Chili, canned: 4 oz / **Hunt Wesson**	100
Chili, hot, canned: ½ cup / **A & P**	140
Chili, hot, canned: 7½ oz / **Luck's**	200
Chili, Mexican, canned: 8 oz / **Van Camp**	210
Chili in meat sauce, canned: 7 oz / **Ezo** Chef's Special	240
Garbanzo, canned: ½ cup / **Old El Paso**	77
Refried, canned: ½ cup / **Del Monte**	130
Refried, canned: ½ cup / **Gebhardt**	145
Refried, canned: ¼ cup / **Old El Paso**	60
Refried, canned: ½ cup / **Rosarita**	130
Refried w green chilis, canned: ¼ cup / **Old El Paso**	25
Refried w sausage, canned: ¼ cup / **Old El Paso**	117
Refried, spicy, canned: ½ cup / **Del Monte**	130
Refried, frozen: ½ cup / **Patio** Boil-in-bag	190
Burritos, frozen: 1 burrito unless noted	
El Charrito Red Hot	350
El Charrito Red Hot, prefried	360
Beef / **El Charrito** Classic Chunky	810
Beef / **El Charrito** Red Hot	340
Beef and bean: 6 oz / **Van de Kamp's**	280
Beef and bean / **El Charrito** Red Hot	390
Beef and bean / **El Charrito,** prefried	350
Beef and bean / **Patio**	190
Beef and bean w green chili / **El Charrito**	350
Beef and bean w red chili / **El Charrito**	350

CALORIES

Beef and bean w red chili / **Patio**	190
Beef and bean w green chili / **Patio**	190
Beef and bean, large / **Patio**	450
Beef and bean, large w green chili / **Patio**	450
Beef and bean, large w red chili / **Patio**	440
Crispy fried w guacamole: 6 oz /	
Van de Kamp's	350
Sirloin: 11 oz / **Van de Kamp's** burrito grande	470
Burrito entrée, frozen: 1 entrée / **El Charrito**	510
Burrito rolls, beef entrée, frozen: 1 entrée /	
El Charrito	820
Burrito filling mix: ½ cup / **Del Monte**	110
Chilies	
Canned / **Del Monte:** ½ cup	20
Canned / **Old El Paso:** 1 chili	7
Canned / **Ortega:** 1 oz	6
Chili con carne, canned	
Chef Boy-ar-dee: ½ can (7½ oz)	370
Dennison's: 7½ oz	300
Gebhardt: 1 cup	433
Health Valley: 4 oz	150
Heinz: 7¾ oz	350
Libby's: 7½ oz	390
Old El Paso: 1 cup	350
Van Camp: 8 oz	390
Chili con carne w beans, canned	
Chef Boy-ar-dee: ½ can (7½ oz)	330
Dennison's: 7½ oz	320
Dennison's hot: 7½ oz	310
Dia-Mel: 8 oz	360
Ezo: 7 oz	340
Ezo, hot: 7 oz	350
Gebhardt: 1 cup	380
Health Valley, mild: 4 oz	150
Health Valley, spicy: 4 oz	180
Heinz, hot: 7¾ oz	330
Libby's: ½ 15-oz can (7½ oz)	270
Libby's: ⅓ 24-oz can (8 oz)	290
Luck's: 7½ oz	350
Old El Paso: 1 cup	423
Van Camp: 8 oz	340

CALORIES

Chili con carne w beans, frozen: 8¾ oz / **Stouffer's**	270
Chili con carne w lentils, canned: ½ cup / **Health Valley**	33
Dips, Mexican-style	
Bean: 4 tbsp / **Hain** Natural	100
Bean w onion: 4 tbsp / **Hain** Natural	90
Bean Jalapeno: 4 tbsp / **Hain** Natural	100
Enchilada: 3⅛ oz / **Fritos**	120
Taco: ¼ cup / **Hain** Natural	20
Enchiladas, frozen	
Beef: 8 oz / **Banquet** International Buffet Supper	264
Beef: 6 oz / **Banquet** International Cookin' Bag	215
Beef: 2 enchiladas / **Patio**	260
Beef: 1 w gravy / **Patio** Boil-in-bag	250
Beef: 7½ oz / **Van de Kamp's** Holiday	250
Beef: 5½ oz / **Van de Kamp's** Holiday	226
Beef: 8½ oz / **Van de Kamp's** Holiday	340
Cheese: 2 enchiladas / **Patio**	170
Cheese: 7½ oz / **Van de Kamp's** Holiday	270
Cheese: 5½ oz / **Van de Kamp's** Holiday	245
Cheese: 8½ oz / **Van de Kamp's** Holiday	370
Cheese w chili gravy: 1 enchilada / **Patio** Boil-in-bag	200
Chicken: 7½ oz / **Van de Kamp's**	250
Chicken: 5½ oz (2 enchiladas) / **Van de Kamp's**	212
Enchilada entrée, frozen: 1 entrée unless noted	
Green Giant Sonora style: 12 oz	700
Beef: 2 enchiladas / **El Charrito**	460
Beef: 6 enchiladas / **El Charrito**	1140
Beef, shredded / **El Charrito** Classic	640
Beef: 11¼ oz / **Swanson**	470
Beef: 16 oz / **Swanson** Hungry Man	660
Beef: 5½ oz / **Van de Kamp's**	175
Beef and bean / **El Charrito** Grande	1010
Beef and cheese / **El Charrito**	880
Cheese: 2 enchiladas / **El Charrito**	350
Cheese / **El Charrito** Classic	630
Cheese: 10 oz / **Health Valley**	340

CALORIES

Cheese: 5½ oz / **Van de Kamp's** Ranchero	252
Chicken / **El Charrito** Classic	520
Chicken: 5½ oz / **Van de Kamp's** Suiza	215
Hot peppers: 1 oz / **Ortega**	8
Jalapeno peppers, canned: ½ cup / **Del Monte**	30
Jalapeno peppers, canned: 2 peppers / **Old El Paso**	12
Mexican-style pastry w chili sauce and cheese filling: 1 pastry / **Pepperidge Farm** Deli's	250
Quesorito entrée, frozen: 1 entrée / **El Charrito**	830
Ranchorito entrée, frozen: 1 entrée / **El Charrito**	770
Salsa, green chile: 1 oz / **Ortega**	6
Taco entrée, beef, frozen: 6 tacos / **El Charrito**	650
Taco and bean entrée, frozen Grande / **El Charrito**	860
Tacos: 1 taco / **Ortega**	150
Tacos, beef, frozen: 2 tacos / **Patio**	240
Tacos, beef, snack, frozen: 4 tacos / **Patio**	130
Taco shell: 1 shell / **Ortega**	50
Taco Starter: 8 oz / **Del Monte**	140
Tamales, canned: 2 tamales / **Old El Paso**	192
Tamales w gravy, frozen: 1 tamale / **Patio** Boil-in-bag	280
Tamalitos w gravy, canned: 7½ oz / **Dennison's**	310
Taquitos, beef, frozen: 1 pkg (6 taquitos) / **El Charrito**	490
Taquitos, beef, frozen w guacamole: 8 oz / **Van de Kamp's**	490
Tomatoes and green chilies, canned: ¼ cup / **Old El Paso**	13
Tomatoes and jalapenos, canned: 1 oz / **Ortega**	7
Tortillas, corn frozen: 2 tortillas / **El Charrito**	45
Tortillas, flour, grozen: 2 tortillas / **El Charrito**	180
Tortillas, frozen: 2 tortillas / **Patio**	100
Tostada shell: 1 shell / **Ortega**	50
Tostada, beef, frozen: 8½ oz / **Van de Kamp's**	530

Milk

	CALORIES
Non-brand name: 8 fl oz (1 cup)	
Whole, 3.3% fat	150
Lowfat, 2% fat	120
Lowfat, 1% fat	100
Nonfat, skim	85
Buttermilk: 8 fl oz (1 cup)	
.5% fat / **A & P**	90
.5% fat / **Borden**	90
.5% fat / **Meadow Gold**	105
1% fat / **Borden**	105
1.5% fat / **Borden**	110
1.5% fat / **Friendship**	120
2% fat / **Borden**	122
3.5% fat / **Borden**	160
Condensed, sweetened	
Borden Dime Brand: ¼ cup	250
Borden Eagle Brand: ¼ cup	250
Carnation: ½ cup	490
Eagle: ⅓ cup	320
Magnolia: ⅓ cup	320
Dry, nonfat	
Fearn: 3 tbsp dry	90
Reconstituted / **Carnation:** 1 cup	80
Reconstituted / **Land O Lakes:** 1 cup	80
Reconstituted / **Lucerne:** 1 cup	80
Evaporated, canned	
Carnation: ½ cup	170
Lucerne: ½ cup	170
Pet: ½ cup	170
Low-fat: ½ cup / **Carnation**	110
Skim: ½ cup / **Carnation**	100
Skim: ½ cup / **Pet**	100
Imitation milk: 8 fl oz / **Lucerne**	150
Low fat: 8 fl oz	
1% fat / **A & P**	100

CALORIES

2% fat / **A & P**	120
2% fat / **Land O Lakes**	120
2% fat / **Lucerne** Two-Ten	140
2% fat / **Meadow Gold** Viva	120
Fortified, 2% fat / **Borden**	140
Skim (.5% fat): 8 fl oz	
A & P	90
Borden	90
Lucerne	90
Meadow Gold	90
Weight Watchers	90
Fortified, skim / **Borden**	100
Whole (3.5% fat): 8 fl oz	
A & P	150
Blossom Time	150
Borden	150
Dairy Land	150
Land O Lakes	150
Lucerne	150
Meadow Gold	150

FLAVORED MILK BEVERAGES

All flavors: 10-fl-oz can/ **Carnation** Slender	220
Chocolate: 8 fl oz / **Borden** Frosted	260
Chocolate, dairy pack: 8 fl oz / **Land O Lakes**	210
Chocolate, dairy pack, low-fat (1.5% fat) / **Lucerne**	170
Chocolate, dairy pack: 8 fl oz / **Meadow Gold**	210
Chocolate, dairy pack, low-fat: 8 fl oz /	
Meadow Gold	160
Chocolate, Dutch, dairy pack: 8 fl oz / **Borden**	210
Chocolate, skim, dairy pack: 8 fl oz /	
Land O Lakes	140
Chocolate mixes	
Alba '77 Fit 'n Frosty: 1 env	70
Carnation Instant Breakfast: 1 env dry	130
Carnation Slender: 1 env dry	110
Lucerne Instant Breakfast: 1 env	130
Ovaltine: ¾ oz (4–5 heaping tsp)	80
Pillsbury Instant Breakfast: 1 pouch dry	130
Quik: 2 tsp	90

CALORIES

Quik prepared w whole milk: 8 fl oz	240
Quik prepared w low-fat milk: 8 fl oz	210
Quik prepared w skim milk: 8 fl oz	170
Chocolate fudge: 1 env dry / **Lucerne** Instant Breakfast	130
Dutch chocolate: 1 env dry / **Carnation** Slender	110
Malt: 1 env dry / **Carnation** Instant Breakfast	130
Malt: 1 env dry / **Lucerne** Instant Breakfast	130
Malt: 1 pouch dry / **Pillsbury** Instant Breakfast	130
Malt: 3 heaping tsp / **Carnation** Instant	85
Coffee, mix: 1 env dry / **Carnation** Instant Breakfast	130
Eggnog	
Dairy case, 4.7% fat: ½ cup / **Borden**	130
Dairy case, 6% fat: ½ cup / **Borden**	150
Dairy case, 8% fat: ½ cup / **Borden**	170
Mix: 6 fl oz (1 pkt prepared) / **Boyd's** Today Instant Hot Nog	110
Mix: 1 env dry / **Carnation** Instant Breakfast	130
Mix: 1 env dry / **Lucerne** Instant Breakfast	130
Malt, mix: ¾ oz (4–5 heaping tsp) / **Ovaltine**	80
Malt, mix: 3 heaping tsp / **Carnation** Instant Natural	90
Strawberry	
Canned: 8 fl oz / **Borden** Frosted	270
Mix: 1 env dry / **Alba** '77 Fit 'n Frosty	70
Mix: 1 env dry / **Carnation** Instant Breakfast	130
Mix: 1 env dry / **Lucerne** Instant Breakfast	130
Mix: 1 pouch / **Pillsbury** Instant Breakfast	130
Mix: 2 tsp / **Quik**	90
Mix: 8 fl oz prepared / **Quik**	240
Mix: 1 env dry / **Alba** '77 Fit 'n Frosty	70
Mix: 1 env dry / **Carnation** Instant Breakfast	130
Mix: 1 env dry / **Lucerne** Instant Breakfast	130
Mix: 1 pouch / **Pillsbury** Instant Breakfast	130
French vanilla, mix: 1 env dry / **Carnation** Slender	110

Muffins: English and Sweet

CALORIES

1 muffin unless noted

Apple cinnamon, mix / **Betty Crocker**	120
Apple, spicy, mix / **Duncan Hines**	120
Banana nut, mix / **Duncan Hines**	130
Blueberry	
Thomas' Toast-r-Cakes	110
Frozen / **Howard Johnson's** Toastees	121
Frozen / **Morton**	120
Frozen / **Morton** Rounds	110
Frozen / **Pepperidge Farm**	180
Mix, prepared / **Duncan Hines**	110
Mix, **Betty Crocker**	120
Bran	
Thomas' Toast-R-Cakes	110
Mix, prepared / **Arrowhead Mills**	135
Mix, prepared / **Duncan Hines**	110
Mix: 3 tbsp dry / **Elam's**	70
w raisins / **Pepperidge Farm**	180
Carrot walnut / **Pepperidge Farm**	170
Cherry, mix / **Betty Crocker**	120
Cinnamon swirl / **Pepperidge Farm**	190
Corn	
Thomas' Toast-R-Cakes	120
Frozen / **Howard Johnson's** Toastees	112
Frozen / **Morton**	130
Frozen / **Pepperidge Farm**	180
Mix, prepared / **Dromedary**	130
Mix / **Flako**	140
English	
Arnold Extra Crisp	150
Earth Grains	160
Merico	120
Pepperidge Farm	135

CALORIES

Thomas'	130
Wonder	130
Bacon and cheese / **Pepperidge Farm**	140
Bran / **Arnold** Bran'nola	160
Cinnamon apple / **Pepperidge Farm**	140
Cinnamon chip / **Pepperidge Farm**	160
Cinnamon raisin / **Merico**	140
Cinnamon raisin / **Pepperidge Farm**	150
Multi-grain / **Merico**	130
Raisin / **Arnold**	170
Raisin / **Earth Grains**	160
Raisin / **Thomas'**	153
Sourdough / **Pepperidge Farm**	140
Wheat / **Pepperidge Farm**	130
Wheat, honey / **Thomas'**	129
Wheatberry / **Earth Grains**	150
Whole wheat / **Earth Grains**	150
Oatmeal, frozen / **Howard Johnson's** Toastees	95
Orange, frozen / **Howard Johnson's** Toastees	127
Orange-cranberry / **Pepperidge Farm**	190
Raisin-bran, frozen / **Howard Johnson's** Toastees	104
Raisin Rounds / **Wonder**	150
Sour dough / **Wonder**	130

Nuts

UNSALTED AND UNFLAVORED

	CALORIES
Almonds	
Dried, in shell: 10 nuts	60
Dried, in shell: 1 cup	185
Dried, shelled, chopped: 1 tbsp	50
Dried, shelled, chopped: 1 cup	775
Dried, shelled, slivered: 1 cup	690
Dried, shelled, whole: 1 cup	850
Roasted, in oil: 1 cup	985
Beechnuts, in shell: 1 lb	1570
Beechnuts, shelled: 1 lb	2575
Brazil nuts, in shell: 1 cup	385
Brazil nuts, shelled: 1 oz (6–8 kernels)	185
Brazil nuts, shelled: 1 cup	915
Butternuts, in shell: 1 lb	400
Butternuts, shelled: 1 lb	2850
Cashew nuts, roasted in oil: 1 cup	785
Cashew nuts, roasted in oil: 1 lb	2545
Chestnuts, fresh	
in shell: 1 cup	190
in shell: 1 lb	715
shelled: 1 cup	310
shelled: 1 lb	880
Filberts, in shell: 1 lb	1325
Filberts, shelled, chopped: 1 cup	730

CALORIES

Filberts, shelled, whole: 1 cup	855
Peanuts, roasted	
in shell: 10 jumbo nuts	105
in shell: 1 lb	1770
Spanish and Virginia: 1 lb	2655
Spanish and Virginia, chopped: 1 cup	840
Hickory nuts, shelled: 1 oz	200
Macadamia nuts, shelled: 1 oz	205
Pecans	
Chopped or pieces: 1 tbsp	50
Chopped or pieces: 1 cup	810
Halves: 10 large (451–550 per lb)	60
Halves: 10 jumbo (301–350 per lb)	95
Halves: 10 mammoth (250 or fewer per lb)	125
Pinenuts, pignolias, shelled: 1 oz	155
Pinenuts, piñon, shelled: 1 oz	180
Pistachio nuts, in shell: 1 lb	1345
Pistachio nuts, shelled: 1 lb	2695
Walnuts	
Black, in shell: 1 lb	625
Black, shelled, chopped or broken kernels: 1 tbsp	50
English or Persian, in shell: 1 lb	1330
English or Persian, shelled, halves: 1 cup	650
English or Persian: 10 large nuts	320
English or Persian, chopped: 1 tbsp	50

ROASTED AND FLAVORED

1 oz unless noted (1 oz equals about ⅕ cup)

Almonds / **Granny Goose**	155
Almonds, dry roasted / **Planters**	170
Cashews / **Granny Goose**	168
Cashews / **Planters** Vacuum Can	170
Cashews, dry roasted / **Planters**	160
Cashews, unsalted / **Planters**	160
Mixed	
Planters Vacuum Can	180
Dry roasted / **Planters**	160
w peanuts / **Planters** Vacuum Can	180
Unsalted / **Planters**	170

Peanuts
    Planters Old Fashioned   170
    Safeway Party Pride   170
    Cocktail / **Planters** Vacuum Can   170
    Cocktail, unsalted / **Planters**   170
    Dry roasted / **Planters**   160
    Redskin Virginia / **Planters** Vacuum Can   170
    Spanish / **Granny Goose**   168
    Spanish / **Planters** Vacuum Can   170
    Spanish, dry roasted / **Planters**   160
    Virginia / **Granny Goose**   166
Pecans / **Granny Goose**   203
Pecans, dry roasted / **Planters**   190
Pistachios / **Granny Goose**   172
Pistachios, dry roasted / **Planters**   170
Sesame Nut Mix / **Planters**   160
Soy nuts / **Planters**   130
Sunflower nuts, unsalted / **Planters**   170
Tavern Nuts / **Planters**   170
Walnuts: ¼ cup shelled (about 5 unshelled) /
    Diamond   192

Oils

CALORIES

1 tbsp unless noted

All varieties / **Health Valley**	120
All Blend / **Hain**	120
Almond / **Hain**	120
Apricot kernel / **Hain**	120
Corn	
Hain	120
Mazola	120
NuMade	120
Scotch Buy	120
Cottonseed / **Hain**	120
Garlic and oil / **Hain**	120
Olive / **Hain**	120
Peanut	
Hain	120
Planters	130
Popcorn / **Orville Redenbacher's**	
Gourmet Popping Oil	120
Popcorn / **Planters**	130
Safflower / **Hain**	120
Safflower / **Hain** SupEr E	120
Salad / **NuMade**	120
Sesame / **Hain**	120
Soy / **Hain**	120
Sunflower / **Hain**	120

	CALORIES
Sunflower / **NuMade**	120
Sunflower / **Sunlite**	120
Vegetable / **Crisco**	120
Vegetable / **Puritan**	120
Vegetable / **Wesson**	120
Vegetable coating / **Mazola** No Stick: 2-second spray	6
Walnut / **Hain**	120
Wheat germ / **Hain**	120

Olives

10 olives

	CALORIES
Green	
10 Small	33
10 Large	45
10 Giant	76
Ripe, black	
Ascolano: 10 extra large	61
Ascolano: 10 giant	89
Ascolano: 10 jumbo	105
Manzanillo: 10 small	38
Manzanillo: 10 medium	44
Manzanillo: 10 large	51
Manzanillo: 10 extra large	61
Mission: 10 small	54
Mission: 10 medium	63
Mission: 10 large	73
Mission: 10 extra large	87
Sevillano: 10 giant	64
Sevillano: 10 jumbo	76
Sevillano: 10 collosal	95
Sevillano: 10 supercolossal	114
Greek style: 10 medium	65
Greek style: 10 extra large	89

Pancakes, Waffles and Similar Breakfast Foods

See also Eggs

	CALORIES
Breakfast, frozen, French toast w sausages: 1 entrée, 6¼ oz / **Swanson**	450
Breakfast, frozen, pancakes and sausages: 1 entrée, 6 oz / **Swanson**	460
Breakfast, frozen, scrambled eggs w sausage: 1 entrée, 6¼ oz / **Swanson**	420
French toast, frozen: 2 slices / **Aunt Jemima**	170
French toast w cinnamon, frozen: 2 slices / **Aunt Jemima**	193
Fritters, apple, frozen: 2 fritters (4 oz) / **Mrs. Paul's**	280
Fritters, corn, frozen: 2 fritters (4 oz) / **Mrs. Paul's**	250

Pancakes

Batter, frozen: 3 cakes, 4-in diam / **Aunt Jemima**	210
Batter, frozen, blueberry: 3 cakes, 4-in diam / **Aunt Jemima**	205
Batter, frozen, buttermilk: 3 cakes, 4-in diam / **Aunt Jemima**	212
Mix, dry: 1 oz / **Health Valley**	105
Mix, dry, buckwheat: ½ cup / **Arrowhead Mills**	270
Mix, dry, buttermilk: ½ cup / **Fearn 7 Grain**	197
Mix, dry, buttermilk: 1 oz / **Health Valley**	105

Mix, dry, griddle lite: ½ cup / **Arrowhead Mills**	260
Mix, dry, multigrain: ½ cup / **Arrowhead Mills**	350
Mix, dry, triticale: ½ cup / **Arrowhead Mills**	270
Mix, dry, whole wheat: ¼ cup / **Elam's** 3 in 1	110
Mix, prepared: 3 cakes, 3-in diam / **Dia-Mel**	100
Mix, prepared: 5 cakes, 4-in diam / **Fearn** Low Sodium	380
Mix, prepared: 4 cakes, 4-in diam / **Fearn** Low Sodium 7 Grain	300
Mix, prepared: 5 cakes, 4-in diam / **Fearn** Rich Earth	380
Mix, prepared: 5 cakes, 4-in diam / **Fearn** Soy-O Triticale	380
Mix, prepared: 3 cakes, 4-in diam / **Golden Blend**	200
Mix, prepared: 3 cakes, 4-in diam / **Golden Blend** Complete	240
Mix, prepared: 3 cakes, 4-in diam / **Hungry Jack** Complete, bulk	190
Mix, prepared: 3 cakes, 4-in diam / **Hungry Jack** Complete, packets	180
Mix, prepared: 3 cakes, 4-in diam / **Hungry Jack** Extra Lights	210
Mix, prepared: 3 cakes, 4-in diam / **Panshakes**	250
Mix, prepared, blueberry: 3 cakes, 4-in diam / **Hungry Jack**	320
Mix, prepared, buttermilk: 3 cakes, 4-in diam / **Betty Crocker**	280
Mix, prepared, buttermilk: 3 cakes, 4-in diam / **Betty Crocker** Complete	210
Mix, prepared, buttermilk: 3 cakes, 4-in diam / **Hungry Jack**	240
Mix, prepared, buttermilk: 3 cakes, 4-in diam / **Hungry Jack** Complete, bulk	190
Mix, prepared, potato: 3 cakes, 3-in diam / **French's**	130
Pancakes and blueberry sauce, frozen: 7 oz / **Swanson**	400
Pancake-waffle mix	
Dry: ½ cup / **Aunt Jemima** Complete	239

	CALORIES
Dry: ¼ cup / **Aunt Jemima** Original	108
Dry, buckwheat: ¼ cup / **Aunt Jemima**	107
Dry, buttermilk: ⅓ cup / **Aunt Jemima**	175
Dry, buttermilk: ½ cup /	
Aunt Jemima Complete	239
Dry, whole wheat: ⅓ cup / **Aunt Jemima**	142
Dry, whole wheat: ½ cup / **Elam's**	220
Mix, prepared: 5 cakes, 4-in diam /	
Fearn Soy-O	390
Mix, prepared, whole wheat: 5 cakes, 4-in diam/	
Fearn Soy-O	370
Waffles, frozen: 1 waffle	
Aunt Jemima Jumbo Original	86
Eggo Homestyle	120
Apple-cinnamon / **Aunt Jemima** Jumbo	86
Apple-cinnamon / **Eggo**	150
Blueberry / **Aunt Jemima** Jumbo	86
Blueberry / **Eggo**	120
Buttermilk / **Aunt Jemima** Jumbo	86
Buttermilk / **Eggo**	110
Strawberry flavor / **Eggo**	120

Pastry

FROZEN AND REFRIGERATOR

	CALORIES
Apple Criss Cross: 2 oz / **Pepperidge Farm**	180
Cobbler, apple: 4.3 oz / **Weight Watchers**	150
Cobbler, black cherry: 4.3 oz / **Weight Watchers**	160
Dumpling, apple: 3 oz / **Pepperidge Farm**	260
Fruit squares, apple: 1 square / **Pepperidge Farm**	230
Fruit squares, blueberry: 1 square /	
Pepperidge Farm	220
Fruit squares, cherry: 1 square / **Pepperidge Farm**	230
Strudel, apple: 3 oz / **Pepperidge Farm**	240
Turnovers: 1 turnover	
Apple / **Pepperidge Farm**	310

	CALORIES
Apple / **Pillsbury**	170
Blueberry / **Pepperidge Farm**	320
Blueberry / **Pillsbury**	170
Cherry / **Pepperidge Farm**	310
Cherry / **Pillsbury**	170
Peach / **Pepperidge Farm**	320
Raspberry / **Pepperidge Farm**	320

TOASTER PASTRY

1 portion

Toaster pastry / **Town House**	200
Pop Tarts / **Kellogg's**	
Blueberry	210
Blueberry, frosted	200
Brown sugar cinnamon	210
Brown sugar cinnamon, frosted	210
Cherry	210
Cherry, frosted	210
Chocolate fudge, frosted	200
Chocolate vanilla, frosted	220
Concord grape, frosted	210
Dutch apple, frosted	210
Raspberry, frosted	210
Strawberry	200
Strawberry, frosted	200
Toaster Strudel / **Pillsbury**	
Blueberry	190
Cinnamon	190
Raspberry	190
Strawberry	190
Toastettes / **Nabisco**	
All varieties	190

Pickles and Relishes

	CALORIES
Capers: 1 tbsp / **Crosse & Blackwell**	6
Chow Chow Mustard Pickles: 1 tbsp / **Crosse & Blackwell**	6
Garden Mix: 1 oz / **Vlasic** Hot & Spicy	4
Onions	
Cocktail: 1 tbsp / **Crosse & Blackwell**	1
Cocktail, lightly spiced: 1 oz / **Vlasic**	4
Spiced: 1 oz / **Heinz**	2
Sweet: 1 oz / **Heinz**	40
Pepperoncini: 1 oz / **Vlasic** Mild Greek	4
Peppers	
Heinz rings or slices: 1 oz	4
Hot / **Heinz** Banana	6
Hot: 1 oz / **Vlasic** Banana Rings	4
Sweet: 1 oz / **Heinz** Mementos	6
Pickles, bread and butter	
Chips: 1 oz / **Vlasic**	27
Chunks: 1 oz / **Vlasic** Deli	25
Chunks: 1 oz / **Vlasic** Old Fashioned	25
Slices: 1 oz / **Heinz**	25
Sticks: 1 oz / **Vlasic** Butter Stix	18
Pickles, dill	
Chips: 1 oz / **Vlasic**	
Half-the-Salt Hamburger Chips	2
Spears: 1 oz / **Vlasic** Kosher	4
Spears: 1 oz / **Vlasic** Kosher Half-the-Salt	4
Gherkins: 1 oz / **Vlasic** Kosher	4
Whole: 1 oz / **Claussen** Kosher	7
Whole: 1 oz / **Vlasic** Kosher Baby	4
Whole: 1 oz / **Vlasic** Kosher Crunchy	4
Whole: 1 oz / **Vlasic** Kosher Crunchy Half-the-Salt	4
Whole: 1 oz / **Vlasic** Kosher Deli Dills	4
Whole: 1 oz / **Vlasic** No Garlic	4
Whole: 1 oz / **Vlasic** Original	2

CALORIES

Pickles, sweet
    Heinz: 1 oz — 35
    Chips: 1 oz / **Vlasic** Half-the-Salt — 30
    Cubes: 1 oz / **Heinz** Salad Cubes — 30
    Gherkins: 1 oz / **Heinz** — 35
    Mixed: 1 oz / **Heinz** — 40
    Slices: 1 slice / **Claussen** Sweet 'n Sour — 3
    Slices: 1 oz / **Heinz** — 35
    Slices: 1 oz / **Heinz** Cucumber Slices — 20
    Sticks: 1 oz / **Heinz** Cucumber Stix — 25
Pimientos: 1 oz / **Dromedary** — 10
Relishes: 1 oz
    Dill / **Vlasic** — 2
    Hamburg / **Vlasic** — 40
    Hamburger / **Heinz** — 30
    Hot Dog / **Heinz** — 35
    Hot Dog / **Vlasic** — 40
    India / **Heinz** — 35
    Picalilli / **Heinz** — 30
    Sweet / **Heinz** — 35
    Sweet / **Vlasic** — 30
Watermelon rind, pickled: 1 tbsp /
    Crosse & Blackwell — 38

Pies

HOME-BAKED

CALORIES

1 pie, 9-in diameter

	CALORIES
Apple	2419
Banana custard	2011
Blackberry	2296
Blueberry	2287
Butterscotch	2430
Cherry	2466
Chocolate chiffon	2125
Chocolate meringue	2293

	CALORIES
Coconut custard	2139
Custard	1983
Lemon chiffon	2028
Lemon meringue	2142
Mince	2560
Peach	2409
Pecan	3449
Pineapple chiffon	1866
Pineapple custard	2002
Pineapple	2390
Pumpkin	1920
Raisin	2551
Rhubarb	2390
Strawberry	1469
Sweet Potato	1938

PIE CRUST, HOME-BAKED

1 pie shell	900

FROZEN

Apple	
Banquet: 3⅓ oz	253
Morton 24 oz: ⅙ pie	290
Mrs. Smith's 46 oz: ⅛ pie	390
Mrs. Smith's Lattice 36 oz: ⅛ pie	350
Mrs. Smith's Natural Juice 36¾ oz: ⅐ pie	420
Mrs. Smith's Old Fashioned 50 oz: ⅛ pie	515
Mrs. Smith's Streusel 41⅛ pie: ⅐ pie	420
Individual: 1 pie / **Banquet** 8 oz	578
Individual: 1 pie /	
Morton Great Little Desserts 8 oz	590
Banana: ⅙ pie / **Morton** 14 oz	160
Banana cream: 2⅓ oz / **Banquet**	177
Banana cream: ⅛ pie / **Mrs. Smith's** 24 oz	240
Banana cream, individual: 1 pie /	
Morton Great Little Desserts 3½ oz	250
Blackberry: 3⅓ oz / **Banquet**	268
Blueberry	
Banquet: 3⅓ oz	266

Morton 24 oz: ⅙ pie	280
Mrs. Smith's 46 oz: ⅛ pie	380
Individual: 1 pie /	
Morton Great Little Desserts 8 oz	580
Boston cream: ⅛ pie / **Mrs. Smith's** 36 oz	260
Cherry	
Banquet: 3⅓ oz	252
Morton 24 oz: ⅙ pie	300
Mrs. Smith's 46 oz: ⅛ pie	400
Mrs. Smith's Lattice 36 oz: ⅛ pie	350
Mrs. Smith's Natural Juice 36¾ oz: ⅐ pie	410
Individual: 1 pie / **Banquet** 8 oz	575
Individual: 1 pie /	
Morton Great Little Desserts	590
Chocolate: ⅙ pie / **Morton** 14 oz	180
Chocolate cream: 2⅓ oz / **Banquet**	185
Chocolate cream: ⅛ pie / **Mrs. Smith's** 24 oz	270
Chocolate cream, individual: 1 pie /	
Morton Great Little Desserts 3½ oz	270
Coconut: ⅙ pie / **Morton** 14 oz	170
Coconut cream: 2⅓ oz / **Banquet**	187
Coconut cream: ⅛ pie / **Mrs. Smith's** 24 oz	270
Coconut cream, individual: 1 pie /	
Morton Great Little Desserts 3½ oz	270
Coconut custard: ⅛ pie / **Mrs. Smith's** 44 oz	330
Coconut custard, individual: 1 pie /	
Morton Great Little Desserts 6½ oz	370
Dutch apple, individual: 1 pie /	
Morton Great Little Desserts 7¾ oz	600
Egg custard: ⅛ pie / **Mrs. Smith's** 44 oz	300
Lemon: ⅙ pie / **Morton** 14 oz	160
Lemon cream: 2⅓ oz / **Banquet**	173
Lemon cream: ⅛ pie / **Mrs. Smith's** 24 oz	245
Lemon cream, individual: 1 pie /	
Morton Great Little Desserts 3½ oz	250
Lemon meringue: ⅛ pie / **Mrs. Smith's** 36 oz	310
Mince: ⅙ pie / **Morton** 24 oz	310
Mincemeat: 3⅓ oz / **Banquet**	258
Peach	
Banquet: 3⅓ oz	244
Morton 24 oz: ⅙ pie	280

Mrs. Smith's 46 oz: ⅛ pie	365
Individual: 1 pie / **Banquet** 8 oz	553
Individual: 1 pie /	
Morton Great Little Desserts	590
Pecan: 5 oz / **Howard Johnson's**	142
Pecan: ⅛ pie / **Mrs. Smith's** 36 oz	510
Pumpkin: 3⅓ oz / **Banquet**	197
Pumpkin: ⅙ pie / **Morton** 24 oz	230
Pumpkin custard: ⅛ pie / **Mrs. Smith's** 46 oz	310
Strawberry cream: 2⅓ oz / **Banquet**	168

PIE MIXES

Boston cream: ⅛ pkg / **Betty Crocker** Classics	260

PIE CRUSTS AND PASTRY SHELLS

Pastry shells: 1 shell / **Stella D'Oro**	147
Patty shells: 1 shell / **Pepperidge Farm**	210
Pie crust	
Mix: ¹⁄₁₆ pkg / **Betty Crocker**	120
Mix: 1⁷⁄₁₀ oz / **Flako**	244
Mix and sticks: ⅙ of double crust pie / **Pillsbury**	270
Refrigerated: ⅛ of double crust pie /	
Pillsbury All Ready	240
Sticks: ⅛ stick / **Betty Crocker**	120
Pie shells, frozen: ⅛ (1 oz) / **Mrs. Smith's**	130
Puff pastry sheets, frozen: ¼ sheet /	
Pepperidge Farm	255

PIE FILLING

Canned, 4 oz unless noted

Apple	
Lucky Leaf	120
Lucky Leaf Deluxe	120
Musselman's	120
Musselman's Deluxe	120
Turnover filling, diced / **Lucky Leaf**	120
Turnover filling, diced / **Musselman's**	120

CALORIES

Apricot / **Lucky Leaf**	150
Apricot / **Musselman's**	150
Banana cream, mix: ⅙ pkg, prepared / **Jell-O**	100
Blackberry / **Lucky Leaf**	120
Blackberry / **Musselman's**	120
Black Raspberry / **Lucky Leaf**	190
Black Raspberry / **Musselman's**	190
Blueberry, cultivated / **Lucky Leaf**	120
Blueberry, cultivated / **Musselman's**	120
Boysenberry / **Lucky Leaf**	120
Boysenberry / **Musselman's**	120
Cherry / **Lucky Leaf**	120
Cherry / **Musselman's**	120
Coconut cream, mix: ⅙ pkg, prepared / **Jell-O**	110
Gooseberry / **Lucky Leaf**	180
Gooseberry / **Musselman's**	180
Lemon	
Lucky Leaf	200
Musselman's	200
French / **Lucky Leaf**	180
French / **Musselman's**	180
Mix: ⅙ pkg, prepared / **Jell-O**	170
Mincemeat	
Crosse & Blackwell	480
Lucky Leaf	190
Musselman's	190
Condensed: ¼ pkg / **Nonesuch**	220
w brandy and rum: ⅓ cup / **Nonesuch**	220
Peach / **Lucky Leaf**	150
Peach / **Musselman's**	150
Pineapple / **Lucky Leaf**	110
Pineapple / **Musselman's**	110
Pumpkin: 1 cup / **Libby's** plain	210
Pumpkin / **Lucky Leaf**	170
Pumpkin / **Musselman's**	170
Raisin / **Lucky Leaf**	130
Raisin / **Musselman's**	130
Red Raspberry / **Lucky Leaf**	190
Red Raspberry / **Musselman's**	190
Strawberry / **Lucky Leaf**	120
Strawberry / **Musselman's**	120

CALORIES

Strawberry-rhubarb / **Lucky Leaf** 120
Strawberry-rhubarb / **Musselman's** 120
Vanilla creme / **Lucky Leaf** 150
Vanilla creme / **Musselman's** 150

PIE AND PASTRY SNACKS

1 piece

Apple pastry, dietetic / **Stella D'Oro** 90
Apple pie
    Drake's 220
    Hostess 390
    Tastykake 362
    French / **Tastykake** 420
    Fried / **Dolly Madison** 490
Berry pie / **Hostess** 390
Blackberry pie / **Tastykake** 371
Blueberry pie / **Hostess** 390
Blueberry pie / **Tastykake** 376
Cherry pie / **Hostess** 390
Cherry pie / **Tastykake** 356
Cherry pie, fried / **Dolly Madison** 470
Coconut cream pie / **Tastykake** 507
Fig pastry, dietetic / **Stella D'Oro** 95
Lemon pie / **Hostess** 400
Lemon pie / **Tastykake** 373
Peach pie / **Hostess** 400
Peach pie / **Tastykake** 333
Peach apricot pastry / **Stella D'Oro** 97
Peach apricot pastry, dietetic / **Stella D'Oro** 90
Pineapple pie / **Tastykake** 369
Prune pastry, dietetic / **Stella D'Oro** 90
Pumpkin pie / **Tastykake** 358
Strawberry pie / **Hostess** 340
Strawberry-rhubarb pie / **Tastykake** 399
Tasty Klair pie / **Tastykake** 446

Pizza

CALORIES

Canadian bacon
Frozen: ¼ pizza / **Celeste** 19 oz	288
Frozen: 1 pizza / **Celeste** 8 oz	483
Frozen: ½ pizza / **Totino's** Party Pizza	340
Frozen: ⅓ pizza / **Totino's** My Classic	440

Cheese
Frozen: 4 oz / **Buitoni** 6-slice	220
Frozen: 2 oz / **Buitoni**	130
Frozen: ¼ pizza / **Celeste** 19 oz	309
Frozen: 1 pizza / **Celeste** 7 oz	472
Frozen: 1 pizza / **Jeno's** 13 oz	840
Frozen: 1 pizza / **Jeno's** Deluxe 20 oz	1470
Frozen: 1 piece (5³⁄₁₆ oz) / **Stouffer's** French Bread	330
Frozen: ½ pizza / **Totino's** Party Pizza	350
Frozen: ⅓ pizza / **Totino's** My Classic Deluxe	490
Frozen: 1 pkg (6 oz) / **Weight Watchers**	350
Frozen, English muffin pizza: ½ pkg / **Chef Boy-ar-dee** 13¼ oz	340
Frozen, English muffin pizza: 1 pizza / **Chef Boy-ar-dee** 6½ oz	340
Mix: ¼ pkg / **Chef Boy-ar-dee**	220
Mix: ⅛ pkg / **Chef Boy-ar-dee** (2 pizzas)	210
Mix: ¼ pkg / **Chef Boy-ar-dee** Pizza in a Skillet	200

Combination
Frozen: ¼ pizza / **Celeste** Chicago style 24 oz	360
Frozen: ¼ pizza / **Celeste** Deluxe 23.5 oz	368
Frozen: 1 pizza / **Celeste** Deluxe 9 oz	563
Frozen: ¼ pizza / **Celeste** Sicilian style 26 oz	408
Frozen: ¼ pizza / **Celeste** Suprema 24 oz	354
Frozen: 1 pizza / **Celeste** Suprema 10 oz	590
Frozen: ¼ pizza / **Celeste** Suprema wo meat 20 oz	272

CALORIES

Frozen: 1 pizza / **Celeste**	
Suprema wo meat 8 oz	434
Frozen: 1 pizza / **Jeno's** Deluxe 23 oz	1680
Frozen: 1/3 pizza / **Totino's** My Classic	610
Frozen: 1 pkg / **Weight Watchers** 7.25 oz	340
Frozen: 6³⁄16 oz / **Stouffer's**	
Deluxe French Bread	400
Hamburger, frozen: 1 pizza / **Jeno's**	880
Hamburger, frozen: 6⅛ oz /	
Stouffer's French Bread	400
Hamburger, frozen: ½ pizza / **Totino's** Party	320
Hamburger, mix: ¼ pkg / **Chef Boy-ar-dee**	300
Mexican style, frozen: ½ pizza / **Totino's** Party	360
Mushroom, frozen: 6 oz (1 piece) /	
Stouffer's French Bread	340
Nacho, frozen: ½ pizza / **Totino's** Party	340
Open face, frozen: 6½ oz / **Buitoni**	310
Pepperoni	
Frozen: ¼ pizza / **Celeste** 20 oz	347
Frozen: 1 pizza / **Celeste** 7.25 oz	568
Frozen: ¼ pizza / **Celeste** Chicago style 24 oz	374
Frozen: ½ pizza / **Fox** Deluxe	280
Frozen / **Jeno's** 13 oz	900
Frozen: 5⅝ oz / **Stouffer's** French Bread	410
Frozen: ½ pizza / **Totino's** Party	370
Frozen: 1/3 pizza / **Totino's** My Classic	560
Frozen, English muffin pizza: ½ pkg /	
Chef Boy-ar-dee 14½ oz	400
Frozen, English muffin pizza: 1 pizza /	
Chef Boy-ar-dee 7¼ oz	420
Mix: ¼ pkg / **Chef Boy-ar-dee**	270
Mix: ⅛ pkg / **Chef Boy-ar-dee** 2-pizza size	250
Mix: ¼ pkg / **Chef Boy-ar-dee** Pizza in a Skillet	240
Sausage	
Frozen: ¼ pizza / **Celeste** 22 oz	359
Frozen: 1 pizza / **Celeste** 8 oz	525
Frozen: ¼ pizza / **Celeste** Chicago style	382
Frozen / **Jeno's** 13 oz	900
Frozen / **Jeno's** Deluxe 21 oz	1500
Frozen: 6 oz (1 piece) /	
Stouffer's French Bread	420

CALORIES

Frozen: ½ pizza / **Totino's** Party	400
Frozen: ⅓ pizza / **Totino's** My Classic	560
Frozen, English muffin: ½ pkg / **Chef Boy-ar-dee** 15½ oz	420
Frozen, English muffin: 1 pizza / **Chef Boy-ar-dee** 7¾ oz	430
Frozen, veal: 1 pkg / **Weight Watchers** 6¾ oz	350
Mix: ¼ pkg / **Chef Boy-ar-dee**	280
Mix: ¼ pkg / **Chef Boy-ar-dee** Pizza in a Skillet	250
w mushrooms, frozen: ¼ pizza / **Celeste** 24 oz	365
w mushrooms, frozen: 1 pizza / **Celeste** 9 oz	555
w mushrooms, frozen: 6½ oz (1 piece) / **Stouffer's** French bread	395
w pepperoni: ½ pizza / **Totino's** Party	400
Vegetable, frozen: 1 pkg / **Weight Watchers** 7¼ oz	350
Pizza crust, mix: 1½ scoops / **Ragu** Pizza Quick	170

Popcorn

CALORIES

Plain
Unpopped: 1 oz	105
Air- or dry-popped: 1 cup	25
Jiffy Pop: 1½ oz (4¾ cups popped)	180
Jolly Time large kernel: 1 cup popped	25
Jolly Time small kernel: 1 cup popped	55
Orville Redenbacher Gourmet: 4 cups popped	90

Popped w oil and salt
Laura Scudder's: 1 oz	130
Orville Redenbacher Gourmet: 4 cups	160
Butter flavor, popped: 1½ oz (4¾ cups) / **Jiffy Pop**	210
Butter flavor, ready to eat: ½ oz (1½ cups) / **Wise**	70

Microwave
Plain, popped: 4 cups / **Orville Redenbacher** Gourmet	140
Plain, popped: 4 cups / **Pillsbury**	260

CALORIES

Plain, popped, no salt: 4 cups / **Pillsbury**	190
Butter flavor, popped: 4 cups /	
Orville Redenbacher Gourmet	140
Butter flavor, popped: 4 cups / **Pillsbury**	260
Cheese flavor: 1 oz / **Laura Scudder's**	145
Cheese flavor: ½ oz / **Wise** Cheez	90
Caramel corn: 1½ oz / **Laura Scudder's**	184
Cracker Jack: 1 oz (1¼ cups)	120
Fiddle Faddle, almond: 1 oz (1¼ cups)	120
Fiddle Faddle, coconut: 1 oz (1¼ cups)	130
Fiddle Faddle, peanut: 1 oz (1¼ cups)	125
Poppycock: 1 oz (1¼ cups)	150
Screaming Yellow Zonkers: 1 oz	121

Pot Pies

CALORIES

Frozen: 1 whole pie

Beef

Banquet 8 oz	557
Banquet Supreme 8 oz	380
Morton 8 oz	320
Stouffer's 10 oz	550
Swanson 8 oz	420
Swanson Chunky 10 oz	580
Swanson Hungry Man 16 oz	700

Chicken

Banquet 8 oz	520
Banquet Supreme 8 oz	430
Morton 8 oz	320
Stouffer's 10 oz	500
Swanson 8 oz	420
Swanson Chunky 10 oz	570
Swanson Hungry Man 16 oz	730
Van de Kamp's 7½ oz	520
Steak burger / **Swanson** Hungry Man 16 oz	830
Tuna / **Banquet** 8 oz	510

CALORIES

Tuna / **Morton** 8 oz	370
Turkey	
Banquet 8 oz	526
Banquet Supreme 8 oz	430
Morton 8 oz	340
Stouffer's 10 oz	460
Swanson 8 oz	430
Swanson Chunky 10 oz	540
Swanson Hungry Man 16 oz	750

Poultry and Poultry Entrées

FRESH

CALORIES

3½ oz unless noted

Chicken, fryer or broiler, batter-fried: ½ chicken	1350
Chicken, fryer or broiler	
Breast, meat and skin, raw: ½ breast (5 oz)	250
Breast, meat and skin, fried: ½ breast	220
Drumstick, meat and skin, raw:	
1 drumstick (2½ oz)	117
Drumstick, meat and skin, fried: 1 drumstick	120
Thigh, meat and skin, raw: 1 thigh (3.3 oz)	200
Thigh, meat and skin, batter-fried: 1 thigh	238
Wing, meat and skin, raw: 1 wing (¾ oz)	109
Wing, meat and skin, batter-fried: 1 wing	159
Wing, meat and skin, roasted: 1 wing	100
Chicken, roasting, meat and skin: ½ chicken (1 lb)	1070
Chicken, roasting	
Dark meat wo skin, roasted	178
Light meat wo skin, roasted	153
Dark meat wo skin: 1 cup (5 oz)	250
Light meat wo skin: 1 cup (5 oz)	215
Chicken, stewed wo skin	177
Chicken, stewed w skin	219

CALORIES

Cornish game hen, roasted w skin	239
Cornish game hen, roasted wo skin	190
Duck, w skin, roasted	337
Duck, wo skin, roasted	201
Goose, roasted, domesticated, wo skin	233
Goose, roasted, domesticated, w skin	441
Goose, roasted, wild	309
Pheasant, cooked	208
Pheasant, cooked: ½ breast	278
Pheasant, cooked, leg	138
Quail, cooked: 1 average-size	364
Squab, cooked: 1 average-size	293
Turkey, dark meat, w skin, roasted	221
Turkey, dark meat, wo skin, roasted	187
Turkey, white meat, w skin, roasted	197
Turkey, white meat, wo skin, roasted	157
Heart, chicken, cooked: 1 oz	42
Heart, turkey, cooked: 1 oz	60
Liver, chicken, cooked: 1 oz	47
Liver, goose, raw: 1 oz	50
Liver, turkey, cooked: 1 oz	50

CANNED, FROZEN AND PROCESSED

See also Dinners

Chicken, chunks or slices	
Canned: 5 oz / **Health Valley**	281
Canned: 1½ oz / **Swanson**	110
Canned chunk style: 2½ oz / **Swanson** Mixin'	130
Canned, white chunk: 2½ oz / **Swanson**	100
Slices, breast: 2 slices /	
Eckrich Calorie Watcher	40
Slices, smoked: 1 oz / **Safeway**	45
Slices, frozen: 5 oz / **Morton** Boil-in-bag	130
Chicken à la King	
Canned: 5¼ oz / **Swanson**	180
Frozen: 5 oz / **Banquet** Cookin' Bag	159
Frozen: 9 oz / **Health Valley**	380
Frozen: 5 oz / **Morton** Boil-in-bag	150
Frozen: 9 oz / **Weight Watchers**	230

CALORIES

w biscuits, frozen: 9 oz / **Green Giant**	370
w rice, frozen: 9½ oz / **Stouffer's**	330
Chicken w barbecue sauce, frozen: 8 oz / **Light and Elegant**	290
Chicken w barbecue sauce, frozen: 1 pkg / **Green Giant**	350
Chicken w broccoli, rice and cheese sauce: 9½ oz / **Green Giant**	330
Chicken, creamed, frozen: 6½ oz / **Stouffer's**	300
Chicken crepes Marco Polo, frozen: 7 oz / **Health Valley**	380
Chicken croquettes, frozen: 6 oz / **Howard Johnson's**	253
Chicken Divan, frozen: 8½ oz / **Stouffer's**	335
Chicken and dumplings, canned: ½ can (7½ oz) / **Luck's**	240
Chicken and dumplings, canned: 7½ oz / **Swanson**	220
Chicken fillets Cacciatore, frozen: 11 oz / **Buitoni**	260
Chicken fillets Marsala, frozen: 11 oz / **Buitoni**	260
Chicken, fried, frozen	
Banquet: 6⅖ oz	325
Morton 32-oz size: 6.4 oz	300
Swanson Entrée: 7¼ oz	390
Weight Watchers Entrée: 6¾ oz	260
Assorted pieces: 3¼ oz / **Swanson**	260
Assorted pieces: 3¼ oz / **Swanson** Take-Out	270
Breast portions: 4⅖ oz / **Banquet**	238
Breast portions: 5½ oz / **Morton** 22 oz	370
Breast portions: 4½ oz / **Swanson**	350
Breast portions: 11¾ oz / **Swanson** Hungry Man	670
Dark portions: 11 oz / **Swanson** Hungry Man	640
Thighs and drumsticks: 5 oz / **Banquet**	277
Thighs and drumsticks: 3¼ oz / **Swanson**	280
Wings: 6¾ oz / **Banquet**	346
Nuggets: 3 oz / **Banquet**	233
Patties: 3 oz / **Banquet**	225
Sticks: 3 oz / **Banquet**	228
Chicken crepes: 8¼ oz / **Stouffer's**	390
Chicken, glazed, frozen: 8 oz / **Light and Elegant**	230

Chicken, glazed, frozen: 8½ oz /
  Stouffer's Lean Cuisine   270
Chicken w herb butter: 1 pkg /
  Green Giant Entrée   430
Chicken Italian, frozen: 8 oz / **Light and Elegant**   240
Chicken Nibbles: 5 oz / **Swanson**   400
Chicken Nibbles: 3¼ oz /
  Swanson Plump and Juicy   300
Chicken and noodles: 5¾ oz / **Stouffer's**   250
Chicken w noodles and vegetables: 9 oz /
  Stouffer's   390
Chicken Paprikash: 10½ oz / **Stouffer's**   385
Chicken w pea pods, rice: 10 oz /
  Green Giant   300
Chicken stew
  Dia-Mel: 8 oz   150
  Canned / **Ezo:** 7 oz   140
  Canned / **Swanson:** 7⅝ oz   170
  w dumplings, canned: 7¼ oz / **Heinz**   210
Chicken w vegetables and vermicelli: 12¾ oz /
  Stouffer's Lean Cuisine   260
Turkey, slices and pieces
  Breast, fresh, cooked: 1 oz / **Louis Rich**   45
  Breast, barbecued: 1 oz / **Louis Rich**   40
  Breast, oven-roasted: 1 slice / **Louis Rich**   30
  Breast, slices, fresh, cooked: 1 oz / **Louis Rich**   40
  Breast, smoked: 1 oz / **Louis Rich**   35
  Breast, smoked: 1 slice / **Louis Rich**   20
  Breast, tenderloin, cooked: 1 oz / **Louis Rich**   40
  Drumsticks, fresh, cooked: 1 oz / **Louis Rich**   60
  Drumsticks, smoked: 1 oz / **Louis Rich**   40
  Ground, fresh, cooked: 1 oz / **Louis Rich**   65
  Slices, frozen w gravy: 5⅓ oz /
    Banquet Buffet Supper   134
  Slices, frozen w gravy: 5 oz /
    Banquet Cookin' Bag   137
  Slices, frozen: 12.3 oz / **Morton**   380
  Slices, frozen: 5 oz / **Morton** Boil-in-Bag   120
  Slices, frozen: 8 oz / **Morton** Family Meal   200
  Slices, smoked: 1 slice / **Louis Rich**   30
  Slices, smoked: 1 oz / **Eckrich** Calorie Watcher   40

CALORIES

Slices, smoked: 1 oz / **Safeway**	40
Slices w wild rice, frozen: 9 oz / **Green Giant**	460
Wings, fresh, cooked: 1 oz / **Louis Rich**	55
Wings, smoked: 1 oz / **Louis Rich** Drumettes	45
Turkey entrée, frozen: 8¾ oz / **Swanson**	230
Turkey entrée, frozen: 13¼ oz / **Swanson** Hungry Man	370
Turkey bologna: 1 slice / **Louis Rich**	60
Turkey breakfast sausage, cooked: 1 oz / **Louis Rich**	65
Turkey casserole, frozen: 9¾ oz / **Stouffer's**	370
Turkey cotto salami: 1 slice / **Louis Rich**	50
Turkey croquettes, frozen: 8 oz / **Morton** Family Meal	440
Turkey franks: 1 link / **Louis Rich**	100
Turkey ham: 1 slice / **Louis Rich**	35
Turkey ham, chopped: 1 slice / **Louis Rich**	40
Turkey luncheon loaf: 1 slice / **Louis Rich**	40
Turkey pastrami: 1 slice / **Louis Rich**	35
Turkey pastry w ham and cheese: 1 pastry / **Pepperidge Farm** Deli's	270
Turkey smoked sausage: 1 oz / **Louis Rich**	55
Turkey summer sausage: 1 slice / **Louis Rich**	50
Turkey tetrazzini, frozen: 6 oz / **Stouffer's**	240
Turkey tetrazzini, frozen: 10 oz / **Weight Watchers**	310

Pretzels

CALORIES

1 oz unless noted

Charles, salted and unsalted	109
Estee: 5 pretzels	25
Mister Salty: 5 pretzels	100
Mister Salty Dutch: 2 pretzels	110
Mister Salty Little Shapes: 19 pretzels	110

CALORIES

Mister Salty Sticks	110
Pepperidge Farm Nugget Style: 25 pretzels	140
Pepperidge Farm Thin Sticks: 30 pretzels	140
Pepperidge Farm Tiny Twists: 15 pretzels	110
Planters Stick	110
Planters Twist	110
Rokeach Baldies or No Salt Dutch	110
Rokeach Party	110

Pudding

CALORIES

½ cup unless noted; all mixes prepared with
   whole milk unless noted

Banana	
Canned, ready to serve: 5 oz / **Del Monte** Pudding Cup	180
Canned, ready to serve: 5 oz / **Hunt's** Snack Pack	210
Canned, ready to serve / **Lucky Leaf**	150
Canned, ready to serve / **Musselman's**	150
Mix, prepared / **Royal**	160
Mix, prepared / **Royal** Instant	180
Mix, prepared / **Safeway**	180
Banana cream, mix, prepared / **Jell-O** Instant	170
Butter pecan, mix, prepared / **Jell-O** Instant	170
Butterscotch	
Canned, ready to serve: 5 oz / **Del Monte** Pudding Cup	180
Canned, ready to serve: 5 oz / **Hunt's** Snack Pack	210
Canned, ready to serve / **Lucky Leaf**	170
Canned, ready to serve / **Musselman's**	170
Mix, prepared w nonfat milk / **Dia-Mel**	50
Mix, prepared w nonfat milk / **D-Zerta**	70
Mix, prepared w nonfat milk / **Estee**	70

Mix, prepared / **Jell-O**	170
Mix, prepared / **Jell-O** Instant	170
Mix, prepared / **My*T*Fine**	143
Mix, prepared / **Royal**	160
Mix, prepared / **Royal** Instant	180
Mix, prepared / **Safeway**	180
Chocolate	
Canned, ready to serve: 5 oz / **Del Monte** Pudding Cup	190
Canned, ready to serve: 5 oz / **Hunt's** Snack Pack	210
Canned, ready to serve / **Lucky Leaf**	180
Canned, ready to serve / **Musselman's**	180
Mix, prepared w nonfat milk / **Dia-Mel**	50
Mix, prepared w nonfat milk / **D-Zerta**	60
Mix, prepared w nonfat milk / **Estee**	70
Mix, prepared / **Jell-O**	160
Mix, prepared / **Jell-O** Instant	180
Mix, prepared / **My*T*Fine**	133
Mix, prepared / **Royal**	180
Mix, prepared / **Royal** Instant	190
Mix, prepared / **Safeway**	190
German, canned, ready to serve: 5 oz / **Hunt's** Snack Pack	220
Milk, mix, prepared / **Jell-O**	170
Milk, mix, prepared / **Jell-O** Instant	180
Chocolate almond, mix, prepared / **My*T*Fine**	169
Chocolate fudge	
Canned, ready to serve: 5 oz / **Del Monte** Pudding Cup	190
Canned, ready to serve: 5 oz / **Hunt's** Snack Pack	200
Canned, ready to serve / **Lucky Leaf**	180
Canned, ready to serve / **Musselman's**	180
Mix, prepared / **Jell-O** Instant	180
Mix, prepared / **My*T*Fine**	151
Chocolate marshmallow, canned, ready to serve: 5 oz/ **Hunt's** Snack Pack	200
Coconut, mix, prepared / **Royal** Instant	170
Coconut cream, mix, prepared / **Jell-O** Instant	180
Coffee, mix, prepared / **Royal** Instant	180

Custard, mix, prepared / **Royal**	150
Dark 'N Sweet, mix, prepared / **Royal**	180
Dark 'N Sweet, mix, prepared / **Royal** Instant	190
Egg custard, golden, mix, prepared /	
Jell-O Americana	160
Flan, mix, prepared / **Royal**	150
Lemon	
Canned, ready to serve: 5 oz /	
Hunt's Snack Pack	180
Canned, ready to serve / **Lucky Leaf**	130
Canned, ready to serve / **Musselman's**	130
Mix, prepared / **Dia-Mel**	14
Mix, prepared / **Estee**	70
Mix, prepared / **Jell-O** Instant	180
Mix, prepared / **My*T*Fine**	164
Mix, prepared / **Royal** Instant	180
Mix, prepared / **Safeway**	180
Pineapple cream, mix, prepared / **Jell-O** Instant	170
Pistachio, mix, prepared / **Jell-O** Instant	180
Pistachio, mix, prepared / **Safeway**	180
Plum, canned, ready to serve: 4 oz /	
Crosse & Blackwell	340
Rice	
Canned, ready to serve: 5 oz /	
Hunt's Snack Pack	220
Canned, ready to serve / **Lucky Leaf**	120
Canned, ready to serve / **Musselman's**	120
Mix, prepared / **Jell-O** Americana	170
Tapioca	
Canned, ready to serve: 5 oz /	
Del Monte Pudding Cup	180
Canned, ready to serve: 5 oz /	
Hunt's Snack Pack	140
Canned, ready to serve / **Lucky Leaf**	140
Canned, ready to serve / **Musselman's**	140
Chocolate, mix, prepared / **Jell-O** Americana	170
Chocolate, mix, prepared / **Royal**	180
Vanilla, mix, prepared / **Jell-O** Americana	160
Vanilla, mix, prepared / **My*T*Fine**	130
Vanilla, mix, prepared / **Royal**	160

CALORIES

Vanilla
  Canned, ready to serve: 5 oz /
    Del Monte Pudding Cup   180
  Canned, ready to serve: 5 oz /
    Hunt's Snack Pack   210
  Canned, ready to serve / **Lucky Leaf**   170
  Canned, ready to serve / **Musselman's**   170
  Mix, prepared w nonfat milk / **Dia-Mel**   50
  Mix, prepared w nonfat milk / **D-Zerta**   70
  Mix, prepared w nonfat milk / **Estee**   70
  Mix, prepared / **Jell-O**   160
  Mix, prepared / **Jell-O** Instant   170
  Mix, prepared / **My*T*Fine**   133
  Mix, prepared / **Royal**   160
  Mix, prepared / **Royal** Instant   180
  Mix, prepared / **Safeway**   180
  French, mix, prepared / **Jell-O**   170
  French, mix, prepared / **Jell-O** Instant   170

Rice and Rice Dishes

RICE, PLAIN

	CALORIES
Brown, long grain, parboiled: ⅔ cup cooked	200
White, instant: 1 cup cooked	180
White, long grain: ⅔ cup cooked	225
White, parboiled: 1 cup cooked	185

RICE DISHES

Frozen

w broccoli in cheese sauce: ½ cup / **Green Giant** Originals	140
French Style: 3.6 oz / **Birds Eye**	120
Chinese Style, fried rice: 3.6 oz / **Birds Eye**	100
w herb butter sauce: ½ cup / **Green Giant** Originals	150
Italian w spinach and cheese: ½ cup / **Green Giant** Originals	160
Italian: 3.6 oz / **Birds Eye**	130
Medley: ½ cup / **Green Giant** Originals	120
Oriental style: 3.6 oz / **Birds Eye**	130
w peas and mushrooms: 2.3 oz / **Birds Eye**	110
Pilaf: ½ cup / **Green Giant** Originals	120
Spanish: 3.6 oz / **Birds Eye**	120
Wild rice and white long grain: ½ cup / **Green Giant** Originals	110

	CALORIES

CANNED OR MIXES

Beef flavor, mix, prepared w margarine or butter: ½ cup / **Lipton** Rice and Sauce	160
Beef flavor, mix: ⅙ pkg dry / Beef **Rice-a-Roni**	130
Beef flavor, mix prepared w butter: ½ cup / **Minute**	150
Chicken flavor, mix, prepared w margarine or butter: ½ cup / **Lipton** Rice and Sauce	150
Chicken flavor, mix: ⅕ pkg dry / **Rice-a-Roni**	160
Chicken flavor, mix, prepared w butter: ½ cup / **Minute**	150
Florentine, mix: ½ cup / **Uncle Ben's**	104
Florentine, mix, prepared w butter or margarine: ½ cup / **Uncle Ben's**	128
Fried, mix, prepared w oil: ½ cup / **Minute**	160
Herb and butter, mix, prepared w butter or margarine: ½ cup / **Lipton** Rice and Sauce	160
Pilaf, mix, prepared w butter or margarine: ½ cup / **Uncle Ben's** Original	133
Pilaf, mix, brown rice: ½ cup / **Pritikin**	90
Spanish, mix, prepared w butter or margarine: ½ cup / **Lipton** Rice and Sauce	140
Spanish, canned: 7¼ oz / **Heinz**	150
Spanish, canned: 8 oz / **Van Camp**	160
Spanish, mix: ⅙ pkg dry / **Rice-a-Roni**	120
Spanish, mix: ½ cup prepared / **Pritikin**	100
Wild and white long grain, mix, prepared w butter: ½ cup / **Minute**	150
Wild and white long grain, mix, prepared: ½ cup / **Uncle Ben's**	97
Wild and white long grain, mix, prepared w butter or margarine: ½ cup / **Uncle Ben's**	114

Rolls, Buns and Bagels

BAGELS

	CALORIES
Frozen: 1 bagel	
Egg / **Lender's**	150
Garlic / **Lender's**	160
Onion / **Lender's**	160
Onion, mini / **Lender's** Bagelettes	70
Plain / **Lender's**	150
Plain, mini / **Lender's** Bagelettes	70
Poppy seed / **Lender's**	150
Pumpernickel / **Lender's**	160
Raisin 'n honey / **Lender's**	200
Raisin 'n wheat / **Lender's**	190
Rye / **Lender's**	150
Sesame seed / **Lender's**	160

BUNS FOR SANDWICHES

1 bun	
Arnold Dutch Egg Sandwich Buns	130
Arnold Francisco Sandwich Rolls	160
Arnold Soft Sandwich	110
w poppyseeds / **Arnold** Soft Sandwich	110
w poppyseeds / **Pepperidge Farm**	130
w sesame seeds / **Arnold** Soft Sandwich	110
w sesame seeds / **Pepperidge Farm**	130
Wheat, cracked / **Pepperidge Farm**	150
Hamburger	
Arnold 8's	110
Butternut	80
Colonial	150
Eddy's	80
Kilpatrick's	150

CALORIES

Millbrook	80
Pepperidge Farm	130
Rainbo	150
Sweetheart	80
Weber's	80
Wonder	120
Hot Dog	
Arnold 6's	110
Butternut	80
Colonial	150
Eddy's	80
Kilpatrick's	150
Millbrook	80
Pepperidge Farm	140
Rainbo	150
Sweetheart	80
Weber's	80
Wonder	120
Mustard bran / **Pepperidge Farm**	130
Onion w poppy seeds / **Pepperidge Farm**	150
Submarine rolls: ½ roll / **Earth Grains**	180

CROISSANTS

1 croissant

Pepperidge Farm	200
Pepperidge Farm Tray	200
Pepperidge Farm Petite	130
Sara Lee	170
Almond / **Pepperidge Farm**	210
Apple / **Sara Lee**	240
Cheese / **Sara Lee**	170
Chocolate / **Pepperidge Farm**	260
Chocolate / **Sara Lee**	290
Cinnamon / **Pepperidge Farm**	210
Cinnamon nut raisin / **Sara Lee**	340
Raisin / **Pepperidge Farm**	200
Strawberry / **Sara Lee**	240
Walnut / **Pepperidge Farm**	210
Wheat 'n honey / **Sara Lee**	170

DINNER AND SOFT ROLLS

1 roll

Arnold Francisco French Style	160
Arnold Francisco Sourdough French	90
Arnold Francisco Sourdough French Brown and Serve	90
Arnold Party Rounds 12's	55
Arnold Party Rounds 24's	55
Butternut Brown 'n Serve	90
Earth Grains Wheat	110
Eddy's Brown 'n Serve	90
Home Pride	85
Millbrook Brown 'n Serve	90
Pepperidge Farm	60
Pepperidge Farm Butter Crescent	110
Pepperidge Farm Finger w poppy seeds	60
Pepperidge Farm Finger w sesame seeds	60
Pepperidge Farm Golden Twist	110
Pepperidge Farm Hearth	50
Pepperidge Farm Old Fashioned	50
Pepperidge Farm Parker House	50
Pepperidge Farm Party	30
Pepperidge Farm Party w poppy seeds	45
Pepperidge Farm Soft Family	100
Sweetheart Brown 'n Serve	90
Weber's Brown 'n Serve	90
Wonder	100
Wonder Buttermilk	85
Wonder Gem Style	85
Wonder Half & Half	80
Wonder Home Bake	85
Wonder Pan	100
Mix, prepared / **Pillsbury** Hot Roll Mix	100

REFRIGERATOR ROLLS

1 roll

Merico Crescent	95
Pillsbury Butterflake	110

CALORIES

Pillsbury Country White, Bakery Style	100
Pillsbury Crescent	100
Pillsbury Parkerhouse	75
Pillsbury Weiner Wrap	60
Pillsbury Weiner Wrap, cheese	60

HARD ROLLS

1 roll

Club / **Pepperidge Farm**	100
French	
Earth Grains	100
Pepperidge Farm	110
Pepperidge Farm	
Brown 'n Serve 2: ½ roll	180
Pepperidge Farm	
Brown 'n Serve 3: ½ roll	120
Wonder Brown 'n Serve	75
Sourdough / **Earth Grains**	100
Kaiser / **Earth Grains**	190
Kaiser / **Wonder**	460
Onion / **Earth Grains**	190
Popovers, mix: 1-oz mix / **Flako**	102
Popovers, mix: 1 popover / **Flako**	170

SWEET ROLLS

1 roll

Bear Claws / **Earth Grains**	250
Cherry / **Dolly Madison**	180
Cinnamon	
Dolly Madison	180
Earth Grains	220
Refrigerated / **Merico**	110
Refrigerated / **Pillsbury** Pipin' Hot	220
Butter flavored, refrigerated / **Merico**	130
w icing, refrigerated / **Hungry Jack**	
Butter Tastin'	145
w icing, refrigerated / **Pillsbury**	115

Danish

Apple / **Earth Grains**	230
Apple / **Hostess**	360
Apple / **Pepperidge Farm**	180
Apple, refrigerated / **Pillsbury** Pipin' Hot	250
Apple, individual / **Sara Lee**	120
Apple / **Tastykake**	310
Apple / **Tastykake** Morning Fresh	321
Blueberry / **Pepperidge Farm**	200
Blueberry / **Tastykake**	307
Butterhorn / **Hostess**	330
Caramel w nuts, refrigerated / **Pillsbury**	155
Cheese / **Pepperidge Farm**	280
Cheese, individual / **Sara Lee**	130
Cheese / **Tastykake**	299
Cheese / **Tastykake** Morning Fresh	290
Cherry / **Earth Grains**	230
Cherry / **Pepperidge Farm**	200
Cherry / **Tastykake**	332
Cherry / **Tastykake** Morning Fresh	328
Cinnamon, refrigerated / **Merico**	125
Cinnamon raisin, refrigerated w icing / **Pillsbury**	145
Lemon / **Tastykake**	306
Orange, refrigerated / **Merico**	130
Orange, refrigerated w icing / **Pillsbury**	145
Raisin, refrigerated / **Merico**	135
Raspberry / **Hostess**	300
Honey buns / **Hostess**	450
Honey buns, frozen / **Morton**	230
Honey buns, frozen, mini / **Morton**	130

Salad Dressings

Bottled unless noted: 1 tbsp unless noted

	CALORIES
A & P	70
Bama	50
Estee, all types	4–6
Mrs. Filbert's	70
NuMade	70
Nutri-Dyne Elwood Zero Dressing: ½ oz	1
P&Q	50
Scotch Buy	60
Avocado: 1 oz / **Health Valley**	160
Bacon and tomato / **NuMade**	60
Bacon and tomato French / **Henri's**	70
Blue cheese	
Dia-Mel	2
Good Seasons	90
Good Seasons Thick 'n Creamy	80
Henri's	60
Henri's Reduced Calorie	30
NuMade Chunky	60
Weight Watchers	20
Wish-Bone Chunky	70
Wish-Bone Lite Chunky	40
Mix, prepared / **Hain** Natural No Oil	14
Mix, prepared / **Weight Watchers**	14
Buttermilk	
Good Seasons	60

Wish-Bone	50
Mix, prepared / **Hain** Natural No Oil	11
Buttermilk Farms / **Henri's**	70
Buttermilk and onion / **Hidden Valley Ranch**	70
Caesar	
NuMade	70
Pfeiffer	70
Pfeiffer Low-Cal	10
Wish-Bone	70
Mix, prepared / **Hain** Natural No Oil	4
Cheddar and bacon / **Wish-Bone**	70
Chopped chive / **Henri's**	60
Cucumber, creamy	
Dia-Mel	2
NuMade	70
Weight Watchers	12
Wish-Bone	80
Wish-Bone Lite	40
Cucumber and onion / **Henri's**	45
Cucumber and onion / **Henri's** Reduced Calorie	35
Dill: ½ oz / **Nutri-Dyne** Elwood	1
Dill / **Weight Watchers**	4
Dill, creamy / **Henri's**	80
French	
Dia-Mel	1
Good Seasons	80
Good Seasons Old Fashioned	80
Good Seasons Riviera	90
Good Seasons Thick 'n Creamy	75
Henri's	60
Henri's Hearty Beefsteak	70
Henri's Sweet 'n Saucy	70
Henri's Reduced Calorie	40
Kraft	60
Kraft Catalina	60
Kraft Reduced Calorie	20
NuMade Savory	60
NuMade Reduced Calorie	30
Nutri-Dyne Elwood: ½ oz	1
Pfeiffer	55
Pfeiffer Low-Cal	18

Pritikin	4
Weight Watchers	10
Wish-Bone Deluxe	50
Wish-Bone Sweet 'n Spicy	70
Wish-Bone Lite	30
Wish-Bone Lite Sweet 'n Spicy	30
Garlic / **Wish-Bone**	60
Herbal / **Wish-Bone**	60
Mix, prepared / **Hain** Natural No Oil	12
Mix, prepared / **Weight Watchers**	4
Garden herb / **Hidden Valley Ranch**	70
Garlic, creamy	
Dia-Mel	1
Henri's	50
Henri's Reduced Calorie	35
Wish-Bone	80
Garlic and cheese, mix, prepared /	
Hain Natural No Oil	6
Green goddess / **NuMade**	60
Herb: 1 oz / **Health Valley**	180
Herb / **Weight Watchers**	2
Herb, mix, prepared / **Hain** Natural No Oil	2
Italian	
Dia-Mel	1
Good Seasons	80
Good Seasons Thick 'n Creamy	80
Kraft Golden Blend	70
Kraft Reduced Calorie	6
Kraft Zesty	80
NuMade	70
NuMade Reduced Calorie	30
Nutri-Dyne Elwood: ½ oz	1
Pfeiffer Chef	60
Pfeiffer Low-Cal	10
Pritikin	4
Wish-Bone	70
Wish-Bone Lite	30
Wish-Bone Robusto	80
Weight Watchers	6
Mix, prepared / **Good Seasons** Low Calorie	8
Mix, prepared / **Hain** Natural No Oil	4

CALORIES

Mix, prepared / **Weight Watchers**	2
Creamy / **Dia-Mel**	1
Creamy / **Kraft**	60
Creamy / **Weight Watchers**	33
Creamy / **Wish-Bone**	60
Creamy / **Wish-Bone** Lite	30
Creamy, mix, prepared / **Weight Watchers**	4
Italian, Herbal / **Wish-Bone**	70
Onion / **Good Seasons**	80
Onion and chive / **Wish-Bone**	40
Ranch Original / **Hidden Valley Ranch**	70
Red wine vinegar / **Dia-Mel**	1
Red wine vinegar and oil / **NuMade**	60
Russian	
Henri's	60
Kraft	60
Kraft Reduced Calorie	30
Nutri-Dyne Elwood: ½ oz	3
Pfeiffer	65
Pfeiffer Low-Cal	15
Pritikin	4
Wish-Bone	45
Wish-Bone Lite	25
Mix, prepared / **Weight Watchers**	4
Russian / Thousand Island / **Weight Watchers**	33
Salad Life Cheese and Herbs / **Health Valley**	80
Slaw dressing / **Henri's**	80
Smoky Bits / **Henri's**	60
Sour cream and bacon / **Wish-Bone**	70
Tahiti / **Dia-Mel**	2
Tas-tee / **Henri's**	60
Thousand Island	
Dia-Mel	2
Good Seasons Thick 'n Creamy	75
Henri's	50
Henri's Reduced Calorie	30
Kraft	70
Kraft Reduced Calorie	30
NuMade Reduced Calorie	30
Pfeiffer	65
Pfeiffer Low-Cal	15

CALORIES

Weight Watchers	16
Wish-Bone	60
Wish-Bone Lite	25
Wish-Bone Southern Recipe	70
w bacon / **Wish-Bone**	60
Mix, prepared / **Hain** Natural No Oil	12
Mix, prepared / **Weight Watchers**	12
Whipped / **Dia-Mel**	24
Whipped / **Weight Watchers**	35
Yogonaise / **Henri's** Reduced Calorie	60
Yogowhip / **Henri's** Reduced Calorie	45
Yogurt buttermilk / **Dia-Mel**	2

Salads, Prepared

Note: You may find these specialty, premade salads at the deli counters of supermarkets, in delicatessens and on buffet tables and salad bars in restaurants. The brand names may or may not be posted.

All portions are 3½ ounces (slightly less than ½ cup)

CALORIES

Antipasto salad / **Signature Salad**	233
Artichoke, marinated salad / **Signature Salad**	143
Barbeque beans / **Orval Kent**	119
California Medley / **Orval Kent**	99
Carrot raisin / **Orval Kent**	181
Chicken salad / **Signature Salad**	234
Coleslaw, creamy / **Orval Kent**	157
Coleslaw, vinegar and oil / **Orval Kent**	115
Corn relish / **Orval Kent**	96
Crabmeat salad / **Signature Salad**	236
Cucumber salad / **Orval Kent**	82
Egg salad / **Signature Salad**	184
German potato salad / **Orval Kent**	117
Ham salad / **Signature Salad**	221
Hawaiian fruit dessert / **Orval Kent**	127

CALORIES

Macaroni salad / **Orval Kent**	189
Mexican shrimp salad Veracruz / **Signature Salad**	58
Mushroom salad, sliced / **Signature Salad**	173
Mushroom salad, button / **Signature Salad**	107
Oriental chicken salad / **Signature Salad**	136
Our Prima pasta salad / **Signature Salad**	203
Pasta pesto w crabmeat salad / **Signature Salad**	156
Pimento spread / **Orval Kent**	416
Pineapple walnut delite / **Orval Kent**	195
Potato salad / **Orval Kent**	117
Red potato and egg salad supreme / **Signature Salad**	140
Shrimp salad / **Signature Salad**	188
Tortellini salad / **Signature Salad**	205
Tuna salad / **Signature Salad**	299
Tri-bean salad / **Orval Kent**	62

Sauces

CALORIES

A la King, mix, prepared: 1 cup / **Durkee**	133
Barbecue, bottled or canned: 1 tbsp unless noted	
Chris' & Pitt's	15
Estee	16
French's Cattlemen's Regular	25
French's Cattlemen's Smoky	25
Heinz Regular	20
Heinz Hickory Smoke	20
Hunt's All Natural Hickory	25
Hunt's All Natural Original	20
Nutri-Dyne Elwood: ½ oz	4
Open Pit	26
Hickory smoke flavor / **Open Pit**	27
Hot / **Heinz**	20
Hot / **Hunt's** All Natural Hot & Zesty	25
Hot / **Open Pit** Hot 'n Spicy	27
Mushroom / **Heinz**	20
Onion / **Heinz**	20

Onion / **Hunt's** All Natural	20
Barbecue, mix, dry: 1 oz / **Nutri-Dyne** Chef Otto	113
Brown, mix, dry: 1 oz / **Nutri-Dyne** Chef Otto	114
Burrito salsa: ¼ cup / **Del Monte**	20
Cheese: 1 oz unless noted	
Land O Lakes Original	40
Cheddar / **Land O Lakes**	50
Cheddar / **Land O Lakes** LaChedda	35
Cheddar, canned / **Lucky Leaf**	60
Cheddar, canned / **Musselman's**	60
Cheddar, mild, canned / **Lucky Leaf**	50
Cheddar, mild, canned / **Musselman's**	50
Cheddar, sharp, canned / **Lucky Leaf**	57
Cheddar, sharp, canned / **Musselman's**	57
Nacho, canned / **Lucky Leaf**	55
Nacho, canned / **Musselman's**	55
Mix, dry / **Nutri-Dyne** Chef Otto	139
Mix, prepared w milk: 1 cup / **Durkee**	316
Mix, prepared: ¼ cup / **French's**	80
Chili: ¼ cup / **Del Monte**	70
Chili: 1 tbsp / **Heinz**	17
Chili hot dog w beef, canned: 1 oz /	
Chef Boy-ar-dee	30
Cocktail: 1 tbsp / **Estee**	10
Cream, mix, dry: 1 oz / **Nutri-Dyne** Chef Otto	105
Dill, creamy, mix for fish: 1 pkg /	
Durkee Roastin' Bag	153
Enchilada: ¼ cup	
Green chili, canned / **Old El Paso**	17
Hot, canned / **Del Monte**	22
Hot, canned / **Old El Paso**	27
Mild, canned / **Del Monte**	22
Mild, canned / **Old El Paso**	25
Mix, prepared / **Durkee**	14
57 Sauce: 1 tbsp / **Heinz**	15
Green chile salsa, mild: ¼ cup / **Del Monte**	20
Hard: 1 tbsp / **Crosse & Blackwell**	64
Hollandaise, mix, prepared: ¾ cup / **Durkee**	173
Hollandaise, mix, prepared: 3 tbsp / **French's**	45
Italian, mix, dry: 1 oz / **Nutri-Dyne** Chef Otto	108

CALORIES

Lemon-butter, mix, prepared: 1 tbsp / **Weight Watchers**	6
Meat marinade, mix, prepared: ½ cup / **Durkee**	47
Mexican: 4 oz / **Pritikin**	60
Pizza, in can or jar: ¼ cup unless noted	
Contadina Original Quick & Easy	40
Ragu Pizza Quick: 3 tbsp	35
Ragu Pizza Quick Chunky: 3 tbsp	45
w cheese: ¼ can (2.63 oz) / **Chef Boy-ar-dee**	70
w cheese / **Contadina**	40
w cheese: ¼ jar (3.88 oz) / **Chef Boy-ar-dee**	90
w pepperoni / **Contadina**	45
w pepperoni: ¼ can (2.6 oz) / **Chef Boy-ar-dee**	110
w sausage: ¼ can (2.6 oz) / **Chef Boy-ar-dee**	90
w tomato chunks / **Contadina**	25
Portovista, in jar	
Chef Boy-ar-dee: 3½ oz	60
w meat: 3½ oz / **Chef Boy-ar-dee**	60
w mushrooms: 3½ oz / **Chef Boy-ar-dee**	60
Salsa picante, hot: ¼ cup / **Del Monte**	20
Salsa picante, hot and chunky: ¼ cup / **Del Monte**	15
Salsa roja, mild: ¼ cup / **Del Monte**	20
Sauce for potatoes, au gratin, mix, dry: ⅙ pkg / **French's**	55
Sauce for potatoes, scalloped, mix, dry: ⅙ pkg / **French's**	40
Sauce for potatoes, sour cream and chives, mix, dry: ⅙ pkg / **French's**	65
Seafood cocktail: ¼ cup / **Del Monte**	70
Sloppy Joe: 5 tbsp / **Hunt's** Manwich Original	40
Sloppy Joe: 5 tbsp / **Hunt's** Manwich Mexican	40
Sour cream, mix, prepared: 2½ tbsp / **French's**	60
Spaghetti	
Canned: ¼ can (3¾ oz) / **Chef Boy-ar-dee**	60
Canned: 4 oz / **Hain** Naturals	70
Canned: 4 oz / **Hunt's** No Salt Added	80
In jar: ¼ jar (4 oz) / **Chef Boy-ar-dee**	60
In jar: ⅐ jar (4.14 oz) / **Chef Boy-ar-dee**	60
In jar: 4 oz / **Prego**	140
In jar: 4 oz / **Prego** No Salt Added	100
In jar: 4 oz / **Pritikin**	60

CALORIES

In jar: 4 oz / **Ragu**	80
In jar: 4 oz / **Ragu** Extra Thick and Zesty	100
In jar: 4 oz / **Ragu** Homestyle	70
In jar: 4 oz / **Ragu** Marinara	90
In jar: ⅓ cup / **Weight Watchers**	40
Mix, prepared: 2½ cup / **Durkee**	224
Mix, prepared: 2½ cup /	
Durkee Extra Thick & Rich	212
Mix, prepared: 5 oz / **French's** Italian Style	100
Mix, prepared: 7 oz (⅞ cup) /	
French's Thick Homemade Style	170
Mix: ⅕ pkg / **McCormick**	26
Mix, prepared: 1 oz / **Spatini**	20
w ground beef, in jar: ¼ jar (4 oz) /	
Chef Boy-ar-dee	90
w ground beef, in jar: ⅐ jar (4.14 oz) /	
Chef Boy-ar-dee	100
w meat, canned: 4 oz / **Chef Boy-ar-dee**	140
w meat, canned: ¼ can (3¾ oz) /	
Chef Boy-ar-dee Original	120
Meat-flavored, in jar: 4 oz / **Prego**	150
Meat-flavored, in jar: 4 oz / **Ragu**	80
Meat-flavored, in jar: 4 oz /	
Ragu Extra Thick and Zesty	100
Meat-flavored, in jar: 4 oz / **Ragu** Homestyle	80
Meat-flavored, in jar: ⅓ cup / **Weight Watchers**	50
w mushrooms, canned: 4 oz / **Chef Boy-ar-dee**	70
w mushrooms, canned: ¼ can (3¾ oz) /	
Chef Boy-ar-dee Original	80
w mushrooms, canned: 4 oz / **Hain** Naturals	80
w mushrooms, in jar: 4 oz / **Chef Boy-ar-dee**	70
w mushrooms, in jar: 4 oz / **Prego**	140
w mushrooms, in jar: 4 oz / **Pritikin**	60
w mushrooms, in jar: 4 oz / **Ragu**	90
w mushrooms, in jar: 4 oz /	
Ragu Extra Thick and Zesty	110
w mushrooms, in jar: 4 oz / **Ragu** Homestyle	70
w mushrooms, in jar: ⅓ cup / **Weight Watchers**	40
w mushrooms, mix, prepared: 2⅔ cup / **Durkee**	208
w mushrooms, mix, prepared: 5 oz / **French's**	100

w mushrooms and cheese, canned: 4 oz /
  Health Valley Bellissimo Regular or No Salt 40
Sparerib, mix w roasting bag: 1 pkg /
  Durkee Roastin' Bag 162
Stroganoff, mix, prepared: ⅓ cup / **French's** 110
Sweet and sour: 4 oz / **Contadina** 150
Sweet and sour, mix, prepared: 1 cup / **Durkee** 230
Sweet and sour, mix, prepared: ½ cup /
  French's 55
Taco
  Hot: ¼ cup / **Del Monte** 15
  Hot: 2 tbsp / **Old El Paso** 11
  Mild: ¼ cup / **Del Monte** 15
  Mild: 2 tbsp / **Old El Paso** 11
Teriyaki, mix, prepared: 2 tbsp / **French's** 35
Tomato, canned
  A & P: ½ cup 45
  Contadina: ½ cup 45
  Contadina Italian Style: ½ cup 40
  Del Monte: 1 cup 70
  Del Monte No Salt: 1 cup 70
  Health Valley Natural: ½ cup 55
  Health Valley No Salt: 1 cup 55
  Hunt's: 4 oz 30
  Hunt's Italian: 4 oz 60
  Hunt's No Salt Added: 4 oz 35
  Hunt's Special: 4 oz 35
  Town House: 8 oz 80
  w bits: 4 oz / **Hunt's** 30
  w cheese: 4 oz / **Hunt's** 45
  Herb: 4 oz / **Hunt's** 80
  w mushrooms: 4 oz / **Hunt's** 25
  w onions: 1 cup / **Del Monte** 100
  w onions: 4 oz / **Hunt's** 40
White, mix, prepared w milk: 1 cup / **Durkee** 317

Seasonings

	CALORIES
1 tsp unless noted	
Ac'cent Flavor Enhancer	10
Bacon, imitation, crumbled: 1 tbsp	
Bac*Os	40
Durkee Bacon Bits	24
Durkee Bacon Chips	44
Lawry's Baconion	40
Libby's Bacon Crumbles	25
McCormick Bacon Chips	28
Barbecue / **French's**	6
Brown Seasoning & Broth: ⅛ pkg /	
G. Washington's	6
Brown Seasoning & Broth: ⅛ pkg /	
G. Washington's Kosher for Passover	6
Chili powder / **Lawry's**	9
Garlic concentrate: 1 tbsp / **Lawry's**	88
Golden Seasoning & Broth: ⅛ pkg /	
G. Washington's	6
Golden Seasoning & Broth: ⅛ pkg /	
G. Washington's Kosher for Passover	6
Herb blend / **Lawry's**	9
Kitchen Bouquet	11
Lemon and Pepper / **French's**	6
Lemon & Pepper / **McCormick**	7
Lemon pepper marinade / **Lawry's**	7
Meat marinade: ⅛ pkg / **French's**	10
Meat tenderizer / **French's**	2
Meat tenderizer, seasoned / **French's**	2
Meat tenderizer / **McCormick**	2
Meat tenderizer, seasoned / **McCormick**	5
Mrs. Dash	12
Mrs. Dash Low-Pepper, No Garlic	12
Onion Seasoning & Broth: ⅛ pkg /	
G. Washington's	12

	CALORIES
Pepper, seasoned / **French's**	8
Pepper, seasoned / **Lawry's**	8
Pizza seasoning / **French's**	4
Potato Toppers: 1 tbsp / **Libby's**	30
Salad Crispins, American, Italian or French	14
Salad Crispins, Country or Swiss	15
Salad Crispins, Home	16
Salad Crunchies: 1 tbsp / **Libby's**	35
Salad Onions, instant: 1 tbsp / **French's**	15
Salad seasoning / **French's**	6
Salad Supreme / **McCormick**	11
Salt	
Butter flavor, imitation / **French's**	8
Celery / **French's**	2
Garlic / **French's**	4
Garlic-flavored / **Lawry's**	5
Garlic, parslied / **French's**	6
Hickory smoke / **French's**	2
Onion / **French's**	6
Onion-flavored / **Lawry's**	4
Salt 'N Spice / **McCormick**	3
Seasoned / **Lawry's** Seasoned Salt-Free	3
Seasoning salt / **French's**	2
Substitute / **Dia-Mel** Salt-It	0
Substitute / **Estee** Salt-Free	0
Seafood seasoning / **French's**	2
Season-All / **McCormick**	4
Soup greens: 2½-oz jar / **Durkee**	216
Stock base, beef flavor / **French's**	8
Stock base, chicken flavor / **French's**	8
Vegetable flakes, dehydrated / **French's**	4
Vegetable Seasoning & Broth: ⅛ pkg / **G. Washington's**	12

SEASONING MIXES

Beef	
Lawry's Beef Ole: 1¼ oz pkg	126
Stew, mix, dry: 1 pkg / **Durkee**	99
Stew, mix, prepared: 1 cup / **Durkee**	379
Stew: ⅙ pkg / **French's**	25

CALORIES

Stew: 1⅔ oz pkg / **Lawry's**	131
Chili: ⅙ pkg / **McCormick**	18
Chili, Texas, mix, dry: 1 pkg / **Durkee**	151
Chili, Texas, mix, prepared: 1 cup / **Durkee**	772
Chili con carne, mix, dry: 1 pkg / **Durkee**	148
Chili con carne, mix, prepared: 1 cup / **Durkee**	465
Chili con carne: 1⅝ oz pkg / **Lawry's**	137
Chili-O: ⅙ pkg / **French's**	25
Chop suey, mix, dry: 1 pkg / **Durkee**	128
Chop suey, mix, prepared: ½ cup / **Durkee**	159
Enchilada: ¼ pkg / **French's**	30
Fried rice, mix, dry: 1 oz / **Durkee**	62
Fried rice, mix, prepared: 1 cup / **Durkee**	215
Ground beef	
Mix, dry: 1 pkg / **Durkee**	91
Mix, prepared: 1 cup / **Durkee**	654
w onions, mix, dry: 1 pkg / **Durkee**	102
w onions, mix, prepared: 1 cup / **Durkee**	659
w onions, mix, dry: ¼ pkg / **French's**	25
Hamburger, mix, dry: 1 pkg / **Durkee**	110
Hamburger, mix, prepared: 1 cup / **Durkee**	663
Hamburger, mix, dry: ¼ pkg / **French's**	25
Lemon butter, for fish, mix: 1 pkg / **Durkee** Roastin' Bag	75
Meatball, mix, dry: ¼ pkg / **French's**	35
Meatball, Italian, mix, dry: 1 pkg / **Durkee**	22
Meatball, Italian, mix, prepared: 1 cup / **Durkee**	619
Meatloaf	
Bells: 4½ oz dry	300
Bells: 4½ oz prepared	300
Contadina: 1 rounded tbsp	35
French's: ⅛ pkg	20
Nutri-Dyne Chef Otto: 1 oz dry	100
Mrs. Dash Crispy Coating Mix: ¼ env	63
Sloppy Joe	
Mix, dry: 1 pkg / **Durkee**	118
Mix, prepared: ½ cup / **Durkee**	291
Mix, dry: ⅛ pkg / **French's**	16
Mix, dry: ⅙ pkg / **McCormick**	17

	CALORIES
Italian, mix, dry: 1 pkg / **Durkee**	99
Italian, mix, prepared: ½ cup / **Durkee**	298
Super Slaw: ½ cup prepared / **Libby's**	240
Taco	
Mix, dry: 1 pkg / **Durkee**	67
Mix, prepared: 1 cup / **Durkee**	642
Mix: ⅛ pkg / **French's**	20
Mix: ⅒ pkg / **McCormick**	12
Mix: 1 pkg / **Old El Paso**	100

Shortening

	CALORIES
Solid	
Lard: 1 cup	1850
1 tbsp	115
Vegetable	
NuMade: 1 tbsp	110
Crisco: 1 tbsp	110
Crisco, butter flavor: 1 tbsp	110
Fluffo: 1 tbsp	110
Snowdrift: 1 tbsp	110

Soft Drinks

Some companies report their diet drinks as having
less than 1 calorie. For convenience, we have
reported those as having 1 calorie.

	CALORIES
6 fl ounces unless noted	
Birch beer / **Canada Dry**	82
Birell, nonalcoholic beverage	39
Bitter lemon / **Canada Dry**	75

CALORIES

Bitter Lemon / **Schweppes**	84
Black cherry / **Cragmont** Diet	1
Black cherry / **Shasta**	80
Black cherry / **Shasta** Sugar Free	1
Bubble Up	73
Bubble Up Sugar Free	1
Cherry	
Cola / **Cragmont** Diet	1
Crush	90
Shasta	68
Shasta Sugar Free	1
Chocolate / **No-Cal**	2
Club soda / **Schweppes**	0
Club soda / **Shasta**	0
Coffee / **No-Cal**	2
Cola	
Coca-Cola	72
Coca-Cola Caffeine Free	76
diet Coke	1
diet Coke Caffeine Free	1
Cragmont Diet	1
Diet-Rite	1
New Natural / **Health Valley**	82
Like	81
Like Sugar Free	1
No-Cal	0
Pepsi-Cola	79
Diet Pepsi	1
Pepsi Free	79
Diet Pepsi Free	1
Pepsi Light	1
RC 100 Caffeine Free	78
Diet RC Caffeine Free	1
Royal Crown	78
Shasta	72
Shasta Sugar Free	1
Tab	1
Cream soda	
Cragmont Diet	1
Crush, red/brown	80
No-Cal	2

CALORIES

Shasta	75
Shasta Sugar Free	1
Diet Skipper / **Cragmont**	1
Dr. Pepper	74
Dr. Pepper Sugar Free	1
Fresca	2
Fruit punch / **Shasta**	84
Ginger ale	
Cragmont Diet	1
Canada Dry	67
Fanta	63
Health Valley	76
No-Cal	2
Schweppes	66
Schweppes Sugar Free	2
Shasta	58
Shasta Sugar Free	1
Ginger beer / **Schweppes**	72
Ginseng root beer / **Health Valley**	95
Grape	
Canada Dry	98
Crush	90
Fanta	86
Hi-C	78
Nehi	87
Schweppes	96
Shasta	86
Shasta Sugar Free	1
Grapefruit	
Cragmont Diet	1
Shasta	79
Shasta Sugar Free	1
Grapefruit, lime / **No-Cal**	2
Iced tea / **Shasta**	60
Lemon / **Hi-C**	75
Lemon / **Schweppes**	62
Lemon-lime	
Cragmont Diet	1
Health Valley	60
No-Cal	2
Shasta	70

CALORIES

Shasta Sugar Free	1
Mandarin lime / **Health Valley**	71
Mello Yello	86
Mineral water / **Schweppes**	0
Mountain Dew	88
Mr Pibb	71
Mr Pibb Sugar Free	1
Orange	
Canada Dry	97
Cragmont Diet	1
Crush	90
Crush Sugar Free	2
Fanta	88
Hi-C	77
Nehi	93
No-Cal	2
Schweppes Sparkling	89
Shasta	86
Shasta Sugar Free	1
Pineapple / **Crush**	90
Punch / **Hi-C**	77
Red Cherry / **No-Cal**	2
Red creme / **Schweppes**	86
Rondo / **Schweppes**	76
Root beer	
A & W	86
A & W Sugar Free	1
Canada Dry Barrelhead	82
Cragmont Diet	1
Dad's	82
Dad's Diet	1
Fanta	78
Health Valley Old Fashioned	76
Health Valley Sarsaparilla	76
Hires	80
Hires Sugar Free	2
Nehi	87
No-Cal	2
Ramblin'	88
Ramblin' Sugar Free	1
Schweppes	79

CALORIES

Shasta	75
Shasta Sugar Free	1
7 Up	72
Diet 7 Up	2
Sprite	71
Sprite, Diet	1
Strawberry	
Canada Dry California	90
Crush	90
Nehi	87
No-Cal	0
Shasta	72
Shasta Sugar Free	1
Sun-Drop	90
Sun-Drop Sugar Free	4
Teem	74
Tonic	
Cragmont Diet	1
Schweppes	66
Schweppes Sugar Free	1
Shasta	59
Vichy water / **Schweppes**	0
Wild Berry / **Health Valley**	71

Soups

CALORIES

Prepared according to package directions, unless noted

Asparagus, cream of, canned: 8 fl oz / **Campbell's**	90
Bean, canned	
Health Valley Chunky: 4 fl oz	100
Health Valley Old Fashioned: 4 fl oz	92
Health Valley Old Fashioned No Salt: 4 fl oz	90
w bacon: 8 fl oz / **Campbell's**	150
Black bean: 8 fl oz / **Campbell's**	110

CALORIES

Black bean w sherry: ½ can / **Crosse & Blackwell**	80
Chowder, pinto bean: 8½ fl oz / **Luck's** Country	210
w ham: 11 fl oz / **Campbell's** Soup for One Old Fashioned	210
w ham, ready to serve: 11 fl oz / **Campbell's** Chunky Old Fashioned	290
w ham: 8½ fl oz / **Luck's** Country Old Fashioned	190
w ham: 9½ fl oz / **Progresso**	170
w ham and onions: 8½ fl oz / **Luck's** Country	170
w sausage: 8½ fl oz / **Luck's** Country	170
Bean barley stew, mix: 1.6 oz dry / **Fearn**	159
Blackbean creole, mix: 1.9 oz dry / **Fearn**	150
Beef, canned	
Campbell's: 8 fl oz	80
Campbell's Chunky: 10¾ fl oz	190
Progresso: 9½ fl oz	150
Cabbage: 8 fl oz / **Manischewitz**	62
Cannelloni, mini, w vegetables: 8¼ fl oz / **Chef Boy-ar-dee** Soup di Pasta	210
Mushroom: 10¾ fl oz / **Campbell's** Chunky Low Sodium	210
Noodle: 8 fl oz / **Campbell's**	70
Noodle: 8 fl oz / **Campbell's** Homestyle	90
Ravioli w vegetables: 8¼ fl oz / **Chef Boy-ar-dee** Soup di Pasta	190
Stroganoff style: 10¾ fl oz / **Campbell's** Chunky	300
Vegetable: 9½ fl oz / **Progresso**	150
Vegetable: 10½ fl oz / **Progresso**	160
Beef flavor, mix: 7 fl oz / **Lipton** Cup-A-Soup Lots-A-Noodles	120
Beef flavor, mix: 6 fl oz / **Lipton** Cup-A-Soup Trim	10
Beef vegetable noodle, mix: 8 fl oz / **Lipton** Hearty ·	80
Borscht, canned or in jars	
Manischewitz: 8 fl oz	80
Manischewitz Low Calorie: 8 fl oz	20
Mother's: 8 fl oz	96
Mother's Lo-Cal: 8 fl oz	29

	CALORIES
Mother's Unsalted: 8 fl oz	103
Rokeach: 8 fl oz	96
Rokeach Diet: 8 fl oz	29
Rokeach Unsalted: 8 fl oz	103
Bouillon	
Beef, cube: 1 cube / **Herb-Ox**	6
Beef, cube: 1 cube / **Maggi**	5
Beef, instant: 1 tsp / **Lite-Line** Low Sodium	12
Beef, instant: 1 tsp / **Maggi**	2
Beef, instant: 1 tsp / **Wyler's**	6
Chicken, cube: 1 cube / **Herb-Ox**	6
Chicken, cube: 1 cube / **Maggi**	5
Chicken, cube: 1 cube / **Wyler's**	8
Chicken, instant: 1 tsp / **Lite-Line** Low Sodium	12
Chicken, instant: 1 tsp / **Maggi**	2
Onion, cube: 1 cube / **Herb-Ox**	10
Onion, cube: 1 cube / **Maggi**	5
Onion, instant: 1 tsp / **Wyler's**	10
Vegetable, cube: 1 cube / **Herb-Ox**	6
Vegetable, cube: 1 cube / **Maggi**	5
Broth	
Beef, canned: 8 fl oz / **Campbell's**	16
Beef, canned: 8 fl oz / **College Inn**	18
Beef, canned: 4 fl oz / **Health Valley**	1
Beef, canned: 4 fl oz / **Health Valley** No Salt	0
Beef, canned: 7¼ fl oz / **Swanson**	20
Beef, mix: 1 packet / **Herb-Ox**	8
Beef, mix: 1 packet / **Herb-Ox** Low Sodium	11
Beef, mix: 1 packet / **Weight Watchers**	10
Chicken, canned: 8 fl oz / **Campbell's**	35
Chicken, canned: 1 can / **Campbell's** Low Sodium	40
Chicken, canned: 8 fl oz / **College Inn**	35
Chicken, canned: 4 fl oz / **Health Valley**	1
Chicken, canned: 4 fl oz / **Health Valley** No Salt	0
Chicken, canned: 6⅞ fl oz / **Pritikin**	14
Chicken, canned: 7¼ fl oz / **Swanson**	30
Chicken, mix: 1 packet / **Herb-Ox**	12

CALORIES

Chicken, mix: 1 packet /
  Herb-Ox Low Sodium   12
Chicken, mix: 6 fl oz / **Lipton** Cup-A-Broth   25
Chicken, mix: 1 packet / **Weight Watchers**   8
Chicken and noodles, canned: 8 fl oz /
  Campbell's   60
Chicken and rice, canned: 8 fl oz / **Campbell's**   50
Onion, mix: 1 packet / **Herb-Ox**   14
Onion, mix: 1 packet / **Weight Watchers**   10
Scotch, canned: 8 fl oz / **Campbell's**   80
Vegetable, mix: 1 packet / **Herb-Ox**   12
Celery, cream of, canned: 8 fl oz / **Campbell's**   100
Celery, cream of, canned: 10 fl oz / **Rokeach**   90
Celery, cream of, canned, prepared w milk: 10 fl oz /
  Rokeach   190
Cheddar cheese, canned: 8 fl oz / **Campbell's**   130
Chickarina w tiny meatballs, canned: 9½ fl oz /
  Progresso   90
Chicken
  Alphabet, canned: 8 fl oz / **Campbell's**   80
  Barley, canned: 8 fl oz / **Manischewitz**   83
  Cream of, canned: 8 fl oz / **Campbell's**   110
  Cream of, mix: 6 fl oz / **Estee**   50
  Cream of, mix: 6 fl oz / **Lipton** Cup-A-Soup   80
  Cream of, mix: 7 fl oz / **Lipton**
    Cup-A-Soup Lots-A-Noodles   150
  'n Dumplings, canned: 8 fl oz / **Campbell's**   80
  Flavor, mix: 7 fl oz /
    Lipton Cup-A-Soup Lots-A-Noodles   120
  Flavor, mix: 6 fl oz /
    Lipton Cup-A-Soup Trim   10
  Gumbo, canned: 8 fl oz / **Campbell's**   60
  Hearty, mix: 6 fl oz /
    Lipton Country Style Cup-A-Soup   70
  Home style, canned: 9½ fl oz / **Progresso**   90
  Home style, canned: 10½ fl oz / **Progresso**   100
  Mushroom, creamy, canned: 8 fl oz /
    Campbell's   110
  Noodle, canned: 8 fl oz / **Campbell's**   70
  Noodle, canned: 10¾ oz / **Campbell's** Chunky   200

Noodle, canned: 8 fl oz /	
Campbell's Homestyle	70
w noodles, canned: 1 can /	
Campbell's Low Sodium	170
and noodles, canned: 11 fl oz /	
Campbell's Soup for One	120
Noodle: 8 fl oz / **Dia-Mel**	50
Noodle, canned: 8 fl oz / **Manischewitz**	46
Noodle, canned: 9½ fl oz / **Progresso**	120
Noodle, canned: 10½ fl oz / **Progresso**	130
Noodle, mix: 8 fl oz / **Lipton**	70
Noodle w meat, mix: 6 fl oz /	
Lipton Cup-A-Soup	45
NoodleO's, canned: 8 fl oz / **Campbell's**	70
Old Fashioned, canned: 10¾ fl oz /	
Campbell's Chunky	170
w pasta, meatballs, and chicken, canned: 8 fl oz/	
Chef Boy-ar-dee Soup di Pasta	110
Ravioli, mini, canned: 8¼ fl oz /	
Chef Boy-ar-dee Soup di Pasta	130
w ribbon pasta, canned: 7¼ fl oz / **Pritikin**	60
Rice, canned: ½ can /	
Campbell's Chunky 19 oz can	140
Rice, canned: 8 fl oz / **Manischewitz**	47
w rice, canned: 8 fl oz / **Campbell's**	60
Rice, mix: 6 fl oz / **Lipton** Cup-A-Soup	45
Rice w vegetables, canned: 9½ fl oz /	
Progresso	140
and stars, canned: 8 fl oz / **Campbell's**	60
Supreme, mix: 6 fl oz / **Lipton**	
Country Style Cup-A-Soup	100
Vegetable, canned: 8 fl oz / **Campbell's**	70
Vegetable, canned: ½ can /	
Campbell's Chunky 19-oz can	170
Vegetable, canned: 1 can /	
Campbell's Chunky Low Sodium	240
Vegetable, canned: 11 fl oz /	
Campbell's Soup for One	120
Vegetable, canned: 8 fl oz / **Manischewitz**	55
Vegetable, canned: 7¼ fl oz / **Pritikin**	70
Vegetable, mix: 6 fl oz / **Lipton** Cup-A-Soup	40

Chili beef, canned: 8 fl oz / **Campbell's**	130
Chili beef, canned: 11 fl oz / **Campbell's** Chunky	290
Chix w vegetables and pasta, canned: 8¼ fl oz / **Chef Boy-ar-dee** Soup di Pasta	110
Clam chowder, canned	
Health Valley: 4 fl oz	80
Health Valley Chunky, Regular or No Salt: 4 fl oz	80
Health Valley No Salt: 4 fl oz	80
Howard Johnson's: 1 cup	177
Manhattan style: 8 fl oz / **Campbell's**	70
Manhattan style: 10¾ oz / **Campbell's** Chunky	160
Manhattan style: ½ can / **Crosse & Blackwell**	50
Manhattan style: 6 fl oz / **Doxsee**	50
Manhattan style: 9½ fl oz / **Progresso**	130
Manhattan style: 7½ fl oz / **Snow's**	70
New England: 8 fl oz / **Campbell's**	80
New England, prepared w milk: 8 fl oz **Campbell's**	150
New England: 10¾ oz / **Campbell's** Chunky	290
New England: 11 fl oz / **Campbell's** Soup for One	130
New England, prepared w milk: 11 fl oz / **Campbell's** Soup for One	200
New England: ½ can / **Crosse & Blackwell**	90
New England: 6 fl oz / **Doxsee**	90
New England: 9½ fl oz / **Hain** Naturals	180
New England, prepared w milk: 7½ fl oz / **Snow's**	140
New England, frozen pouch: 8 fl oz / **Stouffer's**	200
Consomme, beef, canned: 8 fl oz / **Campbell's**	25
Consomme, Madrilene, clear, canned: ½ can / **Crosse & Blackwell**	25
Consomme, Madrilene, red, canned: ½ can / **Crosse & Blackwell**	25
Corn chowder, New England, canned, prepared w milk: 7½ fl oz / **Snow's**	150
Escarole in chicken broth, canned: 9½ fl oz / **Progresso**	35

CALORIES

Fish chowder, New England, canned, prepared w milk: 7½ fl oz / **Snow's**	130
Gazpacho, canned: ½ can / **Crosse & Blackwell**	30
Ham and butter bean, canned: 10¾ oz / **Campbell's** Chunky	280

Lentil
Canned: 9½ fl oz / **Hain** Naturals Regular or No Salt	190
Canned: 4 fl oz / **Health Valley** Regular or No Salt	90
Canned: 9½ fl oz / **Progresso**	170
Canned: 10½ fl oz / **Progresso**	180
Minestrone, mix: 1.9 oz dry / **Fearn**	170
Macaroni and bean, canned: 9½ fl oz / **Progresso**	180
Meatball alphabet, canned: 8 fl oz / **Campbell's**	100

Minestrone
Canned: 8 fl oz / **Campbell's**	80
Canned: ½ can / **Campbell's** Chunky 19-oz can	140
Canned: ½ can / **Crosse & Blackwell**	90
Canned: 9½ fl oz / **Hain** Naturals regular or No Salt	190
Canned: 4 fl oz / **Health Valley**	70
Canned: 4 fl oz / **Health Valley** Chunky	70
Canned: 4 fl oz / **Health Valley** No Salt	70
Canned: 4 fl oz / **Health Valley** No Salt Chunky	70
Canned: 7⅜ fl oz / **Pritikin**	110
Canned: 10½ fl oz / **Progresso**	160
Mix: 6 fl oz / **Manischewitz**	50
Beef, canned: 9½ fl oz / **Progresso**	150
Chicken, canned: 9½ fl oz / **Progresso**	150
w meatballs and pasta, canned: 8¼ fl oz / **Chef Boy-ar-dee** Soup di Pasta	140

Mushroom
Canned: 9½ fl oz / **Hain** Naturals	120
Canned: 4 fl oz / **Health Valley** Regular or No Salt	70
Barley, canned: 8 fl oz / **Manischewitz**	72
Beef flavor, mix: 8 fl oz / **Lipton**	40
Beefy, canned: 8 fl oz / **Campbell's**	60

CALORIES

Bisque, canned: ½ can / **Crosse & Blackwell**	90
Cream of, canned: 8 fl oz / **Campbell's**	100
Cream of, canned: 1 can / **Campbell's** Low Sodium	190
Cream of, canned: 11 fl oz / **Campbell's** Soup for One	180
Cream of, canned: 10 fl oz / **Rokeach**	150
Cream of, prepared w milk: 10 fl oz / **Rokeach**	240
Cream of, mix: 6 fl oz / **Lipton** Cup-A-Soup	80
Cream of, mix: 6 fl oz / **Nutri-Dyne** Med-Diet	90
Cream of, mix: 6 fl oz / **Estee**	50
Golden, canned: 8 fl oz / **Campbell's**	80
Golden w chicken broth, mix: 8 fl oz / **Lipton**	60

Noodle

Mix: 8 fl oz / **Lipton** Giggle Noodle	80
Mix: 8 fl oz / **Lipton** Ring-O-Noodle	60
Mix: 6 fl oz / **Lipton** Cup-A-Soup Ring	50
w beef flavor, mix: 6 fl oz / **Lipton** Cup-A-Soup	45
w chicken, canned: 8 fl oz / **Campbell's** Curly	70
w chicken broth, mix: 8 fl oz / **Lipton**	70
w ground beef, canned: 8 fl oz / **Campbell's**	90
w vegetables and chicken broth, mix: 8 fl oz / **Lipton**	80

Onion

Mix: 8 fl oz / **Lipton**	35
Mix: 6 fl oz / **Lipton** Cup-A-Soup	30
Beefy, mix: 8 fl oz / **Lipton**	35
Cream of, canned: 8 fl oz / **Campbell's**	100
Cream of, canned, prepared w milk and water: 8 fl oz / **Campbell**	140
French, canned: 8 fl oz / **Campbell's**	70
French, canned: 1 can / **Campbell's** Low Sodium	80
French, canned: 9½ fl oz / **Progresso**	120
Golden, w chicken broth, mix: 8 fl oz / **Lipton**	60
Mushroom, mix: 8 fl oz / **Lipton**	45

Oriental style, mix: 7 fl oz / Lipton

Cup-A-Soup Lots-A-Noodles	120
Oyster stew, canned: 8 fl oz / **Campbell's**	70

Oyster stew, canned, prepared w milk: 8 fl oz / **Campbell's**	150
Pea, green, canned: 8 fl oz / **Campbell's**	100
Pea, green, mix: 6 fl oz / **Lipton** Cup-A-Soup	120
Pea, split	
Canned: 1 can / **Campbell's** Low Sodium	240
Canned: 9½ fl oz / **Hain Naturals**	210
Canned: 9½ fl oz / **Hain Naturals** No Salt	220
Canned: 4 fl oz / **Health Valley**	80
Canned: 4 fl oz / **Health Valley** Chunky	70
Canned: 4 fl oz / **Health Valley** No Salt	80
Canned: 4 fl oz / **Health Valley** No Salt Chunky	60
Canned: 8 fl oz / **Manischewitz**	133
Mix: 1.8 oz dry / **Fearn**	169
Mix: 6 fl oz / **Manischewitz**	45
w ham, canned: 10¾ fl oz / **Campbell's** Chunky	230
w ham, frozen pouch: 8¼ fl oz / **Stouffer's**	190
w ham and bacon, canned: 8 fl oz / **Campbell's**	170
Pea, Virginia, mix: 6 fl oz / **Lipton** Country Style Cup-A-Soup	140
Pepper pot, canned: 8 fl oz / **Campbell's**	90
Potato	
Cream of, canned: 8 fl oz / **Campbell's**	70
Cream of, canned, prepared w milk and water: 8 fl oz / **Campbell's**	110
Old-fashioned, canned: 4 fl oz / **Health Valley**	64
Old-fashioned, canned: 4 fl oz / **Health Valley** No Salt	72
Schav, canned: 8 fl oz / **Manischewitz**	11
Seafood chowder, New England, canned, prepared w milk: 7½ fl oz / **Snow's**	130
Shrimp bisque, canned: ½ can / **Crosse & Blackwell**	90
Shrimp, cream of, canned: 8 fl oz / **Campbell's**	90
Shrimp, cream of, canned, prepared w milk: 8 fl oz / **Campbell's**	160

CALORIES

Sirloin burger, canned: 10¾ fl oz /
   Campbell's Chunky   220
Spinach, cream of, frozen pouch:
   8 fl oz / **Stouffer's**   230
Steak and potato, canned: 10¾ fl oz /
   Campbell's Chunky   200
Tomato
   Canned: 8 fl oz / **Campbell's**   90
   Canned, prepared w milk: 8 fl oz / **Campbell's**   160
   Canned: 9½ fl oz / **Hain** Naturals   150
   Canned: 9½ fl oz / **Hain** Naturals No Salt   160
   Canned: 4 fl oz / **Health Valley**   80
   Canned: 4 fl oz / **Health Valley** No Salt   40
   Canned: 8 fl oz / **Manischewitz**   60
   Canned: 10 fl oz / **Rokeach**   90
   Canned, prepared w milk: 10 fl oz / **Rokeach**   190
   Mix: 6 fl oz / **Estee**   60
   Mix: 6 fl oz / **Lipton** Cup-A-Soup   80
   Mix: 6 fl oz / **Nutri-Dyne** Med-Diet   90
   Beefy, mix: 6 fl oz / **Lipton** Cup-A-Soup Trim   10
   Bisque, canned: 8 fl oz / **Campbell's**   120
   w macaroni shells, canned: 10½ fl oz /
      Progresso   130
   w meatballs and pasta, canned: 8¼ fl oz /
      Chef Boy-ar-dee Soup di Pasta   200
   Onion, mix: 8 fl oz / **Lipton**   70
   Rice, canned: 8 fl oz /
      Campbell's Old Fashioned   110
   Rice, canned: 10 fl oz / **Rokeach**   160
   Royale, canned: 11 fl oz / **Campbell's**
      Soup for One   180
   w tomato pieces, canned: 1 can /
      Campbell's Low Sodium   180
   w tomato pieces, canned: 7¼ fl oz / **Pritikin**   70
   Vegetable, mix: 6 fl oz / **Estee**   60
   Vegetable, mix: 7 fl oz / **Lipton**
      Cup-A-Soup Lots-A-Noodles   110
   Vegetable noodle, mix: 8 fl oz / **Lipton** Hearty   80
Turkey noodle, canned: 8 fl oz / **Campbell's**   60
Turkey vegetable, canned: 8 fl oz /
   Campbell's   70

CALORIES

Vegetable

Canned: 8 fl oz / **Campbell's**	80
Canned: 10¾ fl oz / **Campbell's** Chunky	140
Canned: 8 fl oz / **Campbell's** Old Fashioned	60
Canned: 11 fl oz / **Campbell's** Soup for One	130
Canned: 4 fl oz / **Health Valley**	60
Canned: 4 fl oz / **Health Valley** Chunky	60
Canned: 4 fl oz / **Health Valley** No Salt	60
Canned: 4 fl oz / **Health Valley** No Salt Chunky	60
Canned: 8½ fl oz / **Luck's** Country	100
Canned: 8 fl oz / **Manischewitz**	63
Canned: 7⅜ fl oz / **Pritikin**	70
Mix: 6 fl oz / **Manischewitz**	50
Beef, canned: 8 fl oz / **Campbell's**	70
Beef, canned: 10¾ fl oz / **Campbell's** Chunky	180
Beef, canned: 1 can / **Campbell's** Chunky Low Sodium	170
Beef, canned: 8¼ fl oz / **Chef Boy-ar-dee** Soup di Pasta	120
Beef, mix: 6 fl oz / **Lipton** Cup-A-Soup	50
Beef and bacon, canned: 11 fl oz / **Campbell's** Soup for One Burly	150
w beef stock, mix: 8 fl oz / **Lipton**	50
Chicken, canned: 9½ fl oz / **Hain** Naturals Regular or No Salt	130
Country, canned: 8¼ fl oz / **Chef Boy-ar-dee** Soup di Pasta	110
Country, mix: 8 fl oz / **Lipton**	80
Cream of, mix: 6 fl oz / **Estee**	60
Garden, mix: 7 fl oz / **Lipton** Cup-A-Soup Lots-A-Noodles	130
Harvest, mix: 6 fl oz / **Lipton** Country Style Cup-A-Soup	90
Herb, mix: 6 fl oz / **Lipton** Cup-A-Soup Trim	10
Italian, canned: 8¼ fl oz / **Chef Boy-ar-dee** Soup di Pasta	120
Mediterranean, canned: ½ can / **Campbell's** Chunky 19-oz can	160
Soup for dip, mix: 8 oz / **Lipton**	45

CALORIES

Spanish style, canned: 8 fl oz / **Campbell's**	40
Spring, mix: 6 fl oz / **Lipton** Cup-A-Soup	40
Vegetarian, canned: 8 fl oz / **Campbell's**	70
Vegetarian, canned: 9½ fl oz / **Hain** Naturals	180
Vegetarian, canned: 9½ fl oz / **Hain** Naturals No Salt	160
Vichyssoise, cream of, canned: ½ can / **Crosse & Blackwell**	70
Won ton, canned: 8 fl oz / **Campbell's**	40

Spaghetti and Spaghetti Dishes

CALORIES

Spaghetti, plain, enriched, cooked firm, "al dente": 1 cup	192
Spaghetti, plain, enriched, cooked, tender stage: 1 cup	155
Spaghetti, in tomato sauce, canned	
Franco-American UFOs: 7½ oz	180
Franco-American UFOs w meteors: 7½ oz	230
w beef: 7½ oz / **Chef Boy-ar-dee** Spaghetti 'n Beef 15-oz can	220
w beef: 7-oz can / **Ezo**	210
w beef: 7-oz can / **Ezo** Spaghetti 'N Beef	220
w cheese: 7½ oz / **Chef Boy-ar-dee** 15-oz can	150
w cheese: 8 oz / **Chef Boy-ar-dee** 40-oz can	150
w cheese: 7⅜ oz / **Franco-American**	180
w cheese: 7½ oz / **Franco-American** SpaghettiOs	170
w cheese: 7¾ oz / **Heinz**	160
w frankfurters: 7⅜ oz / **Franco-American** SpaghettiOs	220
w meat sauce: 7½ oz / **Franco-American**	210

CALORIES

w meat sauce: 7½ oz / **Heinz**	170
w meatballs: 7½ oz / **Chef Boy-ar-dee** 15-oz can	240
w meatballs: 8 oz / **Chef Boy-ar-dee** 40-oz can	220
w meatballs: 8½ oz / **Chef Boy-ar-dee** Spaghetti & Meatballs 25½-oz can	260
w meatballs: 8 oz / **Dia-Mel**	220
w meatballs: 7-oz can / **Enzo**	200
w meatballs: 7⅜ oz / **Franco-American**	220
w meatballs: 7⅜ oz / **Franco-American** SpaghettiOs	210
w meatballs: 7½ oz / **Lido Club** Spaghetti Rings & Little Meat Balls	220
Spaghetti w sauce, frozen	
Banquet Casserole: 8 oz	270
Light and Elegant: 10¼ oz	290
Morton Casserole: 8 oz	220
Stouffer's: 14 oz	445
Stouffer's Lean Cuisine: 11½ oz	280
w breaded veal: 8¼ oz / **Swanson** Entrée	270
Spaghetti and sauce, mixes	
Chef Boy-ar-dee Dinner w meat sauce (19½ oz): ¼ pkg	240
Chef Boy-ar-dee Dinner w meat sauce (26 oz): ⅛ pkg	270
Chef Boy-ar-dee Spaghetti and Meatball Dinner (21¼ oz): ¼ pkg	310
Chef Boy-ar-dee Dinner w mushroom sauce: (19½ oz): ¼ pkg	210
Hamburger Helper: ⅕ pkg	330
Kraft Dinner: ¾ cup prepared	250
Kraft Dinner, American Style: 1 cup prepared	270
Kraft Tangy Italian Style: 1 cup prepared	270

Spices

	CALORIES
1 teaspoon	
Allspice	5
Anise seed	7
Basil, ground	4
Bay leaf	2
Caraway seed	7
Cardamom, ground	6
Celery seed	8
Chervil, dried	2
Chili powder	8
Cinnamon, ground	6
Cloves, ground	7
Coriander leaf, dried	2
Coriander seed	5
Cumin seed	5
Curry powder	7
Dill seed	7
Dill weed	3
Fennel seed	7
Fenugreek seed	12
Garlic powder	9
Ginger, ground	6
Mace, ground	8
Marjoram, dried	2
Mustard seed	15
Nutmeg, ground	12
Onion powder	7
Oregano, ground	5
Paprika	6
Parsley, dried	1
Pepper, black	5
Pepper, red or cayenne	6
Pepper, white	7
Poppy seed	15

CALORIES

Rosemary, dried	4
Saffron	2
Sage, ground	2
Savory, ground	4
Sesame seeds	16
Tarragon, ground	5
Thyme, ground	4
Turmeric, ground	8

Spreads

CALORIES

1 oz = about ¼ cup

Chicken, canned: 1 oz / **Swanson**	60
Chicken, canned: ½ can (2.4 oz) / **Underwood** Chunky	150
Chicken salad, canned: ¼ can / **Carnation** Spreadables	120
Corned beef, canned: ½ can (2¼ oz) / **Underwood**	120
Ham, deviled, canned: 1½ oz / **Libby's**	130
Ham, deviled, canned: ½ can (2¼ oz) / **Underwood**	220
Ham salad, canned: ¼ can / **Carnation** Spreadables	110
Liverwurst, canned: ½ can (2.4 oz) / **Underwood**	220
Pâté, liver, canned: ½ can (2.4 oz) / **Underwood** Sell's	220
Peanut butter: 1 tbsp unless noted	
Bama Creamy	100
Bama Crunchy	100
Country Pure Chunky: about 1 oz / **Safeway**	190
Country Pure Creamy: about 1 oz / **Safeway**	190
Dia-Mel	100
Jif Creamy	95
Jif Crunchy	95
Laura Scudder's Homogenized	99
Laura Scudder's Old Fashioned	101
NuMade Chunky: about 1 oz	190
NuMade Creamy: about 1 oz	190
Real Roast Chunky / **Safeway**: about 1 oz	190

CALORIES

Real Roast Creamy / **Safeway**: about 1 oz	190
Skippy Creamy	95
Skippy Super Chunk	95
Goober Grape / **Smucker's**	90
Potted meat, canned: 1.83 oz / **Libby's**	100
Roast beef, canned: ½ can (2.4 oz) / **Underwood**	140
Sandwich spread: 1 tbsp unless noted	
Kraft	50
NuMade (whole egg)	60
NuMade (egg yolk)	60
Oscar Mayer: 1 oz	65
Tuna salad, ¼ can (1.9 oz) / **Carnation** Spreadables	100
Turkey salad, canned: ¼ can /	
Carnation Spreadables	110

Sugar and Sweeteners

CALORIES

Honey, strained or extracted: 1 tbsp	64
Honey, strained or extracted: 1 cup	1031
Fructose: 1 tsp	12
Sugar	
Brown, not packed: 1 cup	540
Brown, packed: 1 cup	820
Maple: 1 oz	100
Powdered, unsifted: 1 cup	460
Powdered, unsifted: 1 tbsp	30
White, granulated: 1 cup	770
White, granulated: 1 tbsp	45
White, granulated: 1 tsp	15
Sugar, cinnamon: 1 tsp / **French's**	16
Sugar substitute, granulated	
Equal: 1 pkt	4
Equal: 1 tablet	.5
Weight Watchers: 1 pkt	4
Sweetener, artificial: 6 drops / **Dia-Mel** Sweet 'n It	0

Syrups

	CALORIES
Pancake and waffle	
Aunt Jemima: 1 fl oz	102
Aunt Jemima Lite: 1 fl oz	58
Dia-Mel: 1 tbsp	1
Cary's Lite: 1 tbsp	30
Cary's Low Calorie: 1 tbsp	6
Golden Griddle: 1 tbsp	50
Karo: 1 tbsp	60
Log Cabin, buttered: 1 tbsp	52
Log Cabin Country Kitchen: 1 tbsp	51
Log Cabin Maple-Honey: 1 tbsp	54
Mrs. Butterworth's: 1 tbsp	55
Nutri-Dyne Elwood: ½ oz	3
Corn, dark: 1 tbsp / **Karo**	60
Corn, light: 1 tbsp / **Karo**	60
Fruit: 2 tbsp / **Smucker's**	100
Maple, pure: 1 tbsp	60
Molasses, unsulphured: 1 tbsp / **Grandma's**	60
Sorghum: 1 tbsp	55

Tea

CALORIES

Bags or loose tea prepared

	CALORIES
All flavors, all types (except herbal): 8 fl oz / **Lipton**	2
All flavors, herbal tea: 8 fl oz / **Lipton**	4
Apple Orchard: 5½ fl oz / **Bigelow**	5
Cinnamon Stick: 5½ fl oz / **Bigelow**	1
Constant Comment: 5½ fl oz / **Bigelow**	1
Earl Grey: 5½ fl oz / **Bigelow**	1
Early Riser: 5½ fl oz / **Bigelow**	3
English Teatime: 5½ fl oz / **Bigelow**	1
Feeling Fine: 5½ fl oz / **Bigelow**	1
Fruit and Almond: 5½ fl oz / **Bigelow**	1
I Love Lemon: 5½ fl oz / **Bigelow**	1
Lemon Lift: 5½ fl oz / **Bigelow**	1
Looking Good: 5½ fl oz / **Bigelow**	2
Mint Medley: 5½ fl oz / **Bigelow**	1
Nice over Ice: 5½ fl oz / **Bigelow**	1
Orange Pekoe: 5½ fl oz / **Bigelow**	1
Orange & Spice: 5½ fl oz / **Bigelow**	1
Peppermint Stick: 5½ fl oz / **Bigelow**	1
Plantation Mint: 5½ fl oz / **Bigelow**	1
Sweet Dreams: 5½ fl oz / **Bigelow**	1
Take-a-Break: 5½ fl oz / **Bigelow**	3
Instant w sugar and lemon: 6 fl oz / **Nestea**	70

Thickeners

	CALORIES
Cornstarch: 1 tbsp	
Argo	35
Duryea's	35
Kingsford's	35
Potato starch: 1 oz / **Manischewitz**	100

Toppings

	CALORIES
1 tbsp unless noted	
Blueberry / **Dia-Mel**	0–1
Butterscotch / **Smucker's**	70
Caramel / **Smucker's**	70
Chocolate	
Dia-Mel	6
Hershey's	40
Smucker's	65
Fudge / **Hershey's**	50
Fudge / **Smucker's**	65
Hot caramel / **Smucker's**	75
Hot fudge / **Smucker's**	55
Peanut butter caramel / **Smucker's**	75
Pecans in syrup / **Smucker's**	65
Pineapple / **Smucker's**	65
Strawberry / **Smucker's**	60
Swiss milk chocolate fudge / **Smucker's**	70
Smucker's Magic Shell: 4 tsp	130
Walnuts in syrup / **Smucker's**	65
Whipped	
Nondairy, frozen / **Cool Whip**	14

CALORIES

Nondairy, frozen / **Cool Whip** Extra Creamy	16
Nondairy, frozen / **Dover Farms**	16
Mix, prepared / **Dream Whip**	10
Mix, prepared / **D-Zerta**	8
Mix, prepared / **Estee**	4

V Vegetables

Vegetables

FRESH

	CALORIES
Alfalfa sprouts: 1 cup	10
Amaranth, raw, leaves: 1 lb	163
Amaranth, cooked: ½ cup	14
Artichokes: 1 medium cooked	53
Asparagus	
Raw: 1 lb	118
Raw, cut (1½–2 in), drained: 1 cup	35
Cooked, cut (1½–2 in), drained: 1 cup	22
Spears, cooked: 1 small	8
Spears, cooked: 1 medium	12
Spears, cooked: 1 large	20
Spears, cooked, drained: 1 cup	22
Balsam pear, leafy tips, cooked: ½ cup	10
Balsam pear, pods, cooked: ½ cup	12
Bamboo shoots, raw, ½-in slices: ½ cup	21
Bamboo shoots, cooked: 1 cup	14
Barley, pearled, light: 1 cup	698
Bean curd (tofu): 1 piece (2½ in × 2¾ in × 1 in)	85
Beans	
Great Northern, cooked, drained: 1 cup	212
Lima, immature (green), raw: 1 cup	191
Lima, immature (green), cooked, drained:	
½ cup	104
Lima, dried, cooked, drained: 1 cup	262

CALORIES

Mung, dry, raw: 1 cup	714
Mung, dry, raw: 1 lb	1542
Mung, sprouted seeds, raw: ½ cup	16
Mung, sprouted seeds, cooked, drained: ½ cup	13
Pea (navy) cooked, drained: 1 cup	224
Pinto, dry, raw: 1 cup	663
Pinto or calico or red Mexican, dry, raw: 1 lb	1583
Red, dry, cooked: ½ cup	118
Red, dry, raw: ½ cup	343
Red, kidney, cooked, drained: 1 cup	218
Snap, green, raw, cut: 1 cup	35
Snap, green, cooked, drained: ½ cup	22
Snap, yellow or wax, raw, cut: 1 cup	30
Snap, yellow or wax, cooked, drained: ½ cup	22
White, dry, raw: 1 lb	1542
Beets, common, red, raw, peeled, diced: 1 cup	58
Beets, common, red, peeled, cooked, drained, whole (2-in diam): 2 beets	32
Beets, common, red, peeled, cooked, drained, diced or sliced: ½ cup	27
Beet greens, common, edible leaves and stems, raw: 1 lb	109
Beet greens, common, edible leaves and stems, cooked, drained: ½ cup	20
Broadbeans, raw, immature seeds: 1 lb	476
Broadbeans, raw, mature seed, dry: 1 lb	1533
Broccoli	
Florets, raw: ½ cup	12
Stalks, raw: 1 lb	145
Cooked, drained: 1 small stalk	36
Cooked, drained: 1 medium stalk	47
Cooked, drained: 1 large stalk	73
Cooked, drained, chopped: ½ cup	23
Brussels sprouts, cooked: ½ cup	28
Brussels sprouts, raw: 1 medium	8
Cabbage	
Raw: 1 lb	109
Raw, ground: 1 cup	36
Raw, shredded coarsely or sliced: 1 cup	17
Raw, shredded or chopped: 1 cup	22
Chinese, raw: 1 lb	109

	CALORIES
Chinese, raw, 1-in pieces: 1 cup	11
Red, raw: 1 lb	141
Red, raw, shredded coarsely or sliced: 1 cup	22
Red, raw, shredded finely or chopped: 1 cup	28
Savoy, raw: 1 lb	109
Savoy, raw, shredded coarsely or sliced: 1 cup	17
Spoon, raw, 1-in pieces: 1 cup	11
Spoon, cooked, drained, 1-in pieces: 1 cup	24
Carrots	
Raw: 1 carrot (2⅞ oz)	30
Raw: 1 lb	191
Raw, grated or shredded: 1 cup	46
Raw, strips: 1 oz (6–8 strips)	12
Cooked, drained, diced: 1 cup	45
Cooked, drained, sliced crosswise: 1 cup	48
Cauliflower	
Raw: 1 head (1.9 lb)	232
Raw, flowerbuds, whole: 1 cup	27
Raw, flowerbuds, sliced: 1 cup	23
Raw, flowerbuds, chopped: 1 cup	31
Cooked, drained: 1 cup	28
Celeriac, raw: 4 to 6 roots	40
Celery	
Raw: 1 lb	77
Raw, large outer stalk (8-in long, 1½-in wide): 1 stalk	7
Raw, small inner stalk (5-in long, ¾-in wide): 3 stalks	9
Raw, chopped or diced: 1 cup	20
Cooked, diced: 1 cup	21
Chard, Swiss, raw: 1 lb	113
Chard, Swiss, cooked, drained, leaves: 1 cup	32
Chayote, raw: ½ medium squash	28
Chickpeas or garbanzos, mature seeds, dry, raw: 1 cup	720
Chicory, Witloof, raw: 1 head (5–7-in long)	8
Chicory, Witloof, raw: 1 lb	68
Chicory, Witloof, raw, chopped, ½-in pieces: 1 cup	14
Chives, raw, chopped: 1 tbsp	1
Collards	
Raw, leaves w stems: 1 lb	181

Raw, leaves wo stems: 1 lb	204
Cooked, drained, leaves w stems: 1 cup	42
Cooked, drained, leaves wo stems: 1 cup	63
Corn, sweet, raw, white and yellow, husked: 1 lb	240
Corn, sweet, white and yellow, cooked, drained, kernels only: 1 cup	137
Corn, sweet, white and yellow, cooked, drained, on cob: 1 ear (5 × 1¾ in)	70
Cowpeas (including black eye peas)	
Green, raw: 1 cup	184
Green, cooked, drained: 1 cup	178
Mature, dry, cooked, drained: 1 cup	190
Young pods w seeds, raw: 1 lb	200
Young pods w seeds, cooked, drained: 1 lb	154
Cress, garden, raw, trimmed: 5–8 sprigs	3
Cress, garden, raw, trimmed: ½ lb	72
Cucumbers	
Raw, unpeeled, whole: 1 small	25
Raw, unpeeled, whole: 1 large	45
Raw, unpeeled, sliced: 1 cup	16
Raw, peeled, whole: 1 small	22
Raw, peeled, whole: 1 large	39
Dandelion greens, raw: 1 lb	204
Dandelion greens, cooked, drained: 1 cup	35
Dock or sorrel, raw: ½ lb	45
Eggplant, cooked, drained, diced: 1 cup	38
Endive, raw: 1 lb	91
Endive, raw, small pieces: 1 cup	10
Fennel leaves, raw, trimmed: ½ lb	59
Garlic, cloves, raw: 1 clove	4
Hyacinth-beans, raw, young pods, ½-in pieces: 1 cup	32
Hyacinth-beans, raw, mature, dry: 1 lb	1533
Kale, leaves wo stems, raw: 1 lb	240
Kale, cooked, drained: 1 cup	43
Kohlrabi, raw, diced: 1 cup	41
Kohlrabi, cooked, drained: 1 cup	40
Leeks, raw: 3 leeks (5-in long)	52
Lentils, mature seeds, dry, raw: 1 cup	646
Lentils, mature seeds, cooked, drained: 1 cup	212
Lettuce	
Butternut (Boston types and Bibb): 1 head	23

Butternut (Boston types and Bibb)	
chopped or shredded: 1 cup	8
Cos or romaine: 1 lb	82
Cos or romaine, chopped or shredded: 1 cup	10
Crisphead (including Iceberg):	
1 wedge (¼ head)	18
Crisphead (including Iceberg): 1 head	70
Crisphead (including Iceberg):	
chopped or shredded: 1 cup	7
Looseleaf varieties,	
chopped or shredded: 1 cup	10
Mushrooms: 1 lb	127
Mushrooms, sliced, chopped or diced: 1 cup	20
Mustard greens, raw: 1 lb	141
Mustard greens, cooked, drained: 1 cup	32
Mustard spinach, raw: 1 lb	100
Mustard spinach, cooked, drained: 1 cup	29
New Zealand spinach, raw: 1 lb	86
New Zealand spinach, cooked, drained: 1 cup	23
Okra, slices, cooked, drained: 1 cup	46
Onions	
Raw: 1 lb	172
Raw, chopped: 1 cup	65
Raw, chopped or minced: 1 tbsp	4
Raw, sliced: 1 cup	44
Cooked, drained, whole or sliced: 1 cup	61
Young green, 2 medium or 6 small	14
Young green, chopped: 1 tbsp	2
Young green, chopped or sliced: 1 cup	36
Parsley, raw: 10 sprigs (2½-in long)	4
Parsley, raw, chopped: 1 tbsp	2
Parsnips, raw: 1 lb	293
Parsnips, cooked, drained: 1 large	106
Parsnips, cooked, drained, diced: 1 cup	102
Peas	
Green, immature, raw: 1 cup	122
Green, immature, raw: 1 lb	381
Cooked, drained: 1 cup	114
Mature, dry, split, cooked: 1 cup	230
Peppers, chili, green, raw: ½ lb	62
Peppers, chili, red w seeds: ½ lb	203

	CALORIES
Peppers, chili, red, wo seeds: ½ lb	108
Peppers, hot, red, wo seeds, dried: 1 tbsp	50
Peppers, sweet	
Green, raw, whole: 1 small (about 5 per lb)	16
Green, raw, whole: 1 large (about 2¼ per lb)	36
Green, chopped or diced: 1 cup	33
Green, cooked, drained: 1 large	29
Red, raw, whole: 1 small (aout 5 per lb)	23
Red, raw, whole: 1 large (about 2¼ per lb)	51
Red, chopped or diced: 1 cup	47
Pokeberry (poke) shoots, cooked, drained: 1 cup	33
Potatoes	
Baked in skin: 1 potato (2⅓ × 4¾ in)	145
Boiled in skin: 1 potato (2⅓ × 4¾ in)	173
Boiled in skin: 1 potato, round 2½-in diam	104
Boiled in skin, diced or sliced: 1 cup	100
Peeled, boiled: 1 potato (2⅓ × 4¾ in)	146
Peeled, boiled: 1 potato, round, 2½-in diam	88
Peeled, boiled, diced or sliced: 1 cup	100
French fried: 10 strips, 2–3½-in long	137
Fried from raw: 1 cup	455
Mashed w milk and butter or margarine: 1 cup	195
Pumpkin, pulp: 8 oz	40
Purslane leaves and stems, raw: ½ lb	48
Radishes, raw, whole: 10 medium	8
Radishes, raw, whole: 10 large	14
Radishes, raw, sliced: 1 cup	20
Rutabagas, cooked, drained, cubed or sliced: 1 cup	60
Shallot bulbs, raw, chopped: 1 tbsp	7
Soybeans	
Mature seeds, dry, cooked: 1 cup	235
Sprouted seeds, raw: 1 cup	48
Sprouted seeds, cooked, drained: 1 cup	48
Spinach, raw: 1 lb	118
Spinach, raw, chopped: 1 cup	40
Spinach, leaves, cooked, drained: 1 cup	40
Squash	
Acorn, baked: ½ squash	97
Acorn, baked, mashed: 1 cup	115
Butternut, baked, mashed: 1 cup	140
Butternut, boiled, mashed: 1 cup	100

Crookneck and straightneck, yellow, raw, sliced: 1 cup	25
Crookneck and straightneck, yellow, cooked, sliced: 1 cup	27
Crookneck and straightneck, yellow, cooked, mashed: 1 cup	35
Hubbard, baked, mashed: 1 cup	105
Hubbard, boiled, mashed: 1 cup	75
Hubbard, boiled, diced: 1 cup	70
Scallop varieties, white and pale green, raw, sliced: 1 cup	25
Scallop varieties, white and pale green, raw: 1 lb	95
Summer, all varieties, cooked, sliced: 1 cup	25
Summer, all varieties, cooked, cubed, or diced: 1 cup	30
Summer, all varieties, cooked, mashed: 1 cup	130
Winter, all varieties, cooked, baked, mashed: 1 cup	130
Winter, all varieties, cooked, boiled, mashed: 1 cup	95
Zucchini and Cocozelle, green, raw, sliced: 1 cup	95
Zucchini and Cocozelle, green, raw: 1 lb	75
Zucchini and Cocozelle, green, cooked, sliced: 1 cup	20
Zucchini and Cocozelle, green, cooked, mashed: 1 cup	30
Sweet potatoes, baked in skin: 1 potato (5 × 2 in)	160
Sweet potatoes, boiled in skin: 1 potato (5 × 2 in)	170
Sweet potatoes, mashed: 1 cup	290
Tofu (bean curd): 1 piece (2½ × 2¾ × 1 in)	85
Tomatoes, raw: 1 small (3½ oz)	20
Tomatoes, raw: 1 large (4¾ oz)	27
Tomatoes, boiled: 1 cup	63
Turnips, raw: 1 cup	40
Turnips, cooked, drained, cubed: 1 cup	35
Turnips, cooked, mashed: 1 cup	53
Turnip greens, raw: 1 lb	125
Turnip greens, cooked, drained: 1 cup	30
Water chestnuts, peeled: 4 chestnuts	20

CALORIES

Watercress, raw, whole: 1 cup	7
Watercress, raw, finely chopped: 1 cup	24

CANNED AND FROZEN

½ cup unless noted; 3.3 ounces is usually about ½ cup.

Artichoke hearts, frozen: 3 oz (5 or 6 hearts) / **Birds Eye Deluxe**	30
Asparagus, canned	
Cut / **Green Giant**	20
Spears and tips / **Del Monte**	20
Spears / **Le Sueur**	30
Tipped / **Del Monte**	20
Asparagus, frozen	
Cut: 3.3 oz / **Bel-Air**	25
Cut: 3.3 oz / **Birds Eye**	25
Cut, in butter sauce / **Green Giant**	70
Spears: 3.3 oz / **Bel-Air**	25
Spears: 3.3 oz / **Birds Eye**	25
Beans, baked, canned, pea: 8 oz / **B & M**	330
Beans, baked, canned, red kidney: 8 oz / **B & M**	330
Beans, baked, canned, yellow eye: 8 oz / **B & M**	330
Beans, baked style, canned: ½ cup unless noted	
Campbell's Home Style: 8 oz	270
Campbell's Old Fashioned: 8 oz	270
Howard Johnson's: 1 cup	340
Van Camp: 8 oz	260
Van Camp Brown Sugar: 8 oz	290
w frankfurters: 8 oz / **Van Camp** Beanee Weenee	300
w frankfurters: 8 oz / **Van Camp** Chilee Weenee	290
w frankfurters: 7¾ oz / **Heinz** Beans 'n' Franks	330
w pork: 8 oz / **Campbell's**	250
w pork: 8 oz / **Heinz**	250
w pork: 4 oz / **Hunt's**	140
w pork: 8 oz / **Van Camp**	220
w pork and molasses / **Libby's**	140
w pork and molasses / **Seneca**	140
w pork and tomato sauce / **A & P**	150

CALORIES

w pork and tomato sauce / **Libby's**	140
w pork and tomato sauce / **Seneca**	140
Vegetarian / **A & P**	130
Vegetarian: 8 oz / **Heinz**	230
Vegetarian / **Libby's**	130
Vegetarian / **Seneca**	130
Vegetarian: 8 oz / **Van Camp**	210
Beans, barbecue: 7⅞ oz / **Campbell's**	250
Beans, black turtle, canned: 8 oz / **Progresso**	205
Beans, cannellini (white kidney), canned: 8 oz / **Progresso**	180
Beans, fava, canned: 8 oz / **Progresso**	180
Beans, great northern, canned, w pork: 7¼ oz / **Luck's** 29 oz	220
Beans, great northern, canned, w pork: 7½ oz / **Luck's** 15 oz	230
Beans, great northern, canned, w pork: 7 oz / **Luck's** 7 oz	220
Beans, green, canned: ½ cup unless noted	
Cut / **A & P** Regular or No Salt	20
Cut / **Del Monte** Regular or No Salt	20
Cut / **Green Giant**	20
Cut / **Libby's** Regular or No Salt	20
Cut / **Seneca** Regular or No Salt	20
Cut, w pork: 8 oz / **Luck's**	200
French style / **A & P** Regular or No Salt	20
French style / **Del Monte** Regular or No Salt	20
French style / **Libby's** Regular or No Salt	20
French style / **Seneca** Regular or No Salt	20
French style, cut / **Green Giant**	18
French style, seasoned / **Del Monte**	20
Italian, cut / **Del Monte**	25
Kitchen cut / **Green Giant**	20
Whole / **A & P**	20
Whole / **Del Monte**	20
Whole / **Libby's** Regular or No Salt	20
Whole / **Seneca** Regular or No Salt	20
Beans, green, frozen	
Cut: 3 oz / **A & P**	25
Cut: 3 oz / **Bel-Air**	25
Cut: 3 oz / **Birds Eye**	25

CALORIES

Cut / **Green Giant**	20
Cut / **Green Giant** Harvest Fresh	25
French style: 3 oz / **A & P**	25
French style: 3 oz / **Bel-Air**	25
French style: 3 oz / **Birds Eye**	25
French style: about 3½ oz / **Health Valley**	30
French style, in butter sauce / **Green Giant**	40
French style, w toasted almonds: 3 oz / **Birds Eye**	50
Italian: 3 oz / **Bel-Air**	30
Italian: 3 oz / **Birds Eye**	30
Whole: 3 oz / **Bel-Air**	25
Whole: 3 oz / **Birds Eye** Deluxe	25
in cream sauce w mushrooms: ½ cup / **Green Giant**	80
w corn, carrots, and pearl onions: 3.2 oz / **Birds Eye** Farm Fresh	45
w cauliflower and carrots: 3.2 oz / **Birds Eye** Farm Fresh	25
Mushroom casserole: 4¾ oz / **Stouffer's**	150
Beans, kidney, red, canned	
A & P: ½ cup	110
Hunt's: 4 oz	120
Luck's Special Cook: 7½ oz	190
Progresso: 8 oz	190
Van Camp: 8 oz	180
Light: 8 oz / **Van Camp**	180
Seasoned w pork: 7½ oz / **Luck's**	220
Beans, kidney, New Orleans style, canned: 8 oz / **Van Camp**	180
Beans, lima, canned: ½ cup unless noted	
A & P	80
Del Monte	70
Libby's Regular or No Salt	80
Seneca Regular or No Salt	80
w ham: 7½ oz / **Dennison's**	250
Giant, seasoned w pork: 7½ oz / **Luck's** 15-oz can	230
Giant, seasoned w pork: 7 oz / **Luck's** 7-oz can	230

Small, seasoned w pork / **Luck's**: 7½ oz	220
Beans, lima, frozen	
Green Giant: ½ cup	100
Green Giant Harvest Fresh: ½ cup	100
Baby: 3.3 oz / **A & P**	130
Baby: 3.3 oz / **Bel-Air**	130
Baby: 3½ oz / **Health Valley**	120
Fordhook: 3.3 oz / **A & P**	100
Fordhook: 3.3 oz / **Bel-Air**	100
Fordhook: 3.3 oz / **Birds Eye**	100
Tiny: 3.3 oz / **Birds Eye** Deluxe	110
In butter sauce: ½ cup / **Green Giant**	120
Beans, navy, canned, seasoned w pork: 7½ oz / **Luck's**	230
Beans, October, canned, seasoned w pork: 7¼ oz / **Luck's** 29 oz can	230
Beans, October, canned, seasoned w pork: 7½ oz / **Luck's** 15 oz can	220
Beans, pinto, canned	
Progresso: 8 oz	165
Seasoned w pork: 7¼ oz / **Luck's** 29-oz can	220
Seasoned w pork: 7½ oz / **Luck's** 15-oz can	220
Seasoned w pork: 7 oz / **Luck's** 7-oz can	220
w onions, seasoned w pork: 7½ oz / **Luck's**	230
and great northern, seasoned w pork: 7¼ oz / **Luck's** 29 oz can	200
and great northern, seasoned w pork: 7½ oz / **Luck's** 15 oz can	220
Beans, red, canned: ½ cup / **A & P**	120
Beans, red, canned: 8 oz / **Van Camp**	190
Beans, Roman, canned: 8 oz / **Progresso**	210
Beans, wax, canned: ½ cup	
Cut / **A & P**	20
Cut / **Del Monte**	20
Cut / **Libby's** Regular or No Salt	20
Cut / **Seneca** Regular or No Salt	20
French / **Del Monte**	20
Beans, western style, canned: 8 oz / **Van Camp**	210
Beans, yelloweye, canned, seasoned w pork: 7½ oz / **Luck's**	220

Bean salad, canned: ½ cup /
  Green Giant Three Bean   80
Beets, canned: ½ cup
  Cut / **Libby's** Regular or No Salt   35
  Cut / **Seneca** Regular or No Salt   35
  Diced / **Libby's** Regular or No Salt   35
  Diced / **Seneca** Regular or No Salt   35
  Harvard / **Libby's** Regular or No Salt   80
  Harvard / **Seneca** Regular or No Salt   80
  Pickled, crinkle sliced / **Del Monte**   80
  Pickled, sliced / **Libby's** Regular or No Salt   80
  Pickled, sliced / **Seneca** Regular or No Salt   80
  Pickled, sliced, w onions /
    Libby's Regular or No Salt   80
  Pickled, sliced, w onions /
    Seneca Regular or No Salt   80
  Pickled, whole / **Libby's** Regular or No Salt   80
  Pickled, whole / **Seneca** Regular or No Salt   80
  Shoestring / **Libby's** Regular or No Salt   25
  Shoestring / **Seneca** Regular or No Salt   25
  Sliced / **A & P**   40
  Sliced / **A & P** No Salt   35
  Sliced / **Del Monte** Regular or No Salt   35
  Sliced / **Libby's** Regular or No Salt   35
  Sliced / **Seneca** Regular or No Salt   35
  Whole / **A & P**   40
  Whole / **Del Monte**   35
  Whole / **Libby's** Regular or No Salt   35
  Whole / **Seneca** Regular or No Salt   35
Broccoli, frozen: ½ cup unless noted
  Baby spears: 3.3 oz / **Birds Eye** Deluxe   30
  Chopped: 3.3 oz / **A & P**   25
  Chopped: 3.3 oz / **Bel-Air**   25
  Chopped: 3.3 oz / **Birds Eye**   25
  Cut: 3.3 oz / **A & P**   25
  Cut: 3.3 oz / **Bel-Air**   25
  Cut: 3.3 oz / **Birds Eye**   25
  Cut / **Green Giant**   16
  Cut / **Green Giant** Harvest Fresh   30
  Florets: 3.3 oz / **Birds Eye** Deluxe   25
  Mini-spears / **Green Giant** Frozen Like Fresh   16

Spears: 3.3 oz / **A & P**	25
Spears: 3.3 oz / **Bel-Air**	25
Spears, cut: 3.3 oz / **Bel-Air**	25
Spears: 3.3 oz / **Birds Eye**	25
Spears / **Green Giant** Harvest Fresh	30
Spears: 3½ oz / **Health Valley**	30
w almonds: 3.3 oz / **Birds Eye**	50
In butter sauce / **Green Giant**	40
w carrots / **Green Giant** Fanfare	25
w carrots and pasta twists: 3.3 oz / **Birds Eye** Blue Ribbon	90
w carrots and water chestnuts: 3.2 oz / **Birds Eye** Farm Fresh	30
w cauliflower / **Green Giant** Medley	60
w cauliflower / **Green Giant** Supreme	20
w cauliflower: 3.2 oz / **Kohl's** Blend	25
w cauliflower and carrots: 3.2 oz / **Birds Eye** Farm Fresh	25
w cauliflower and carrots in cheese sauce: 5 oz / **Birds Eye**	100
w cauliflower and carrots in cheese sauce / **Green Giant**	60
w cauliflower and red peppers: 3.3 oz / **Birds Eye** Deluxe	25
w cheese sauce: 5 oz / **Birds Eye**	120
w cheese sauce / **Green Giant**	70
w cheese sauce (white cheddar) / **Green Giant**	70
w cheese sauce: 4½ oz / **Stouffer's**	130
w corn and red peppers: 3.2 oz / **Birds Eye** Farm Fresh	50
w green beans, pearl onions, and red peppers: 3.2 oz / **Birds Eye** Farm Fresh	25
w water chestnuts: 3.3 oz / **Birds Eye**	30
Brussels sprouts, frozen: ½ cup unless noted	
A & P: 3.3 oz	35
Bel-Air: 3.3 oz	35
Birds Eye: 3.3 oz	35
Green Giant	30
Baby: 3.3 oz / **Birds Eye**	40
In butter sauce / **Green Giant**	60

w cauliflower and carrots: 3.2 oz / **Birds Eye** Farm Fresh	30
w cheese sauce: 4½ oz / **Birds Eye**	120
w cheese sauce / **Green Giant**	80
Butterbeans, canned / **A & P**	110
Butterbeans, canned: 7½ oz / **Luck's**	230
Butterbeans, canned: 8 oz / **Van Camp**	160
Carrots, canned	
Diced / **Del Monte**	30
Diced / **Libby's** Regular or No Salt	20
Diced / **Seneca** Regular or No Salt	20
Sliced / **A & P**	30
Sliced / **A & P** No Salt	25
Sliced / **Del Monte**	30
Sliced / **Libby's** Regular or No Salt	20
Sliced / **Seneca** Regular or No Salt	20
Whole / **Del Monte**	30
Carrots, frozen	
A & P: 3.3 oz	40
Bel-Air: 3.3 oz	40
Birds Eye Deluxe: 3.3 oz	40
Baby, w sweet peas and pearl onions: 3.3 oz / **Birds Eye** Deluxe	50
Crinkle cut, in butter sauce: ½ cup / **Green Giant**	80
Cauliflower, frozen	
A & P: 3.3 oz	25
Bel-Air: 3.3 oz	25
Birds Eye: 3.3 oz	25
Green Giant	16
Kohl's: 3 oz	20
w almonds: 3.3 oz / **Birds Eye**	40
w carrots / **Green Giant** Bonanza	60
w cheese sauce: 5 oz / **Birds Eye**	120
w cheese sauce / **Green Giant**	60
w cheese sauce (white cheddar) / **Green Giant**	70
w green beans / **Green Giant** Festival	16
w green beans and corn: 3.2 oz / **Birds Eye** Farm Fresh	35
Chick peas (garbanzos), canned / **A & P**	100
Chick peas (garbanzos), canned: 8 oz / **Progresso**	200

Collard greens, canned, seasoned w pork:

7½ oz / **Luck's**	100
Collard greens, frozen: 3.3 oz / **Bel-Air**	25

Corn, golden, canned: ½ cup

Cream style / **A & P**	100
Cream style / **Del Monte**	80
Cream style / **Del Monte** No Salt	80
Cream style / **Green Giant**	100
Cream style / **Libby's** Regular or No Salt	80
Cream style / **Seneca** Regular or No Salt	80
Shoepeg / **Green Giant**	90
Whole kernel / **A & P**	80
Whole kernel / **A & P** No Salt	80
Whole kernel / **A & P** Vacuum-Packed	100
Whole kernel / **Del Monte**	70
Whole kernel / **Del Monte** No Salt	80
Whole kernel / **Del Monte** Vacuum-Packed	90
Whole kernel / **Del Monte** Vacuum-Packed No Salt	90
Whole kernel / **Green Giant** Vacuum-Packed	90
Whole kernel / **Le Sueur**	80
w peppers / **Mexicorn**	80

Corn, golden, frozen: ½ cup unless noted

On cob: 1 ear / **A & P**	120
On cob: 2 ears / **A & P** Cob Treats	130
On cob: 1 ear / **Bel-Air**	120
On cob: 2 ears / **Bel-Air** Short Ears	130
On cob: 1 ear / **Birds Eye**	120
On cob: 1 ear / **Birds Eye** Big Ears	160
On cob: 2 ears / **Birds Eye** Little Ears	130
On cob: 1 ear / **Green Giant** Nibblers	80
On cob: 1 ear / **Green Giant** Niblet Ears	140
On cob: 4½ oz / **Ore-Ida**	150
Whole kernel: 3.3 oz / **A & P**	80
Whole kernel: 3.3 oz / **Bel-Air**	80
Whole kernel: 3.3 oz / **Birds Eye**	80
Whole kernel, sweet: 3.3 oz / **Birds Eye** Deluxe	80
Whole kernel / **Green Giant** Harvest Fresh Niblets	100
w broccoli / **Green Giant** Bounty	60

CALORIES

w butter sauce / **Green Giant** Niblets	100
Cream style / **Green Giant**	120
w cream sauce / **Green Giant** Niblets	130
w green beans and pasta curls: 3.3 oz / **Birds Eye**	110
w white corn / **Green Giant** Niblets and White Corn	80
Corn, white: ½ cup	
Cream style, canned / **Del Monte**	90
Whole kernel, canned / **Del Monte**	70
Whole kernel, canned / **Green Giant** Vacuum-Packed	90
Whole kernel, canned / **Libby's** Regular or No Salt	80
Whole kernel, canned / **Seneca** Regular or No Salt	80
In butter sauce, frozen / **Green Giant**	100
Eggplant parmigiana, frozen: 11 oz / **Mrs. Paul's**	540
Eggplant sticks, fried, frozen: 3½ oz / **Mrs. Paul's**	240
Green peppers, frozen, diced: 1 oz / **Bel-Air**	6
Green peppers, frozen, stuffed: ½ pkg / **Green Giant**	200
Hominy, golden, canned: 8 oz / **Van Camp**	120
Hominy, golden, canned, w red and green peppers: 8 oz / **Van Camp**	120
Hominy, white, canned: 8 oz / **Van Camp**	125
Kale, frozen, cut leaf: 3.3 oz / **Bel-Air**	25
Mixed, canned: ½ cup	
A & P (Eastern label)	45
A & P (Western label)	40
A & P No Salt	40
Del Monte	40
Libby's Regular or No Salt	40
P & Q Chunky	40
Seneca Regular or No Salt	40
Mixed, frozen: ½ cup unless noted	
A & P: 3.3 oz	65
A & P California Blend: 3.3 oz	25
Bel-Air: 3.3 oz	65
Bel-Air Rancho Fiesta Style: 3.3 oz	70
Birds Eye: 3.3 oz	60

Green Giant	50
Green Giant Harvest Fresh	60
Health Valley: 3½ oz	300
Bavarian style beans and spaetzle /	
Birds Eye: 3.3 oz	110
w butter sauce / **Green Giant**	80
Chinese style: 3.3 oz / **Birds Eye**	80
Chinese style: 3.3 oz / **Birds Eye** Stir-Fry	30
Chinese style / **Green Giant**	60
Far Eastern style: 3.3 oz / **Birds Eye**	80
Italian blend: 3.3 oz / **A & P**	40
Italian style: 3.3 oz / **Birds Eye**	110
Japanese style: 3.3 oz / **Birds Eye**	100
Japanese style: 3.3 oz / **Birds Eye** Stir-Fry	30
Japanese style / **Green Giant**	45
Mexicana style: 3.3 oz / **Birds Eye**	120
New England style: 3.3 oz / **Birds Eye**	130
w onion sauce: 2.6 oz / **Birds Eye**	100
Oriental blend: 3.3 oz / **A & P**	25
San Francisco style: 3.3 oz / **Birds Eye**	100
Winter blend: 3.3 oz / **A & P**	24
Mushrooms, canned	
B in B: 2 oz	25
Green Giant: 2 oz	14
Libby's Regular or No Salt: ¼ cup	35
Seneca Regular or No Salt: ¼ cup	35
In butter sauce: 2 oz / **Green Giant**	30
Mushrooms, frozen, in butter sauce: ½ cup /	
Green Giant	70
Mustard greens, canned / **Town House:** 1 cup	40
Mustard greens, frozen, chopped: 3.3 oz / **Bel-Air**	20
Okra, frozen	
Cut: 3.3 oz / **Bel-Air**	25
Cut: 3.3 oz / **Birds Eye**	25
Whole: 3.3 oz / **Bel-Air**	30
Whole: 3.3 oz / **Birds Eye**	30
Onions, frozen	
Chopped: 1 oz / **Bel-Air**	8
Chopped: 2 oz / **Ore-Ida**	20
Pearl: 3.3 oz / **Birds Eye** Deluxe	35
Small, whole: 4 oz / **Birds Eye**	40

CALORIES

Small, w cream sauce: 3 oz / **Birds Eye**	110
Onion rings, fried, frozen: 2¼ oz / **Mrs. Paul's**	150
Onion rings, fried, frozen: 2 oz /	
Ore-Ida Onion Ringers	150
Peas, black-eye, canned	
A & P	120
Progresso: 8 oz	165
Seasoned w pork: 7¼ oz / **Luck's** 29-oz can	210
Seasoned w pork: 7½ oz / **Luck's** 15-oz can	200
Seasoned w pork: 7 oz / **Luck's** 7-oz can	200
w corn, seasoned w pork: 7½ oz / **Luck's**	220
Peas, black-eye, frozen: 3.3 oz / **Bel-Air**	130
Peas, Crowder, canned, seasoned w pork:	
7½ oz / **Luck's**	200
Peas, field, canned, w snaps, seasoned w pork:	
7½ oz / **Luck's**	200
Peas, green, canned: ½ cup unless noted	
A & P	70
A & P No Salt	60
Del Monte	60
Del Monte No Salt	60
Del Monte Small	50
Green Giant	60
Le Sueur	60
Le Sueur Mini	60
Libby's Regular or No Salt	60
Seneca Regular or No Salt	60
Seasoned / **Del Monte**	60
w carrots / **Del Monte**	50
w carrots / **Kohl's**	50
w carrots / **Libby's** Regular or No Salt	50
w carrots / **Seneca** Regular or No Salt	50
w onions / **Green Giant**	60
w snaps, seasoned w pork: 7½ oz / **Luck's**	200
Peas, green, frozen: ½ cup unless noted	
A & P: 3.3 oz	80
Bel-Air: 3.3 oz	80
Birds Eye: 3.3 oz	80
Birds Eye Deluxe Tiny: 3.3 oz	60
Green Giant	60
Green Giant Harvest Fresh	80

CALORIES

Health Valley: 3½ oz	330
In butter sauce / **Green Giant**	90
w carrots: 3.3 oz / **A & P**	60
w carrots: 3.3 oz / **Bel-Air**	60
w carrots and pearl onions: 3.2 oz / **Birds Eye** Farm Fresh	60
w cream sauce: 2.6 oz / **Birds Eye**	130
w cream sauce / **Green Giant**	100
w cauliflower / **Green Giant** Medley	40
w onions: 3.3 oz / **Birds Eye**	70
w onions and carrots, in butter sauce / **Le Sueur**	90
w onions and cheese sauce: 5 oz / **Birds Eye**	140
w pea pods and water chestnuts in butter sauce / **Green Giant**	80
w potatoes, in cream sauce: 2.6 oz / **Birds Eye**	140
Potatoes, canned: ½ cup	
A & P	45
Del Monte	45
Libby's	45
Seneca	45
Potatoes, frozen	
Au gratin: 3¹³⁄₁₆ oz / **Stouffer's**	135
French-fried: 3½ oz / **A & P**	140
French-fried: 3½ oz / **A & P** Crinkle Cut	140
French-fried: 3½ oz / **A & P** Potato Morsels	140
French-fried: 3½ oz / **A & P** Shoestrings	170
French-fried: 3 oz / **Bel-Air** Crinkle Cut	120
French-fried: 3 oz / **Bel-Air** Shoestrings	140
French-fried: 2.8 oz / **Birds Eye** Cottage Fries	120
French-fried: 3 oz / **Birds Eye** Crinkle Cuts	110
French-fried: 3 oz / **Birds Eye** French Fries	110
French-fried: 3.3 oz / **Birds Eye** Shoestrings	140
French-fried: 2½ oz / **Birds Eye** TastiFries	140
French-fried: 3 oz / **Ore-Ida** Cottage Fries	140
French-fried: 3 oz / **Ore-Ida** Country Style Dinner Fries	120
French-fried: 3 oz / **Ore-Ida** Crispers	240
French-fried: 3 oz / **Ore-Ida** Crispy Crowns	150
French-fried: 3 oz / **Ore-Ida** Golden Crinkles	120

CALORIES

French-fried: 3 oz / **Ore-Ida** Golden Fries	130
French-fried: 3 oz / **Ore-Ida** Pixie Crinkles	160
French-fried: 3 oz / **Ore-Ida** Shoestrings	160
Fried: 3½ oz / **A & P** Steak Fries	140
Fried: 2 oz / **Bel-Air** Patties	100
Fried: 3 oz / **Birds Eye** Steak Fries	110
Fried: 3.2 oz / **Birds Eye** Tiny Taters	200
Fried: 2½ oz / **Ore-Ida** Golden Patties	130
Fried: 3 oz / **Ore-Ida** Tater Tots	160
Fried, w bacon flavor: 3 oz / **Ore-Ida** Tater Tots	160
Fried, w onions: 3 oz / **Ore-Ida** Tater Tots	160
Hash browns: 3½ oz / **A & P**	80
Hash browns: 4 oz / **Bel-Air**	80
Hash browns: 4 oz / **Birds Eye**	70
Hash browns: 3 oz / **Birds Eye** Shredded	60
Hash browns: 6 oz / **Ore-Ida** Shredded	130
Hash browns: 3 oz / **Ore-Ida** Southern Style	70
O'Brien: 3 oz / **Ore-Ida**	80
w onions: 3 oz / **Ore-Ida** Crispy Crowns	170
Puffs: 2½ oz / **Birds Eye** TastiPuffs	190
Scalloped: 4 oz / **Stouffer's**	125
Stuffed: 1 potato / **Larry's** Deluxe	200
Stuffed, w cheese topping: 5 oz / **Green Giant**	200
Stuffed, w cheese: 1 potato / **Larry's** Deluxe	190
Stuffed, w chives: 1 potato / **Larry's** Deluxe	190
Stuffed, w sour cream and chives: 5 oz / **Green Giant**	230
w peas in bacon cream sauce: ½ cup / **Green Giant**	110
Sliced: 3 oz / **Bel-Air**	120
Sliced: 3 oz / **Ore-Ida** Home Style	110
Sliced: 3 oz / **Ore-Ida** Home Style Potato Planks	110
Sliced: 3 oz / **Ore-Ida** Potato Thins	130
Sliced, in butter sauce: ½ cup / **Green Giant**	80
Wedges: 3 oz / **Birds Eye** Farm Style	110
Wedges: 3 oz / **Ore-Ida** Home Style	100
Whole, peeled: 3.2 oz / **Birds Eye**	60
Whole, peeled: 3 oz / **Ore-Ida**	80

Potatoes, mix, prepared: ½ cup unless noted

Au gratin / **Betty Crocker**	150
Au gratin / **French's** Tangy	150
Au gratin: ¾ cup / **Libby's** Potato Classics	130
Chicken 'n herb / **Betty Crocker**	120
Creamed, oven / **Betty Crocker**	170
Creamed, saucepan / **Betty Crocker**	180
Hash browns w onions / **Betty Crocker**	150
Hickory smoke cheese / **Betty Crocker**	150
Julienne / **Betty Crocker**	130
Mashed / **Betty Crocker** Potato Buds	130
Mashed / **French's** Big Tate	140
Mashed / **French's** Idaho	120
Mashed / **Hungry Jack**	140
Mashed / **Idaho** Naturally	128
Mashed / **Mr. Spud**	128
Mashed: 4 oz / **Town House**	60
Scalloped / **Betty Crocker**	140
Scalloped / **French's** Crispy Top	160
Scalloped: ¾ cup / **Libby's** Potato Classics	130
Scalloped, cheese / **French's**	160
Sour cream and chives / **French's**	170
Potatoes, sweet, canned, in syrup: ½ cup / **Kohl's**	110
Pumpkin, canned: ½ cup / **Del Monte**	35
Pumpkin, canned: 1 cup / **Libby's** Solid Pack	80
Ratatouille, frozen: 5 oz / **Stouffer's**	60
Salad greens, canned, seasoned w pork: 7½ oz / **Luck's**	100
Sauerkraut, canned or in jar: ½ cup	
A & P	20
Claussen	17
Del Monte	25
Libby's	20
Seneca	20
Vlasic Old Fashioned: 1 oz	4
Spinach, canned: ½ cup	
A & P	20
Del Monte Regular or No Salt	25
Libby's Regular or No Salt	25
Seneca Regular or No Salt	25
Spinach, frozen	
Chopped: 3.3 oz / **A & P**	20

CALORIES

Chopped: 3.3 oz / **Bel-Air**	20
Chopped: 3.3 oz / **Birds Eye**	20
Chopped: 3½ oz / **Health Valley**	110
Creamed: 3 oz / **Birds Eye**	60
Creamed / **Green Giant**	70
Creamed: 4½ oz / **Stouffer's**	190
Leaf: 3.3 oz / **A & P**	25
Leaf: 3.3 oz / **Bel-Air**	20
Leaf: 3.3 oz / **Birds Eye**	20
Leaf: 3½ oz / **Health Valley**	110
Leaf, in butter sauce: ½ cup / **Green Giant**	50
Mushroom casserole: 7½ oz / **Health Valley**	380
Souffle: 4 oz / **Stouffer's**	135
w water chestnuts: 3.3 oz / **Birds Eye**	25
Squash, cooked, frozen: 4 oz / **Bel-Air**	45
Squash, cooked, frozen: 4 oz / **Birds Eye**	45
Squash, cooked, frozen: 4 oz / **Kohl's**	45
Squash, yellow, sliced, frozen: 3.3 oz / **Bel-Air**	18
Stew vegetables, frozen: 4 oz / **A & P**	60
Stew vegetables, frozen: 3.3 oz / **Kohl's**	50
Stew vegetables, frozen: 3 oz / **Ore-Ida**	60
Succotash, canned: ½ cup / **Libby's** Regular or No Salt	80
Succotash, canned: ½ cup / **Seneca** Regular or No Salt	80
Succotash, frozen: 3.3 oz / **Bel-Air**	100
Tomato paste, canned	
A & P: 6 oz (¾ cup)	150
Contadina: 6 oz	150
Del Monte: ¾ cup	150
Del Monte No Salt: 6 oz	150
Hunt's: 2 oz	45
Hunt's No Salt: 2 oz	45
Town House: ⅔ cup	150
Italian: 2 oz / **Contadina**	70
Italian: 2 oz / **Hunt's**	50
Italian w mushrooms: 2 oz / **Contadina**	60
Tomato puree, canned / **A & P**	60
Tomato puree, canned / **Contadina**	50
Tomato puree, canned: 4 oz / **Hunt's**	45
Tomatoes, canned: ½ cup unless noted	
Baby sliced / **Contadina**	50
Italian style / **Contadina**	25

Kosher: 1 oz / **Claussen**	5
Stewed / **A & P**	35
Stewed / **Contadina**	35
Stewed / **Del Monte**	35
Stewed / **Del Monte** No Salt	35
Stewed: 4 oz / **Hunt's**	35
Stewed: 4 oz / **Hunt's** No Salt	35
Stewed / **Town House**	35
Wedges / **Del Monte**	30
Whole / **A & P**	25
Whole / **Contadina**	25
Whole / **Del Monte**	25
Whole: 4 oz / **Hunt's**	20
Whole: 4 oz / **Hunt's** No Salt	20
Whole / **Town House**	25

Turnip greens, canned, w diced turnips:
7½ oz / **Luck's** — 90
Turnip greens, frozen, chopped: 3.3 oz / **Bel-Air** — 20
Turnip greens, frozen, chopped, w diced turnips:
3.3 oz / **Bel-Air** — 20

Yams
Canned: ½ cup / **Town House**	105
Frozen, candied: 4 oz / **Mrs. Paul's**	181
Frozen, candied, w apples: 4 oz / **Mrs. Paul's**	150
Frozen, w apples: 5 oz / **Stouffer's**	160

Zucchini
Canned, in tomato sauce: ½ cup / **Del Monte**	30
Frozen, baby sliced: 3.3 oz / **Birds Eye** Deluxe	16
Frozen, crinkle cut: 3.3 oz / **Bel-Air**	16
Frozen, sticks, in light batter: 3 oz / **Mrs. Paul's**	180

VEGETABLES IN PASTRY

1 piece

Asparagus w mornay sauce / **Pepperidge Farm** Vegetable in Pastry	250
Broccoli w cheese / **Pepperidge Farm** Vegetable in Pastry	250

CALORIES

Cauliflower and cheese sauce / **Pepperidge Farm** Vegetable in Pastry	220
Green beans w mushroom sauce / **Pepperidge Farm** Vegetable in Pastry	270
Mexican style / **Pepperidge Farm** Vegetable in Pastry	220
Mushrooms Dijon / **Pepperidge Farm** Vegetable in Pastry	230
Oriental Garden / **Pepperidge Farm** Vegetable in Pastry	230
Ratatouille w cheese / **Pepperidge Farm** Vegetable in Pastry	230
Spinach almondine / **Pepperidge Farm** Vegetable in Pastry	260
Zucchini Provencal / **Pepperidge Farm** Vegetable in Pastry	210

Vegetable Juices

CALORIES

6 fl oz unless noted

Tomato	
A & P	30
Campbell's	35
Hunt's	30
Hunt's No Salt	30
Libby's	35
Sunkist: 4 oz in portion cup	24
Town House: 5½ fl oz	35
Welch's	35
Tomato cocktail / **Snap-E-Tom**	40
Vegetable cocktail	
Town House	35
V-8	35
V-8 No Salt	40
V-8 Spicy Hot	35

Wines and Distilled Spirits

4 fl oz unless noted

	CALORIES
Almonetta: 3½ fl oz / **Manischewitz**	125
Aurora / **Great Western**	96
Aurora Blanc / **Great Western**	92
Baco Noir / **Great Western**	96
Barbera / **Sebastiani** Vineyards (1978)	90
Beaujolais, Gamay / **Almaden**	89
Blackberry: 3½ fl oz / **Manischewitz**	175
Bordeaux	
Red / **B&G** Margaux	83
Red / **B&G** Prince Noir	81
Red / **B&G** St. Emilion	84
White / **B&G** Graves	87
White / **B&G** Haut Sauternes	132
White / **B&G** Prince Blanc	83
White / **B&G** Sauternes	127
Burgundy	
Almaden Monterey	86
Almaden Mountain	91
Charles Fournier American	86
Charles Fournier Personal Selection Superieur	84
Great Western	96
Manischewitz: 3½ fl oz	80
Sebastiani Mountain	85
Taylor	92
Red / **B&G** Beaujolais St. Louis	80
Red / **B&G** Nuits St. George	93
Red / **B&G** Pommard	89

CALORIES

Red / **Gallo**	88
Red / **Gallo** Hearty	92
Sparkling / **Great Western**	108
Sparkling / **Henri Marchant** American	104
Sparkling / **Taylor**	100
White / **B&G** Chablis	80
White / **B&G** Pouilly Fuisse	85
White / **B&G** Puligny Montrachet	81
Cabernet Pfeffer / **Almaden**	86
Cabernet Sauvignon	
Almaden	90
Sebastiani Country	90
Sebastiani Vineyards (1980)	95
Sebastiani Vineyards (1981)	92
Wine Cellars of Ernest and Julio Gallo	88
Catawba	
Pink / **Great Western**	144
Pink / **Mountain Lake**	142
Pink / **Taylor**	128
Red / **Mountain Lake**	135
White / **Mountain Lake**	135
Cayuga White / **Great Western**	88
Chablis	
Almaden Monterey	88
Almaden Mountain	85
Charles Fournier American	85
Charles Fournier Personal Selection Superieur	87
Gallo Chablis Blanc	80
Great Western	88
Manischewitz: 3½ fl oz	80
Paul Masson Light: 3.4 fl oz	49
Sebastiani Mountain	88
Taylor	92
Pink / **Gallo**	80
Champagne	
Almaden Blanc de Blancs	92
Almaden Eye of the Partridge	93
Almaden LeDomaine Brut	93
Almaden LeDomaine Extra Dry	105
Almaden Vintage Brut	95
Almaden Vintage Extra Dry	102

Charles Fournier Special Selection American Blanc de Blancs	91
Charles Fournier Special Selection American Blanc de Noirs	91
Gold Seal New York State Brut	92
Gold Seal New York State Extra Dry	102
Gold Seal New York State Naturel	85
Great Western Brut	96
Great Western Extra Dry	100
Great Western Naturel	92
Henri Marchant American Brut	94
Henri Marchant American Extra Dry	104
Henri Marchant American Naturel	85
Mumm's Cordon Rouge Brut	87
Mumm's Extra Dry	109
Pierre Corbeau American Brut	94
Pierre Corbeau American Extra Dry	104
Taylor Brut	96
Taylor Extra Dry	100
Pink / **Gold Seal** New York State	102
Pink / **Great Western**	104
Pink / **Henri Marchant** American	102
Pink / **Taylor**	100
Chardonnay	
Almaden	89
Charles Fournier (1982)	91
Charles Fournier (1981)	92
Sebastiani Country	90
Sebastiani Vineyards (1982)	93
Sebastiani Vineyards (1983)	93
Wine Cellars of Ernest and Julio Gallo	88
Chenin Blanc	
Almaden	92
Sebastiani Country	86
Sebastiani Vineyards (1984)	97
Wine Cellars of Ernest and Julio Gallo	88
Cherry: 3½ fl oz / **Manischewitz**	175
Claret, red / **Almaden** Mountain	89
Cold Duck / **Henri Marchant**	104
Cold Duck / **Taylor**	108
Cold Duck, pink / **Great Western**	112

Colombard, French / **Almaden**	89
Colombard, French / **Sebastiani** Country	86
Colombard, French / **Wine Cellars of Ernest and Julio Gallo**	88
Concord	
Manischewitz: 3½ fl oz	175
Cream red: 3½ fl oz / **Manischewitz**	175
Cream white: 3½ fl oz / **Manischewitz**	125
Medium dry: 3½ fl oz / **Manischewitz**	100
Pink: 3½ fl oz / **Manischewitz**	125
Red / **Gold Seal**	137
DeChaunac / **Great Western**	92
DeChaunac, Rose of / **Great Western**	96
Delaware / **Great Western**	96
Diamond / **Great Western**	92
Dutchess / **Great Western**	88
Elderberry: 3½ fl oz / **Manischewitz**	175
Fumé Blanc / **Almaden**	89
Fumé Blanc / **Sebastiani** Country	90
Gamay Rose / **Sebastiani** Country	95
Gewurztraminer / **Almaden**	90
Gewurztraminer / **Sebastiani** Vineyards (1984)	97
Gewurztraminer / **Wine Cellars of Ernest and Julio Gallo**	88
Green Hungarian / **Sebastiani** Vineyards (1984)	86
Labrusca, red / **Gold Seal**	133
Lake Country	
Chablis / **Taylor**	100
Gold / **Taylor**	108
Pink / **Taylor**	112
Pink, soft / **Taylor**	96
Red / **Taylor**	104
Red, soft / **Taylor**	100
White / **Taylor**	104
White, soft / **Taylor**	88
Loganberry: 3½ fl oz / **Manischewitz**	175
Maison Blanc / **Almaden**	86
Maison Rouge / **Almaden**	85
Moselle / **Julius Kayser's** Graacher Himmelreich	80
Moselle / **Julius Kayser's** Piesporter Reisling	76
Moselle / **Julius Kayser's** Zeller Schwarze Katz	76

CALORIES

Pina Coconetta: 3½ fl oz / **Manischewitz**	125
Pinot Noir / **Almaden**	89
Pinot Noir / **Sebastiani Vineyards** Blanc (1984)	93
Pinot St. George / **Almaden**	90

Port

Almaden Solera	180
Gallo	172
Great Western	172
Taylor	184
Taylor Light	172
Tawny / **Great Western**	188
Tawny / **Taylor**	180
Tawny / **Taylor Light**	168
White / **Gallo**	172

Rhine

Almaden Mountain	103
Charles Fournier American	90
Gallo	80
Great Western	92
Julius Kayser's Liebfraumilch Glockenspiel	76
Julius Kayser's Bereich Nierstein	72
Paul Masson Light: 3.4 fl oz	50
Sebastiani Mountain	87
Taylor	92

Riesling

Almaden California	89
Charles Fournier Personal Selection Dry	67
Charles Fournier Personal Selection Johannisberg (1980 Late Harvest)	104
Sebastiani Vineyards Johannisberg	88
Wine Cellars of Ernest and Julio Gallo Johannisberg	84

Rosé

Almaden Carafe	89
Almaden Gamay	92
Almaden Grenache	90
Almaden Mountain Nectar Vin	104
Charles Fournier American Vin	93
Charles Fournier Personal Selection Superieur	87
Gallo Vin Rosé	88
Great Western	100

CALORIES

Paul Masson Light: 3.4 fl oz	54
Sebastiani Mountain Vin	89
Taylor	100
Wine Cellars of Ernest and Julio Gallo	88
Red / **Gallo**	112
Rose of Isabella / **Great Western**	108
Sangria / **Taylor**	140
Sauterne / **Almaden** Mountain	82
Sauterne / **Charles Fournier** American Dry	94
Sauterne / **Taylor**	104
Sauvignon Blanc / **Almaden**	92
Sauvignon Blanc / **Sebastiani** Vineyards (1982)	93
Sauvignon Blanc /	
Wine Cellars of Ernest and Julio Gallo	80
Seyval Blanc / **Great Western**	88
Sherry	
Gallo	128
Great Western Solera Dry	136
Great Western Solera Regular	156
Taylor Dry	136
Taylor Light Dry	132
Cocktail / **Almaden**	137
Cream / **Almaden**	187
Cream / **Gallo** Livingston Cellars	156
Cream / **Great Western** Solera	188
Cream / **Taylor**	192
Cream / **Taylor** Empire	180
Cream / **Taylor** Light	184
Golden / **Almaden**	159
Golden / **Taylor**	164
Golden / **Taylor** Light	144
Very Dry / **Gallo** Livingston Cellars	120
Strawberry Coconetta: 3½ fl oz / **Manischewitz**	125
Verdelet / **Great Western**	96
Vermouth	
Dry / **Gallo**	112
Dry / **Great Western**	112
Dry / **Taylor**	128
Sweet / **Gallo**	180
Sweet / **Great Western**	176
Sweet / **Taylor**	168

Vidal Blanc / **Great Western**	88
Wine Coolers: 3½ fl oz / **Manischewitz**	70
Zinfandel	
Almaden	89
Sebastiani Country	92
Sebastiani Vineyards (1980)	104
Sebastiani Vineyards (1981)	94
Wine Cellars of Ernest and Julio Gallo	92
White / **Sebastiani** Country	82

Yeast

	CALORIES
Bakers: 1 oz	24
Brewer's, debittered: 1 tbsp	23
Brewer's, debittered: 1 oz	80
Dry, active: ¼ oz pkg / **Fleischmann's**	20
Dry, active, in jar: ¼ oz / **Fleischmann's**	20
Fresh, active: .6 oz pkg / **Fleischmann's**	15
Household: .5 oz / **Fleischmann's**	15

Yogurt

	CALORIES
8 ounces equals ⅞ to ⁹⁄₁₀ of a cup	
All flavors: 3½ oz / **Colombo**	130
All flavors: 1 cup / **Lucerne** Low-Fat	260
Apple cinnamon: 6 oz / **Yoplait** Breakfast	240
Berries: 6 oz / **Yoplait** Breakfast	230
Blueberry: 6 oz / **Weight Watchers** European Style Nonfat	150
Blueberry: 8 oz / **Weight Watchers** Nonfat	150
Cherry: 1 cup / **Dannon**	260
Cherry vanilla: 8 oz / **Borden**	270
Citrus fruits: 6 oz / **Yoplait** Breakfast	250

CALORIES

Coffee: 1 cup / **Dannon**	200
Coffee: 1 cup / **Friendship** Low-Fat	210
Coffee: 6 oz / **Yoplait** Custard Style	180
Fruit: 1 cup / **Friendship** Low-Fat	230
Fruit flavors, all varieties: 6 oz / **Y.E.S.**, **Yogurt Extra Smooth**	190
Fruit flavors: 6 oz / **Yoplait** Custard Style	190
Fruit flavors: 6 oz / **Yoplait** Original	190
Lemon: 8 oz / **Borden**	320
Lemon: 1 cup / **Dannon**	200
Orchard fruits: 6 oz / **Yoplait** Breakfast	240
Peach: 1 cup / **Dannon**	260
Pineapple: 8 oz / **Borden**	260
Plain	
Colombo Natural Lite: 8 oz	110
Dannon: 1 cup	150
Friendship: 1 cup	170
Lite-Line: 8 oz	180
Lucerne: 1 cup	160
Weight Watchers European Style: 6 oz	90
Weight Watchers Nonfat: 8 oz	90
Yoplait Original: 6 oz	130
w honey: 6 oz / **Yoplait** Custard Style	160
Raspberry: 6 oz / **Weight Watchers** European Style Nonfat	150
Raspberry: 8 oz / **Weight Watchers** Nonfat	150
Strawberry	
Borden: 8 oz	230
Dannon: 1 cup	260
Meadow Gold Sundae Style: 1 cup	270
Weight Watchers European Style Nonfat: 6 oz	150
Weight Watchers Nonfat: 8 oz	150
Tropical fruits: 6 oz / **Yoplait** Breakfast	250
Vanilla: 1 cup / **Dannon**	200
Vanilla: 1 cup / **Friendship** Low-Fat	210
Vanilla: 6 oz / **Yoplait** Custard Style	180

FROZEN YOGURT

Regular: 1 cup	
Blueberry / **Danny**	210

CALORIES

Chocolate / **Danny**	190
Piña Colada / **Danny**	230
Raspberry / **Danny**	210
Strawberry / **Danny**	210
Vanilla / **Danny**	180
Soft, all varieties: 3½ oz / **Danny-Yo**	115
Bars: 1 bar	
Boysenberry, carob-coated / **Danny**	140
Chocolate, chocolate-coated / **Danny**	130
Chocolate, uncoated / **Danny**	60
Piña Colada, uncoated / **Danny**	70
Raspberry, chocolate-coated / **Danny**	130
Strawberry, chocolate-coated / **Danny**	130
Vanilla, chocolate-coated / **Danny**	130
Vanilla, uncoated / **Danny**	60

Restaurant Calorie Guide

Here, for the first time, is what many readers have asked for: a dining-out calorie guide, listing not only fast foods, but also many typical foods served in various types of restaurants including American, French, Mexican, Latin American, Chinese, Japanese, Indian, Greek, Middle Eastern and Italian. We have obtained the calorie counts for these typical restaurant foods from the U.S. Department of Agriculture's nationwide food consumption surveys. Most of the calorie counts come from the 1985–1986 continuing food consumption survey; a few come from the 1977–78 ten-year survey. Agriculture officials use these figures in estimating the nutritional value of the American diet.

It is important to point out that these government figures for restaurant foods are *approximate*—typical of what experts expect to find in restaurant dishes. Obviously, the calorie counts for restaurant foods cannot be precise because recipes and portions vary. Agriculture nutritionists calculate the calories in typical serving sizes, using classic recipes from standard cookbooks. The ingredients are quite similar from restaurant to restaurant in a dish like chicken curry or a reuben sandwich or paella, for example. Often, restaurant recipes are primarily distinguished not by a difference in basic high-calorie ingredients, but by spices, flavoring and other ingredients of little caloric importance.

Although these calorie counts are not absolute, they are the most authoritative available and fill a critical gap for calorie watchers who frequently eat out. At very least, the figures help guide you to dishes that are traditionally lower in calories and enable you to compare the over-all caloric expectations in various types of restaurants. Governmental authorities have enough confidence in the general accuracy of the figures to use them in assessing the nation's caloric energy intakes. Additionally, the author made further calculations for Japanese sushi and tempura, using basic information from the USDA and measurements obtained in a typical Japanese restaurant.

All of the portions are *average*, the size government analysts expect typical restaurants to serve. More precise measurements, such as one cup, 3 ounces, etc., are given when available to help you better judge the serving size.

The calorie counts in fast foods, obtained from the companies, are based on standardized restaurant chain recipes and serving sizes and vary only slightly, if at all, throughout the country.

Restaurants

AMERICAN

Includes regional cooking and delicatessen Jewish foods

	CALORIES
Apple cobbler: ½ cup	235
Baked Alaska: 1 piece	350
Banana split	80
Boston baked beans: ½ cup	155
Blintz, cheese: 1 blintz	139
Blintz, fruit: 1 blintz	125
Caesar salad: 1 cup	160
Carrot cake: ¹⁄₁₂ of 10-inch cake	550
Cheesecake: ¹⁄₁₂ of 9-inch cake	406
Chicken a la king: ¾ cup	345
Chicken croquettes: 3 oz	222
Chicken fricasse: ¾ cup	290
Chicken w dumplings: 1 cup	373
Chicken and noodles: ¾ cup	275
Chicken salad: ¾ cup	314
Clams, raw: 1 clam	12
half dozen on half shell	72
Clams, breaded, fried: 3 oz (about ½ cup)	158
Codfish balls: 1 piece	227
Codfish, creamed: ¾ cup	250
Coleslaw: ½ cup	115
Corned beef hash: 1 cup	344
Crabs, steamed	
1 medium, Chesapeake Bay	17

CALORIES

Crab cake: 1 cake (4 oz)	203
Crab Imperial: ¾ cup	281
Crab salad: ¾ cup	205
Crayfish tails: 3 oz	88
1 tail	5
Deviled crab: ¾ cup	250
Flounder, stuffed w crab: 7½ oz	310
Green pepper, stuffed: ½ pepper	200
Ham salad: ¾ cup	298
Hush puppies: 1 piece	73
Julienne salad wo dressing: 1 cup	73
Julienne salad, wo dressing: 1 salad	300
Julienne salad w dressing: 1 salad	510
Kidney bean salad: ½ cup	175
Knish, cheese: 1 knish	208
Knish, potato: 1 knish	204
Liver, chopped with egg and onion: ¾ cup	225
Lobster, steamed or broiled in shell:	
1-pound lobster	105
Lobster tail: 1 small	45
1 medium	95
1 large	170
Lobster, stuffed and baked: 14 oz without shell	750
Lobster Newburg: ¾ cup	454
Lobster Norfolk: ¾ cup	333
Lobster salad: ¾ cup	102
Matzo balls: 1 matzo ball	50
Matzo ball soup: 1 cup	120
Meat loaf: 1 medium slice (3½ oz)	240
Mussels, cooked: 1 small	10
½ cup	120
Oysters, fried, breaded: 1 medium	25
Potato, baked: 1 medium	130
Salmon croquettes: 1 croquette	272
Salmon salad: ¾ cup	320
Shoe-fly pie: ⅛ of 9-in pie	392
Shrimp, stuffed: 1 shrimp	30
Shrimp creole: 1 cup	300
Shrimp gumbo w rice: 1 cup	300
Shrimp jambalaya w rice: 1 cup	300
Shrimp salad: ¾ cup	210

Smoked salmon: 1 piece, about ⅔ oz	35
Sundae, fruit	330
Tuna salad: ¾ cup	290
Turkey salad: ¾ cup	314
Vegetables, batter-fried	
Broccoli: 1 cup	160
Cauliflower: ½ cup	83
Eggplant: 1 stick	45
Okra: ½ cup	88
Onion rings: 1 large ring	40
1 medium ring	25
Zucchini: 1 slice	25

Breakfast or Brunch Foods

Eggs, fried: 1 egg	100
Eggs, hard or soft boiled: 1 egg	80
Eggs, poached: 1 egg	80
Eggs, scrambled: 1 egg	110
Eggs benedict: 1 egg	335
Omelets—2 eggs	
Plain	215
Cheese	295
Ham	350
Ham and cheese	450
Spanish	328
Western	358
Corn meal mush, fried: 1 slice	85
Croissant, fresh: 1 croissant	205
Danish pastry: 1 piece	270
Grits: ⅔ cup	83
Pancakes: 1 cake, 6-in diam	162
Quiche lorraine: ⅛ of 9-in diam	593
Spinach quiche: ⅛ of 9-in diam	335
Waffles: 2 pieces, 4-in squares	204

Salad Bar

Bacon bits: 1 tbsp	27
Beets, pickled, canned: ⅛ cup	18
Broccoli: ⅛ cup	3
Carrots: ⅛ cup	6

CALORIES

Cheese

cheddar: 2 tbsp	56
cottage: ½ cup	116
parmesan: 2 tbsp	45
Chickpeas: 2 tbsp	21
Cucumber: 2 tbsp	2
Egg, chopped: 2 tbsp	27
Lettuce: ¼ cup	18
Mushrooms, sliced: 2 tbsp	3
Onions: 2 tbsp	3
Pepper, green: 2 tbsp	3
Potato salad: ½ cup	180
Sprouts, alfalfa: 2 tbsp	2
Tomato: 2 slices	3

Salad Dressings:

Blue: 1 tbsp	75
French: 1 tbsp	79
Italian: 1 tbsp	78
Italian, low calorie: 1 tbsp	7
Oil / vinegar: 1 tbsp	72
Thousand Island: 1 tbsp	56

Sandwiches

Bacon and cheese	439
Bacon and egg	391
Bacon, lettuce and tomato	346
Bologna	260
Cheese	275
Cheeseburger, plain on bun	323
Chicken salad	279
Chili dog	413
Club (bacon, tomato, chicken)	502
Corn dog	278
Corned beef	250
Crabcake	318
Egg	230
Egg salad	290
Fish on bun	375
Ham	260

Ham and cheese	381
Ham and cheese grilled	417
Ham and egg	269
Ham salad	258
Hero, ham and cheese	445
Hoagie, cheese	440
Hot dog, plain	263
Hot dog with condiments	296
Pastrami	338
Peanut butter	280
Peanut butter and jelly	315
Pig in blanket	278
Reuben	535
Roast beef	341
Salami	238
Sausage	345
Sloppy Joe on bun	387
Steak	438
Steak and cheese	543
Submarine, regular	560
Submarine, steak, w tomato	438
Turkey salad	218
Tuna salad	374

CHINESE

Bean sprouts, fried: ¼ cup	40
Beef chow mein w noodles: 1 cup	405
Beef chop suey w noodles: 1 cup	405
Beef chow mein wo noodles: ¾ cup	204
Beef and broccoli: ¾ cup	185
Beef and green beans: ½ cup	130
Beef and vegetables, stir-fried: ¾ cup	115
Bird's nest soup: 1 cup	30
Chicken chow mein w noodles: 1 cup	287
Chicken chow mein wo noodles: ¾ cup	145
Chinese barbecue pork or roast pork: ¾ cup	340
Chinese pancake: 1 cake	60
Chow mein noodles: ½ cup	110
Dim sum: 1 dumpling	55
Egg drop soup: 1 cup	65

CALORIES

Egg foo yung, pork: 1 patty	100
Egg foo yung, shrimp: 1 patty	175
Egg roll w meat: 1 (2¼ oz)	120
Egg roll w shrimp: 1 (2¼ oz)	106
Egg roll, vegetarian: 1 (2¼ oz)	103
Fried rice w bean sprouts: ½ cup	160
Fried rice w shrimp: ¾ cup	215
Hot and sour soup: 1 cup	100
Lo mein w meat: 1 cup	285
Lychee, fresh: 1 fruit	8
Pancake: 1 pancake	60
Pepper beef: 1 cup	240
Pork chop suey w noodles: 1 cup	430
Pork chop suey wo noodles: ¾ cup	223
Rice cake: 1 oz	80
Shrimp chop suey w noodles: 1 cup	235
Shrimp chow mein w noodles: 1 cup	265
Shrimp chow mein wo noodles: ¾ cup	141
Shrimp w lobster sauce: ¾ cup	216
Stir fried vegetables: ½ cup	85
Sweet and sour shrimp w sauce: ¾ cup	460
Sweet and sour pork w pineapple: ¾ cup	475
Sweet and sour soup: 1 cup	30
Won ton chips: 1 piece	10
Won ton, fried: 1 piece	20
Won ton, meat-filled, fried: 1 piece	60
Won ton soup: 1 cup	210

ENGLISH

Beef Wellington, 1 slice (4 oz)	325
Brunswick stew: ¾ cup	300
Scone: 1 regular size	150
Shepherd's pie: 1 cup	304
Welsh rarebit: ½ cup	205
Yorkshire pudding: 3-in square	170

FRENCH AND CONTINENTAL

Beef Bourguignon: ¾ cup	194
Beef burgundy: ¾ cup	230

CALORIES

Beef stroganoff: ¾ cup	308
Beef stroganoff w noodles: 1 cup	342
Bouillabaisse: 1 cup	230
Brioche: 1 medium	270
Cheese fondue: ¼ cup	125
Cheese souffle: 1 cup	205
Chicken cordon bleu: (8 oz)	437
Chocolate eclair: 1 eclair	220
Chocolate mousse: ½ cup	175
Crepe, fruit-filled: 1 crepe	95
Crepe, filled w poultry or meat and sauce: 1 crepe	250
Escargots: 1 snail	8
Fish timbale or mousse: ¾ cup	272
French horn: 1 piece	135
Frog legs: 1 leg fried	60
Hollandaise sauce: 2 tbsp	135
Meringue: 1 piece (4 × 2 × 2 in)	85
Swedish meatballs: ¾ cup	275

GERMAN

Apple strudel: 1 piece (about 3 oz)	280
Frankfurters and sauerkraut: 1 frank w kraut	158
German potato salad: ½ cup	110
Sauerbraten: 1 piece 3 × 2 × ¾ in (3½ oz)	190
Weiner schnitzel: 1 piece (about 3½ oz)	280

GREEK

Baklava: 1 piece	332
Gyros sandwich	215
Pita bread: 1 small	165
1 large	265
Spanakopita: 1 serving	255

INDIAN

Chapati: 1 piece	73
Chutney: 1 tbsp	28
Curry, beef: ¾ cup	345
Curry, shrimp: ¾ cup	232

CALORIES

Curry, chicken: ¾ cup	302
Curried chick peas and potatoes: ½ cup	111
Paratha (fried bread): 1 piece (about 1 oz)	96
Puri bread: 1 piece	115

ITALIAN

Antipasto: small	125
large	250
1 cup	150
Bread sticks: 1 medium	40
Calzone, meat and cheese: ½ calzone (about 7½ oz)	736
Cannoli: 1 piece	234
Chicken cacciatore: ¾ cup	345
Chicken tetrazzini: 1 cup	210
Clams casino: 1 large	100
1 small	50
Eggplant parmesan: ½ cup	190
Garlic bread: 1 medium slice	100
Gnocchi, cheese: 1 cup	125
Fettucine Alfredo: 1 cup	270
Manicotti, cheese w meat sauce: 1 manicotti	235
Manicotti, cheese w tomato sauce: 1 manicotti	223
Lasagna: 1 cup	350
Lasagna, meatless: 1 piece 2½ in × 4 in	317
Pasta salad, vegetable: ¾ cup	253
Pizza, cheese, thin crust: ⅛ of 12-inch pizza	163
Pizza, cheese, thick crust: ⅛ of 12-inch pizza	203
Pizza, meat, cheese, thin crust: ⅛ of 12-inch pizza	210
Pizza, meat, cheese, thick crust: ⅛ of 12-inch pizza	250
Pizza, vegetarian, thin crust: ⅛ of 12-inch pizza	150
Pizza, vegetarian, thick crust: ⅛ of 12-inch pizza	192
Polenta: ⅔ cup	165
Ratatouille: ½ cup	73
Ravioli, cheese-filled w tomato sauce: 1 cup	338
Ravioli, cheese-filled w tomato beef sauce: 1 cup	360
Ravioli, meat-filled w tomato sauce: 1 cup	386
Rigatoni w sausage: ¾ cup	260
Rissoto: ½ cup	180
Spaghetti w meat sauce: 1 cup	255

CALORIES

Spaghetti w tomato sauce: 1 cup	155
Spaghetti w meatballs and tomato sauce: 1 cup	330
Spaghetti w meatballs, tomato sauce and cheese: 1 cup	225
Spaghetti w red clam sauce: 1 cup	225
Spaghetti carbonara: 1 cup	372
Tortellini (meat filled) w tomato sauce: 1 cup	262
Veal parmigiana: 1 piece (about 6 oz)	350
Veal scallopini: 1 slice (about 3½ oz)	255
Ziti: 1 cup	350

JAPANESE

Japanese pickles (tsukemono): ¼ cup	7
Japanese pickled cabbage: ¼ cup	7
Japanese radish (Daikon): ½ cup	14
Kim chee: 1 cup	30
Miso soup: 1 cup	78
Sashimi, tuna: 1 cubic inch	25
Sashimi, 1 2-inch piece (⅓ oz)	12
Sukiyaki: ¾ cup	130
Sushi, roll: 1 piece (⅙ roll usually)	
w cucumber (kappa maki)	30
w tuna (tekka maki)	32
California roll	35
Sushi: 1 piece	
Eel (anago)	80
Flounder	55
Salmon	50
Shrimp (ebi)	45
Tuna (maguro)	50
Yellowtail	54
Seaweed and soy sauce: ½ cup	20
Tempura, fish cake: (10 oz.)	466
Tempura, shrimp: 1 jumbo shrimp	70
Tempura, softshell crab: 1 crab (2¼ oz)	215
Tempura, vegetable: 1 cup or (about 2¼ oz)	100
1 small piece	20
1 large piece	40
Teriyaki, chicken: 6½ oz	257
Teriyaki, steak: 6½ oz	317

CALORIES

Tofu, stir fried: ½ cup	66
Tofu, deep fried: 1 oz	75
Tofu w beef and vegetables: ¾ cup	200

LATIN AMERICAN

Arroz con pollo: 1 cup without bones	185
Black bean soup: 1 cup	116
Cheese, white (queso del pais blanco): 1 cubic inch	25
Cuban sandwich	672
Diplomat pudding: ½ cup	395
Flan: 1 custard cup	195
Gazpacho: 1 cup	56
Guava nectar: ½ cup	65
Guava paste: 1 medium piece (1 oz)	90
Octopus salad: ¾ cup	277
Paella: 1 cup	350
Plantain, fried (tostones): ½ cup	210
Plantain, ripe, fried: 2-in piece	50
Pumpkin pudding, Puerto Rican: 1 piece 2½ in × 2 in × 1 in	185
Red beans, stewed: ½ cup	185
Rice and beans: ⅔ cup	150
Seviche: ¾ cup	122
Veal marengo: 1 cup	200
Yucca, white, boiled: ½ cup	110
Zarzuela: ¾ cup	310

MEXICAN

1 whole item unless otherwise noted:

Burrito, beef and beans	290
Burrito, beef, beans and cheese	388
Burrito, bean and cheese	286
Chalupe, chicken and cheese	311
Chiles rellenos	218
Chili con carne, beans: 1 cup	311
Chili con carne, beans and rice: 1 cup	308
Chili con carne, beans: 1 cup	331
Chili con queso: ¼ cup	135
1 tbsp	35

CALORIES

Chimichanga, beef and cheese: about 4 oz	282
Chimichanga, chicken and sour cream: about 4 oz	214
Enchilada, cheese	164
Enchilada, beef and beans	192
Enchilada, beef and cheese	235
Enchilada, chicken	168
Enchilada, chicken and cheese	214
Guacamole: ½ cup	240
Nachos, cheese and bean: 1 piece	50
Quesadilla	190
Refried beans: ½ cup	210
Taco, bean and cheese	144
Taco, beef and cheese	180
Taco, chicken and cheese	148
Taco salad: 1 cup	202
Tamale	183
Taquito	185
Tortilla, corn, plain	32
Tortilla, flour plain	118
Tostado, bean and cheese	144
Tostado, beef and cheese	180
Tostado, chicken and cheese	148

MIDDLE EASTERN

Cabbage rolls: 1 roll	100
Grape leaves, stuffed w rice: 1 roll	145
Hummus: 1 oz (about 1¾ tbsp)	45
Kibbe: 1 cup	375
Lamb shishkabob: 1 medium	115
1 large	225
Turkish coffee: 4 fl oz	45

MIDDLE EUROPEAN

Noodles, Romanoff: 1 cup	270
Pierogi: 1 pastry	105
Potato pancakes: 1 medium	105
Rice pilaf: ¾ cup	200
Shav soup: 1 cup	60

CALORIES

Veal Goulash: 1 cup	200
Veal Paprikash: ½ cup	230

WINE AND BAR DRINKS

1 typical drink

Bacardi	118
Black Russian	255
Bloody Mary	125
Bourbon and soda	105
Brandy, straight, 1 fl oz	65
Brandy Alexander	180
Daiquiri	113
Gibson	158
Gimlet	132
Gin: 1 jigger	110
Gin and tonic	170
Gin rickey	115
Grasshopper	165
Hot buttered rum	180
Mai Tai	310
Manhattan	130
Margarita	170
Martini	160
Mint julep	155
Old fashioned	155
Piña colada	230
Rum: 1 jigger	100
Sangria	155
Scotch and soda	105
Screwdriver	182
Singapore sling	228
Sloe gin fizz	120
Stinger	282
Tequila sunrise	190
Tom Collins	120
Vodka: jigger	100
Whiskey: 1 jigger	105
Whiskey sour	122
White Russian	268

Wine

Dry, dinner wines
    1 wine glass: 3½ fl oz   70
Dessert wines (Marsala, port, tokay, madeira, sherry, sweet vermouth)
    1 wine glass: 3½ fl oz   150
Wine spritzer   60

Fast Foods

Fast Foods

ARBY'S

	CALORIES
Arby's Sub (no dressing)	484
Beef 'N Cheddar Sandwich	484
Chicken Breast Sandwich	584
French Dip	386
French Fries: 2½-oz serving	216
Ham 'N Cheese Sandwich	484
Potato Cakes: 2 cakes	190
Roast Beef, Deluxe, Sandwich	486
Roast Beef, Junior, Sandwich	220
Roast Beef, Regular, Sandwich	350
Roast Beef, Super, Sandwich	620
Sauce, Arby's: 1 oz	34
Sauce, Horsey: 1 oz	120
Turnover, Apple	310
Turnover, Blueberry	340
Turnover, Cherry	320

ARTHUR TREACHER'S FISH & CHIPS

Chicken: 2 pieces	370
Chicken Sandwich	410
Chips: 1 serving	280
Chowder: 1 serving	110
Coleslaw: 1 serving	120

Fish: 2 pieces	360
Fish Sandwich	444
Krunch Pup	200

BURGER CHEF

Big Shef	556
Biscuit Sandwich w Sausage	418
Cheeseburger	278
Cheeseburger, Double	402
Chicken Club	521
Fisherman's Filet	534
Fries, Large: 1 serving	285
Fries, Regular: 1 serving	204
Hamburger	235
Hash Rounds: 1 serving	235
Mushroom Burger	520
Scrambled Eggs and Bacon Platter	567
Scrambled Eggs and Sausage Platter	668
Shake, Chocolate	403
Shake, Vanilla	380
Sunrise w Bacon	392
Sunrise w Sausage	526
Super Shef	604
Top Shef	541
Turnover, Apple	237

BURGER KING

Apple Pie	240
Bacon Double Cheeseburger	600
Cheeseburger	350
Cheeseburger, Double	530
Chicken Sandwich	690
French Fries, Regular: 1 serving	210
Hamburger	290
Onion Rings, Regular: 1 serving	270
Shake, Chocolate: 10 oz	340
Shake, Vanilla: 10 oz	340
Veal Parmigiana	600
Whaler	540

	CALORIES
Whaler w Cheese	590
Whopper	630
Whopper w Cheese	740
Whopper, Double Beef	850
Whopper, Double Beef w Cheese	950
Whopper Junior	370
Whopper Junior w Cheese	420

CARL'S JR.

Bacon: 2 strips	70
California Roast Beef Sandwich	300
Carrot Cake: 1 piece	350
Charbroiler Chicken Sandwich	450
Charbroiler Steak	230
Charbroiler Steak Sandwich	630
Cheese Sandwich, American	70
Cheese Sandwich, Swiss	70
Chicken Breasts: 2 pieces	200
Crispirito	670
Eggs, scrambled: 1 serving	150
English Muffin w Butter and Jelly	228
Famous Star Hamburger	530
Filet of Fish Sandwich	570
French Fries, Regular: 1 serving	250
Garlic Bread: 1 serving	130
Ground Beef: 1 serving	520
Happy Star Hamburger	330
Hashed Brown Potatoes: 2	280
Hot Cakes w Syrup and Butter: 1 serving	480
Hot Chocolate: 1 serving	110
Old Time Star Hamburger	450
Omelette, Bacon 'n Cheese	290
Omelette, California	310
Omelette, Cheese	280
Onion Rings: 1 serving	330
Onion Ring Garnish: 1 serving	110
Potato, Baked	167
Potatoes, Wedge Cut: 1 serving	252
Salad, Regular	210
Salad Dressing, Bleu Cheese: 2 oz	160

Salad Dressing, Low-Cal Italian: 2 oz	80
Salad Dressing, Thousand Island: 2 oz	240
Sausage: 1 patty	110
Shake, Regular	490
Sunrise Sandwich w Bacon	410
Sunrise Sandwich w Sausage	450
Super Star Hamburger	780
Sweet Roll w Butter	420
Tartar Sauce: ¾ oz	NA
Top Sirloin Steak	210
Trout w Lemon Garlic Butter	200
Turnover, Apple	400
Western Bacon Cheeseburger	670
Zucchini: 1 serving	311

CHURCH'S FRIED CHICKEN

Chicken	
Dark Meat: 1 average portion	305
White Meat: 1 average portion	327
Breast	283
Leg	172
Thigh	319
Wing	279
Chicken Snack	
Chicken: 1 large piece	316
Dinner Roll: 1	83
Coleslaw: 3 oz	83
Corn on the Cob: 9 oz buttered	165
French Fries: 3 oz	256
Jalapeno Pepper: 1	4
Pie, Apple: 3 oz	300
Pie, Pecan: 3 oz	367

DAIRY QUEEN / BRAZIER

Banana Split	540
Buster Bar	460
Chicken Sandwich	670
Cone, Large	340
Cone, Regular	240

	CALORIES
Cone, Small	140
Cone, Dipped, Chocolate, Large	510
Cone, Dipped, Chocolate, Regular	340
Cone, Dipped, Chocolate, Small	190
Dilly Bar	210
Double Delight	490
DQ Sandwich	140
Fish Sandwich	400
Fish Sandwich w Cheese	440
Float	410
Freeze	500
French Fries, Large: 1 serving	320
French Fries, Regular: 1 serving	200
Hamburger, Double	530
Hamburger, Double w Cheese	650
Hamburger, Single	360
Hamburger, Single w Cheese	410
Hamburger, Triple	710
Hamburger, Triple w Cheese	820
Hot Dog	280
Hog Dog w Cheese	330
Hot Dog w Chili	320
Hot Dog, Super	520
Hot Dog, Super w Cheese	580
Hot Dog, Super w Chili	570
Hot Fudge Brownie Delight	600
Malt, Chocolate, Large	1060
Malt, Chocolate, Regular	760
Malt, Chocolate, Small	520
Mr. Misty Float	390
Mr. Misty Freeze	500
Mr. Misty Kiss	70
Mr. Misty, Large	340
Mr. Misty, Regular	250
Mr. Misty, Small	190
Onion Rings: 1 serving	280
Parfait	430
Peanut Buster Parfait	740
Shake, Chocolate, Large	990
Shake, Chocolate, Regular	710
Shake, Chocolate, Small	490

	CALORIES
Strawberry Shortcake	540
Sundae, Chocolate, Large	440
Sundae, Chocolate, Regular	310
Sundae, Chocolate, Small	190

DUNKIN' DONUTS

Cake and Chocolate Cake Donuts (includes rings, sticks, crullers)	240
Fancies (includes coffee rolls, danish, etc.)	215
w filling and topping	add 45
Glazed Yeast-Raised Donuts	168
Munchkins—Cake and Chocolate Cake	66
w filling and topping	add 13
Munchkins—Yeast-Raised	26
Yeast-Raised Donuts	160

HARDEE'S

Bacon Cheeseburger	686
Bacon & Egg Biscuit	405
Biscuit	275
Biscuit w Egg	383
Cheeseburger	335
Chicken Fillet	510
Cookie, Big	278
Fisherman Fillet	469
French Fries, Large: 1 serving	381
French Fries, Small: 1 serving	239
Ham Biscuit	349
Ham Biscuit w Egg	458
Ham and Cheese Sandwich, Hot	376
Hamburger	305
Hashrounds: 1 serving	200
Hot Dog	346
Milkshake	391
Mushroom 'N' Swiss	512
Roast Beef Sandwich	376
Roast Beef Sandwich, Big	418
Sausage Biscuit	413
Sausage Biscuit w Egg	521

Steak Biscuit	419
Steak Biscuit w Egg	527
Turkey Club	426
Turnover, Apple	282

JACK IN THE BOX

Bacon Cheeseburger Supreme	724
Bacon Croissant	480
Breakfast Jack	307
Cheeseburger	323
Chicken Strips Dinner	689
Chicken Supreme	601
Croissant Supreme	547
French Fries: 1 serving	221
Hamburger	276
Ham Croissant	447
Jumbo Jack	485
Jumbo Jack w Cheese	630
Moby Jack	444
Nachos, Cheese: 1 serving	571
Nachos, Supreme: 1 serving	718
Onion Rings: 1 serving	382
Pancake Breakfast	630
Pita Pocket Supreme	284
Sausage Croissant	584
Scrambled Eggs Breakfast	720
Shake, Chocolate	360
Shake, Strawberry	380
Shake, Vanilla	340
Shrimp Dinner	731
Shrimp Salad Supreme	116
Sirloin Steak Dinner	699
Swiss and Bacon Burger	643
Taco, Regular	191
Taco, Super	288
Taco Salad	377
Turnover, Apple	410

KENTUCKY FRIED CHICKEN

Chicken Breast Filet Sandwich	436
Chicken Dinner, Extra Crispy: 2 pieces of chicken w mashed potatoes, gravy, cole slaw and roll	
Combination	902
Dark	765
White	755
Chicken Dinner, Original Recipe: 2 pieces of chicken w mashed potatoes, gravy, cole slaw and roll	
Combination	661
Dark	643
White	604
Coleslaw: 1 serving	121
Corn: 5½-in piece	169
Gravy: 1 serving	23
Individual Chicken Pieces, Extra Crispy	
Drumstick	155
Keel	297
Side Breast	286
Thigh	343
Wing	201
Individual Chicken Pieces, Original Recipe	
Drumstick	117
Keel	236
Side Breast	199
Thigh	257
Wing	136
Kentucky Fries: 1 serving	184
Mashed potatoes: 1 serving	64
Roll	61

LONG JOHN SILVER'S SEAFOOD SHOPPES

Catfish Fillet: 1 piece	203
Catfish Fillet Dinner	980
Chicken Plank: 1 piece	104
Chicken Planks: 4 pieces w Fryes	662
Chicken Plank Dinner w Slaw	844
Chicken Sandwich	562
Clam Chowder: 6 fl oz	128

CALORIES

Clams, Breaded: 1 serving	526
Clams, Fried, w Fryes, Slaw: 1 serving	955
Coleslaw: 3½ oz serving drained on fork	182
Corn on the Cob: 1 ear	176
Fish, Baked, w Sauce: 5½ oz serving	151
Fish, Baked, w Sauce, Slaw, Mixed Vegetables	387
Fish w Batter: 1 piece	202
Fish, Kitchen-Breaded: 1 piece	122
Fish Dinner	1180
Fish Dinner, Kitchen-Breaded, 2-Piece	816
Fish Dinner, Kitchen-Breaded, 3-Piece	938
Fish & Chicken	838
Fish & Fryes, 2-Piece	651
Fish & Fryes, 3-Piece	853
Fish & More	976
Fish Sandwich	555
Fish Sandwich Platter	984
Fryes, Bigger Better: 3-oz serving	247
Hush Puppies: 2 pieces	145
Oyster, Breaded: 1 piece	60
Oysters w Fryes, Slaw	787
Peg Leg w Batter: 1 piece	91
Peg Legs w Fryes	703
Pie, Apple: 4-oz serving	280
Pie, Cherry: 4-oz serving	294
Pie, Lemon meringue: 3½-oz serving	200
Pie, Pecan: 4-oz serving	446
Pie, Pumpkin: 4-oz serving	251
Sauce, Seafood: 1.2 oz	34
Sauce, Tartar: 1 oz	119
Scallop w Batter: 1 piece	53
Scallops w Fryes, Slaw	746
Seafood Combo, Chilled	437
Seafood Platter	974
Seafood Salad: 5.8-oz serving	386
Seafood Salad w Lettuce, Tomato, Crackers	471
Shrimp, Battered: 1 piece	47
Shrimp, Battered, w Fryes, Slaw	709
Shrimp, Breaded: 4.7-oz serving	388
Shrimp, Breaded, Platter	962
Shrimp, chilled: 1 piece	6

Shrimp Dinner, chilled	354
Treasure Chest	1015
Vegetables, mixed: 4-oz serving	54
Children's Menu	
1 Piece Fish, Fryes	449
2 Chicken Planks, Fryes	455
3 Peg Legs, Fryes	521
1 Piece Fish, 1 Peg Leg, Fryes	540

McDONALD'S

Big Mac	563
Biscuit, Plain	312
Biscuit, Buttered	342
Biscuit w Bacon, Egg and Cheese	509
Biscuit w Sausage	522
Biscuit w Sausage and Egg	612
Cheeseburger	307
Chicken McNuggets: 1 serving	314
Cone (soft ice cream)	185
Cookies, Chocolaty Chip: 2½-oz serving	342
Cookies, McDonaldland: 2½-oz serving	308
Egg McMuffin	330
Eggs, Scrambled	180
English Muffin w Butter	186
Filet-O-Fish	432
Fries, Regular: 1 serving	220
Hamburger	255
Hash Brown Potatoes: 1 serving	125
Hotcakes w Butter and Syrup	500
Pie, Apple	253
Pie, Cherry	260
Quarter Pounder	424
Quarter Pounder w Cheese	524
Sauce, Barbeque (for McNuggets): 1 serving	60
Sauce, Honey (for McNuggets): 1 serving	50
Sauce, Hot Mustard (for McNuggets): 1 serving	63
Sauce, Sweet and Sour (for McNuggets): 1 serving	64
Sausage: 1 serving	206
Sausage McMuffin	417
Sausage McMuffin w Egg	507

Shake, Chocolate	383
Shake, Strawberry	362
Shake, Vanilla	352
Sundae, Caramel	328
Sundae, Hot Fudge	310
Sundae, Strawberry	289

PIZZA HUT

One-half of a 10-inch pizza (3 slices)

Thin 'N Crispy Pizza	
Beef	490
Cheese	450
Pepperoni	430
Pork	520
Supreme	510
Thick 'N Chewy Pizza	
Beef	620
Cheese	560
Pepperoni	560
Pork	640
Supreme	640

PONDEROSA

Baked Fish	268
Baked Fish, w potato, garnishes, roll, butter or margarine, tartar sauce	1061
Chicken Strips	282
Chicken Strips, w baked potato, garnishes, roll, butter or margarine	785
Chopped Beef	209
Chopped Beef, w baked potato, garnishes, roll, butter or margarine	712
Chopped Beef, Big	295
Chopped Beef, Big, w baked potato, garnishes, roll, butter or margarine	798
Double Deluxe	560
Double Deluxe, w garnishes, fries	791
Filet Mignon	152

CALORIES

Filet Mignon, w baked potato, garnishes, roll, butter or margarine	655
Filet of Sole Dinner	918
Filet of Sole Sandwich	605
Filet of Sole Sandwich w Fries	836
Ham 'n Cheese	509
Ham 'n Cheese w Fries	739
Imperial Prime Rib	572
Imperial Prime Rib, w baked potato, garnishes, roll, butter or margarine	1079
King Prime Rib	409
King Prime Rib, w baked potato, garnishes, roll, butter or margarine	912
New York Strip	362
New York Strip, w baked potato, garnishes, roll, butter or margarine	865
Prime Rib	286
Prime Rib, w baked potato, garnishes, roll, butter or margarine	789
Ribeye	197
Ribeye, w baked potato, garnishes, roll, butter or margarine	700
Ribeye & Shrimp	336
Ribeye & Shrimp, w baked potato, garnishes, roll, butter or margarine, cocktail sauce	901
Salad Bar: 1-oz serving each item	
Bean sprouts	13
Beets	5
Broccoli	9
Cabbage, red	9
Carrots	12
Cauliflower	8
Celery	4
Chickpeas (garbanzos)	102
Cucumber	5
Green Pepper	6
Lettuce	4
Mushrooms	8
Onions, White	11
Radish	5
Tomato	6

Salad dressings: 1 oz	
Blue Cheese	129
Creamy Italian	138
Low Calorie	14
Oil-Vinegar	124
Sweet 'n Tart	129
Thousand Island	117
Shrimp Dinner	785
Sirloin	197
Sirloin, w baked potato, garnishes, roll, butter or margarine	700
Sirloin Tips	192
Sirloin Tips, w baked potato, garnishes, roll, butter or margarine	695
Steakhouse Deluxe	380
Steakhouse Deluxe w Fries	610
Super Sirloin	383
Super Sirloin, w baked potato, garnishes, roll, butter or margarine	886
T-Bone	240
T-Bone, w baked potato, garnishes, roll, butter or margarine	743
Children's Items	
Chicken Strips	141
French Fries	230
Gelatin: ½ cup	97
Hot Dog	248
Pudding, Butterscotch	200
Pudding, Chocolate	213
Pudding, Vanilla	195
Square Shooter	216
Whipped Topping: ¼ oz	19

ROY ROGERS

Bacon Cheeseburger	603
Cheeseburger	570
Double-R-Bar Burger	672
Egg Sandwich	290
English Muffin	130
Bacon	54

CALORIES

Ham	102
Sausage	196
French Fries: 3-oz serving	240
French Fries, large: 4-oz serving	321
Fried Chicken	
Breasts: 8 oz	241
Drumsticks: 4 oz	136
Thighs: 6½ oz	276
Wings: 3½ oz	151
Hamburger	516
Hash Browns: 1 serving	137
Pancakes: 1 serving	229
Roast Beef Sandwich	459
Roast Beef Sandwich, Large	505
Roast Beef Sandwich w Cheese	511
Roast Beef Sandwich w Cheese, Large	557
Salad Bar and Fixins Bar Items	
Bacon Bits: ¼ oz	29
Bean Sprouts: 1 oz	8
Blue Cheese Dressing: 1 oz	143
Carrots: ¼ oz	3
Chick Peas: 1 oz	102
Chow Mein Noodles: ½ oz	77
Cucumbers: ½ oz	2
Diced Egg: ½ oz	23
French Dressing: 1 oz	116
Lettuce: 2 oz	7
Lo-Cal Italian dressing: 1 oz	15
Onions: 1 oz	11
Parmesan Cheese: ¼ oz	28
Peppers: ¾ oz	5
Potato Salad: 2 oz	74
Radishes: ¾ oz	4
Red Beets: 1 oz	10
Tomato: 2 oz	13
Scrambled Eggs: 1 serving	104
Shake, Chocolate	364
Shake, Vanilla	323

TACO BELL

Bean Burrito	343
Beef Burrito	466
Beefy Tostado	291
Bellbeefer	221
Bellbeefer w Cheese	278
Burrito Supreme	457
Combination Burrito	404
Enchirito	454
Taco	186
Tostada	179

WENDY'S

Bacon: 2 strips	110
Bacon Cheeseburger on White Bun	460
Breakfast Sandwich	370
Chicken Sandwich on Multigrain Wheat Bun	320
Chili: 8 oz	260
Danish	360
French Fries, regular: 1 serving	280
French Toast: 2 slices	400
Frosty: 12 fl oz	400
Garden Spot Salad Bar	
Alfalfa Sprouts: 2 oz	20
American Cheese, Imitation: 1 oz	70
Bacon Bits: ⅛ oz	10
Bell Peppers: ¼ cup	4
Blueberries: 1 tbsp	8
Breadsticks: 1	20
Broccoli: ½ cup	14
Cantaloupe: 2 pieces	4
Carrots: ¼ cup	12
Cauliflower: ½ cup	14
Cheddar Cheese, Imitation: 1 oz	90
Chow Mein Noodles: ¼ cup	60
Cole Slaw: ½ cup	90
Cottage Cheese: ½ cup	110
Croutons: 18	30
Cucumbers: ¼ cup	4

Eggs: 1 tbsp	14
Green Peas: ½ cup	60
Jalapeno Peppers: 1 tbsp	9
Lettuce, Iceberg: 1 cup	8
Lettuce, Romaine: 1 cup	10
Mild Pepperoncini or Banana Peppers: 1 tbsp	18
Mozzarella Cheese, Imitation: 1 oz	90
Mushrooms: ¼ cup	6
Oranges: 2 pieces	10
Pasta Salad: ½ cup	134
Peaches in Syrup: 2 pieces	17
Pineapple Chunks in Juice: ½ cup	80
Red Onions: 1 tbsp	4
Saltine Crackers: 4 pieces	45
Swiss Cheese, Imitation: 1 oz	80
Sunflower Seeds and Raisins: ¼ cup	180
Tomatoes: 1 oz	6
Turkey Ham: ¼ cup	46
Watermelon: 2 pieces	3
Dressings: 1 tbsp	
Bleu Cheese	60
Celery Seed	70
Golden Italian	45
Oil	130
Ranch	80
Red French	70
Reduced Calorie Bacon & Tomato	45
Reduced Calorie Creamy Cucumber	50
Reduced Calorie Italian	25
Reduced Calorie Thousand Island	45
Thousand Island	70
Wine Vinegar	2
Hamburger, Double, on White Bun	560
Hamburger, Single, on Multi-grain Wheat Bun	340
Hamburger, Single, on White Bun	350
Home Fries: 1 serving	360
Hot Stuffed Baked Potatoes	
Bacon & Cheese	570
Broccoli & Cheese	500
Cheese	590
Chicken à la King	350

Chili & Cheese	510
Plain	250
Sour Cream & Chives	460
Stroganoff & Sour Cream	490
Kids' Meal Hamburger	220
Light Menu	
Chicken Sandwich on Multi-grain Wheat Bun	320
Garden Spot Salad Bar (*see individual items*)	
Hamburger, Single, on Multi-grain Wheat Bun	340
Multi-grain Wheat Bun	135
Pick-up Window Side Salad	110
Plain Baked Potato	250
Omelet #1—Ham & Cheese	250
Omelet #2—Ham, Cheese, & Mushroom	290
Omelet #3—Ham, Cheese, Onion, Green Pepper	280
Omelet #4—Mushroom, Onion, Green Pepper	210
Pick-up Window Side Salad	110
Sausage: 1 patty	200
Scrambled Eggs: 1 serving	190
Taco Salad: 1 serving	390
Toast w margarine: 2 slices	250

WHITE CASTLE

Cheeseburger	185
Fish (wo tartar sauce)	190
French Fries	225
Hamburger	160

Index

317

ABOUT THE AUTHOR

JEAN CARPER is an independent writer and broadcaster, specializing in health, nutrition and consumer subjects. She has written numerous articles for national publications including *Reader's Digest* and the *Washington Post*. She is the author of eleven other books: *Stay Alive! Bitter Greetings: The Scandal of the Military Draft, The Dark Side of the Marketplace* (co-authored with Jacqueline Verrett), *The All-In-One Carbohydrate Counter, The All-In-One Low Fat Gram Counter, The Revolutionary 7-Unit Low Fat Diet, The Brand Name Nutrition Counter, The National Medical Directory, Jean Carper's Total Nutrition Guide,* and most recently, *The Food Pharmacy*. She was formerly a national consumer reporter for Westinghouse Broadcasting (Group W) and the Washington medical correspondent for Cable News Network (CNN). She lives in Washington, D.C.

INVEST IN THE POWERS OF YOUR MIND
WITH SUBLIMINAL SELF-HELP TAPES
FROM BANTAM AUDIO PUBLISHING

The Bantam Audio Self-Help series, produced by Audio Activation, combines sophisticated psychological techniques of behavior modification with subliminal stimulation to help you get what you want out of life.

For Women

☐	45004	SLIM FOREVER	$8.95
☐	45035	STOP SMOKING FOREVER	$8.95
☐	45041	STRESS-FREE FOREVER	$8.95
☐	45172	DEVELOP A PERFECT MEMORY	$8.95
☐	45130	DEVELOP YOUR INTUITION	$7.95
☐	45022	POSITIVELY CHANGE YOUR LIFE	$8.95
☐	45106	GET A GOOD NIGHT'S SLEEP...EVERY NIGHT	$7.95
☐	45094	IMPROVE YOUR CONCENTRATION	$7.95
☐	45016	PLAY TO WIN	$7.95
☐	45081	YOU'RE IRRESISTIBLE	$7.95
☐	45112	AWAKEN YOUR SENSUALITY	$7.95

For Men

☐	45005	SLIM FOREVER	$8.95
☐	45036	STOP SMOKING FOREVER	$8.95
☐	45042	STRESS-FREE FOREVER	$8.95
☐	45173	DEVELOP A PERFECT MEMORY	$8.95
☐	45131	DEVELOP YOUR INTUITION	$7.95
☐	45023	POSITIVELY CHANGE YOUR LIFE	$8.95
☐	45107	GET A GOOD NIGHT'S SLEEP...EVERY NIGHT	$7.95
☐	45095	IMPROVE YOUR CONCENTRATION	$7.95
☐	45017	PLAY TO WIN	$7.95
☐	45082	YOU'RE IRRESISTIBLE	$7.95
☐	45113	AWAKEN YOUR SENSUALITY	$7.95

Look for them at your local bookstore or use this handy page for ordering:

Bantam Books, Dept. BAP4, 414 East Golf Road, Des Plaines, IL 60016

Please send me _____ copies of the tapes the items I have checked. I am enclosing $_____ (please add $2.00 to cover postage and handling). Send check or money order, no cash or C.O.D.s please.

Mr/Ms _____

Address _____

City/State _____ Zip _____

Please allow four to six weeks for delivery.
Prices and availability subject to change without notice.

BAP4–11/89

Special Offer
Buy a Bantam Book
for only 50¢.

Now you can have Bantam's catalog filled with hundreds of titles plus take advantage of our unique and exciting bonus book offer. A special offer which gives you the opportunity to purchase a Bantam book for only 50¢. Here's how!

By ordering any five books at the regular price per order, you can also choose any other single book listed (up to a $5.95 value) for just 50¢. Some restrictions do apply, but for further details why not send for Bantam's catalog of titles today!

Just send us your name and address and we will send you a catalog!

BANTAM BOOKS, INC.
P.O. Box 1006, South Holland, Ill. 60473

Mr./Mrs./Ms. _____
(please print)

Address _____

City _____ State _____ Zip _____

FC(A)-11/89

Please allow four to six weeks for delivery.

RECEIVED
JUL 1993
Mission College
Learning Resource
Services